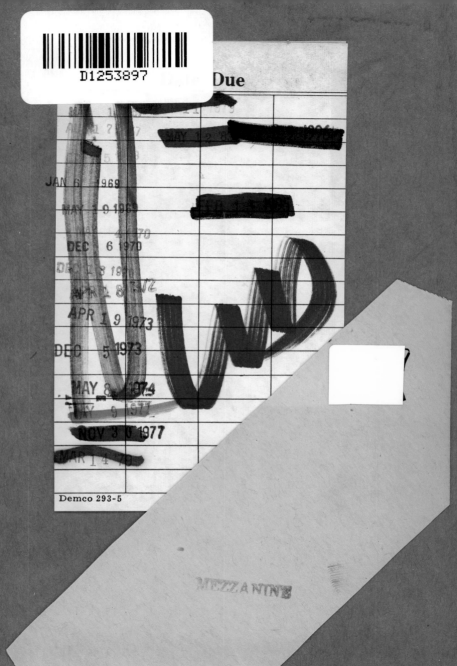

Notorious Literary Attacks

Edited With An Introduction

By

ALBERT MORDELL

AUTHOR OF "THE EROTIC MOTIVE IN LITERATURE," "THE
LITERATURE OF ECSTASY," ETC.

NEW YORK
BONI & LIVERIGHT
1926

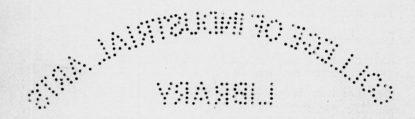

CONTENTS

v

INTRODUCTION

This volume comprises curious and hostile articles and reviews on great English and American authors and books of the nineteenth century; these notices made a great noise in their time, and the echoes have come down to us. I have preserved these inaccessible essays because they have never been gathered in book form, except for extracts here and there. There have, however, been slashing reviews that were collected by their authors which have permanently and deservedly damaged literary reputations. The best known instance is of Macaulay's essay flaying Robert Montgomery. Another famous instance is Anatole France's attack on George Ohnet's novel, *Volonté*, in the article called "Beyond Literature." I have not collected articles previously gathered together. I have not, for instance, given anything by Poe, who was always with a scourge in his hand. Poe's attacks have been collected by his editors. His *Letter to Thomas Dunn English* should be mentioned as a notable violent piece of invective. A legal suit was also instituted by Poe in which he vindicated himself from a charge of forgery.

I have not collected any of the abusive articles on Wordsworth and Keats, because the attacks are well known now, and have been reprinted. Professor Harper in his biography of Wordsworth and Sidney Colvin, in his book on Keats, have gone into these matters. Jeffrey reprinted from the *Edinburgh Review,* in his collected works, his notorious notice of Wordsworth's *Excursion,* beginning "This will never do," and of *The White Doe of Ryle- stone.* He also included his slight belated appreciation of Keats.

Dr. J. L. Haney and Mr. E. Stevenson have reprinted in their collections of early reviews the attacks on the *Lyrical Ballads* from the *Monthly Review* and the *Crit- ical Review,* respectively, and the articles on Words- worth's poems from the *Edinburgh Review* and *Black- wood's Magazine,* respectively. These editors have also preserved for us the two famous assaults on Keats's *Endymion,* Haney the one in *Blackwood's* and Stevenson the one in the *Quarterly Review.*

I have collected the articles in this volume, not just because they are "curiosities of criticisms," which they may or may not be. We have seen so many shiftings in literary valuations that we cannot even say we are abso- lutely certain that posterity may not again take up the viewpoint of some of these reviews. In fact, sometimes the reviewers hit very effectively on real weaknesses of great writers, the cumulative effect of whose fame has ob- scured for us those faults. The fact remains that the reviewers were right when they complained of the puerili- ties of some of Wordsworth's ballads, of the strained metaphors of Shelley, of the Germanic style of Carlyle, of the automatons and caricatures of Dickens, of the immoralities of Byron, of the catalogues of Whitman; their judgment was correct in a large measure upon Keats's *Endymion* and Byron's *Hours of Idleness.* They, however, failed to recognize that all these authors had such merits that to a great degree nullified their deficiencies.

We need not scoff too much at the curious judgments of reviewers, for every great writer, from Shakespeare down, has had his detractors from highly respected sources. Yet when a critic belittles geniuses and extols nonentities, we may regard his views as curious. Every critic from Dr. Johnson to Matthew Arnold, has been guilty of such lapses. Poe, for example, once wrote that his private as well as public opinion of Carlyle was that he was an ass because he wrote intending to be understood with the result that he was not understood. Poe, however, considered one William A. Jones, the most analytic if not best, American critic, except possibly Whipple. No contemporary reviewer has written more contemptuously of Shelley than has Carlyle.

Reprints of adverse reviews on great writers give consolation to abused contemporary authors. The scurrilous attacks on Wagner, Whistler, Rodin and the Impressionists, and the subsequent fame of these men, have encouraged many artists and musicians into thinking that they too, being the subject of castigation, would be deified by posterity. The stories of the abuse of Keats have brought balm to many poets. I imagine that the late Amy Lowell, who identified herself with Keats, derived great comfort from the assaults upon her verse, by reading the life of Keats, and the story of his abuse by critics. Her *Life of Keats* shows this.

But a very unblushing effort at self consolation was made public recently, by an English poetess. She cited

an attack upon *her* poetic efforts by a critic, and a laudatory notice of another poet, and exclaims with womanly
candor that such criticism might have been written a
hundred years ago, and that modern critics *will not* learn
anything from the death of Keats or the exile of Shelley
or the persecution and final triumph of Wordsworth and
Coleridge. Her article cites a few passages in which the
contemporary reviews unjustly dealt with *The Ancient
Mariner, Endymion, The Excursion* and *Prometheus Unbound*. Thus fortified, she went out to battle for her own
verses. She overlooked a slight item in carrying out the
analogy; like these writers she was attacked, but was she
sure that like them, she has genius?

However, poets will comfort themselves and why not?
It is now known that Southey was greatly consoled in his
belief that his lengthy epics would be read by posterity,
but they are not, and he does not know it, anyhow.

I have been compelled to exclude some notorious un-
collected articles because of their length. For example,
there is James Fenimore Cooper's attack on Scott in his
review on Lockhart's *Life of Scott*, in the *Knickerbocker
Magazine*, an article which brought out replies both in
that magazine and in the *Quarterly Review*, which had
already attacked him before for his book on England.

To the captious gentlemen who always want things to
remain buried and not revived, who think that a notorious
article is entombed even when it is in print in a periodical,
I would say that everything that helps us to understand
an author is valuable. Hostile reviews about an author's
books define the gaps between him and his contemporaries,

and indeed often have a value and interest *per se*. Further, the assaults upon such geniuses as Shelley and Whitman *have* taught a lesson to literary critics, and have instructed them somewhat in learning how to welcome great men, though there have been blunders since. We have also learned that the literary innovations of the day may become the commonplaces of criticism of to-morrow. We have seen that a man may have very radical views and actually be a virtuous man, or write a good book. We have discovered that we may have a great writer in one whose methods or views we disapprove.

Books that were once considered immoral have become required reading for high school girls.

Again, these notorious articles and scurrilous reviews are as surely part of literary history as despatches written in battle are of a nation's chronicles. Sometimes the reviews have influenced the author into changing his course, and sometimes they have urged him into greater defiance of the critics than ever. Sometimes they have improved and, sometimes, they have impaired public taste. You can no more take the books that provoked these reviews from out of their setting than you can think of Johnson without Boswell or Napoleon without Las Cases. When you think of Poe, you must remember Griswold. It is futile to say, "Let the controversy be forgotten." Shelley's poem *Adonais* preserves within its stanzas a curse upon the *Quarterly Reviewer*, for his articles on *Endymion*, which had such destructive effect on Keats. You cannot read Byron and forget the effect of Brougham's revilement of the *Hours of Idleness* in the *Edinburgh Review*, which drove the poet to pen his famous satire *English Bards and Scotch Reviewers*, to forego his resolution to abandon poetry and finally achieve a work like *Don Juan*. The letters of Shelley don't let you forget his personal life was attacked by the *Quarterly*.

Hazlitt's *Letter to William Gifford* keeps in your mind the fact that the *Quarterly* attacked three of his masterpieces. So examples may be multiplied. A poet like Whitman must almost be read with the hostile reviews about him in hand.

The nineteenth century writers and critics took themselves very seriously. To-day we are amused at the stupendous claims once made for writers like George Eliot and Tennyson. Two or three centuries hence, it is possible that nearly all the great poets of the nineteenth century will be known by some lyrics and select passages preserved only in anthologies. Perhaps, the ponderous long poems of the nineteenth century will not be read and Ward's *English Poets* has already preserved most of what ultimately will be remembered of poets who are constantly put next to Shakespeare by the admirers of Wordsworth, Coleridge, Byron, Shelley, Keats, Tennyson, Browning, Swinburne. I myself, however, hope that at least *The Prelude* and *Don Juan* will survive.

I believe there has been no book of the nature of the one here set forth. The nearest approach to it are the two volumes of early book reviews previously cited. The first volume of this nature was issued about thirty-five years ago in the Camelot Series, and edited by E. Stevenson under the title *Early Reviews*. It contained seventeen reviews originally published from 1786 to 1832, but only a few that really made literary history like the *Edinburgh Review* notice of Byron's first poems, the *Quarterly* article on *Endymion*, and the *Monthly Review* attacks on the *Lyrical Ballads* and on *Christabel*. Some of the reviews in the book had already been collected like those taken from Jeffrey's collected works. The book also included almost as many favourable reviews as unfavourable ones, notices like the *Westminster Review* articles by Sir John Bowring on Tennyson's first poems. It also had notices of three prose works, De Staël's *L'Allemagne*, Austen's *Emma* (by Scott) and Scott's *Waverley*. A really excellent and indispensable collection of *Early Reviews of English Poets* with an informative introduction about the history of English periodical literature and valuable notes was brought out by John Louis Haney in 1904, and privately printed by him in a limited edition. Dr. Haney was then Assistant Professor of English at the Central High School of Philadelphia, of which school he is now President, succeeding Dr. Robert Ellis Thompson. Dr. Haney's book contains twenty-nine reviews from Gray's *Odes* to Browning's *Men And Women* (1855). About a half dozen of these are very brief not covering a page each. He reprints two found in Stevenson's collection, the historic Byron and Keats items. His book is valuable for reprinting some very important reviews like the attacks of *Blackwood's* on *Endymion*, of the *Edinburgh* on *Christabel* (attributed to Hazlitt), of the *Saturday Review* on Browning's *Men and Women*, of Lockhart on

Tennyson's second volume in the *Quarterly*, of Southey on his friends' *Lyrical Ballads* in the *Critical Review*, and of the *Literary Gazette* on Shelley's *Adonais*. Some of the notices Haney reprints are favourable.

I wish here to thank him for some suggestions he made after reading the proofs of this Introduction.

I have included nothing that has already been reprinted in the two volumes alluded to. I have reprinted hostile notices exclusively, and not only on poems but on prose works like those of Coleridge, Hazlitt, Carlyle, Hawthorne, Hardy. I have gathered together attacks on the most significant English writers in the nineteenth century, from Hazlitt to Stevenson. I have given two of the most discussed critical articles in the latter part of the nineteenth century, Buchanan's *Fleshly School of Poetry* and Henley's essay on Robert Louis Stevenson. It is singular that articles that made so much literary history like the *Blackwood's* attacks on Coleridge, Hunt and Byron, and the *Quarterly's* blasts against Hazlitt, Shelley and Brontë, should never have been collected. I have remedied the defect and place these inaccessible articles in the reader's hands.

I have not chosen as a rule, as did Stevenson or Haney, only early reviews of an author's first works. On the contrary, I have often given reviews of authors written when the best of their work had been done, though the reviews are contemporary. The critical summings up made, of Dickens and Whitman, in the articles I have collected are probably more interesting than the earliest notices of these writers' first books. Similarly,

Coleridge, Hazlitt, Byron, Carlyle, Hawthorne, Tennyson, Rossetti, Swinburne and Hardy, had already won their laurels when the strange reviews I give were published. The reviewers knew exactly what they were doing and they tried ineffectually to stem the growing reputation of the men criticised.

Moreover I devote most of my reprints to the latter part of the nineteenth century.

I have included only one article about a living writer, Thomas Hardy. I have reprinted only one not written in the lifetime of the subject, Henley's article on Stevenson.

The present editor has felt that the true lover of literature after reading a great literary masterpiece wants to know what reaction an author's contemporaries experienced. In view of the fact that literary values shift, those reactions are of interest to the future reader, and also help him to comprehend the work. It was Professor John Bach McMaster who formed the plan of writing history by taking into consideration the newspapers and periodicals of the period under survey and getting public opinion as reflected in them. Another American, Professor Lounsbury, has been one of the first to study seriously the contemporary notices of authors he treated of and it is this fact that makes his *Life of James Fenimore Cooper* in the American Men of Letters Series probably the best work in that series, with the possible exception of Woodberry's Hawthorne. Lounsbury's book on the first half of Tennyson's Life and Times, also gives a study of early reviews of Tennyson, notably the *Black-*

wood's and *Quarterly* articles of Tennyson's first two volumes, by Wilson and Lockhart, respectively.

The essays I have collected represent almost a running commentary on some of the leading works and writers in the nineteenth century.

Hostile articles and reviews have always been with us, and some of them have achieved more notoriety than the works they noticed. I suppose the most infamous attack in the literature of the nineteenth century has been Griswold's on Poe. Griswold first wrote the notice of Poe's death in the *New York Tribune* and the major part of it was reprinted in Willis's reply to it and can be found in some editions and biographies of Poe. Griswold's enlargement on his first article is in the fourth volume he edited of Poe's works two years later, and he reprints almost word for word the conclusion of the *Tribune* article. It is too long for reprinting, but can be found in the first edition of Poe's collected works. It formed the basis of an even more violent article on Poe in the *Edinburgh Rview* some years later.

Then there have been books made up of almost undiluted attacks on writers like Byron's famous verse satire on the *English Bards and Scotch Reviewers,* Hunt's poem *Feast of the Poets* with its attacks on Scott and others in the prose notes, and Hazlitt's able volume *The Spirit of the Age,* with his malevolent animadversions on some writers. Alfred Austin achieved notoriety with a book called *Poetry of the Period* (1870) where Tennyson, Browning and Swinburne came in for very severe strictures. The most violent condemnation of literary men in a group of the last generation, was Nordau's *Degeneration*. Churton Collins was an atrabiliar critic and his handling of Edmund Gosse in *Ephemera Critica* is still remembered.

Almost every great author has been subjected to literary attacks. Possibly this is better than being the victim of log-rolling. Many of us smile now when we read how the most respected critics of the nineties saw in Stephen Phillips a Milton or a Sophocles, more than when we read some of the scurrilous attacks on great men.

Contemporary predictions which assume to speak for posterity are often amusing. The most flagrant instance is the well known conjecture of Jeffrey written in 1829, and collected by him in 1843, in his essay on Hemans that Keats, Shelley, Wordsworth and Byron would fade away and that the two who had longest withstood the decay of fame were Rogers and Campbell. To-day Rogers is not read at all and Campbell is only known for a few patriotic poems.

I do not consider attacks notorious when the reviewers unanimously spiked a famous author, because his work was far beneath his usual standard, as they thought in the case of, say, Thackeray's *Virginians,* though I personally believe they erred as regards his *Adventures of Philip.* Every great English writer produced some things of a low order of merit that were deservedly criticised. Yet it is singular that every great poet of the nineteenth century has received abuse for what are now accepted as his masterpieces.

Sometimes an important periodical ignored a writer

altogether. For example, Shelley never got a notice in the *Edinburgh Review* in his lifetime. Sometimes a review was certainly inconsistent in its acceptance of writers. *Blackwood's,* for example, berated Hunt and Keats, but accepted Shelley, first praised and then insulted Hazlitt, admired Lamb, maligned Coleridge and blew hot and cold for Wordsworth. The *Edinburgh* was hostile to Wordsworth, but praised Hunt and Keats, and it opened its pages to Hazlitt. It criticised severely the early works of Moore, Lamb, Southey, Byron and Scott.

The *Quarterly Review* praised Wordsworth; one article, that on *The Excursion,* being written by Lamb, though it was much mutilated by Gifford. The *Quarterly* was largely friendly to Byron. Its abuse of Hazlitt, Hunt, Shelley and Keats, is literary history.

Scott was praised all around. Over two hundred reviews appeared in the leading reviews of his works in his lifetime, among them the lengthy one he himself wrote for the *Quarterly,* January, 1817, on *Old Mortality.* Scott had helped to found the *Quarterly.*

Next to Scott the most reviewed writer was Byron.

The most famous single issue of any English magazine is the seventh issue of *Blackwood's,* October, 1817, which contained the article on Coleridge's *Biographia Literaria,* the first of the Cockney School of Poetry Series on Hunt, and the Chaldee Manuscript concoction satirising Edinburgh notabilities.

It will be noticed that in the present volume the periodicals from which articles predominate are *Blackwood's* (four articles), the *Quarterly* (three articles) and the *Saturday Review* (three articles) or more than half of the articles in this book. This is as it should be. These periodicals are intimately connected with the history of English literature. Conservative, they fought against books that have since become classics. They were severe, but ably edited. They attacked a writer because they did not like his politics. Accounts of the history of these periodicals are easily accessible.

It will also be observed that some of the articles were in the nature of personal attacks, a kind of book reviewing that is not much indulged in to-day. Coleridge, Hunt, Byron and Shelley, were criticised as bad writers because they were supposed to have been bad husbands. The most violent of all the personal attacks were on Hunt and Hazlitt. Both, as well as Coleridge, threatened lawsuits against *Blackwood's*, which, however, were never prosecuted. Lengthy replies to their critics were written by Byron, Rossetti and Hazlitt, and these replies have become classics, and can be found in the collected editions of their works. Swinburne's pamphlet reply was not only to the *Saturday Review* article, but to some of the other attacks. Hunt's reply appeared in the pages of the *Examiner*. Two of the writers attacked, Shelley and Brontë, interlard much of their correspondence with references to their reviewers. *Blackwood's* article on Hunt and Hazlitt led to the murder in a duel of John Scott, editor of the *London Magazine*.

The articles that have produced the most prolonged controversies were the Buchanan and Henley articles, the former also leading to several pamphlets and a lawsuit, and, as some charged, the death of the poet. Henley's article is still a subject of controversy.

The names of the writers of most of the infamous review articles have been preserved for posterity. Nearly all of these men have done other things to save them from infamy. The most notorious names still are those of Wilson and Lockhart. Their work in *Blackwood's* cannot often be separated, but we know that Wilson libelled Coleridge, and ridiculed Tennyson; Lockhart has gone down to immemorial infamy by the attack on Keats, and also on Tennyson (in the *Quarterly*), while both had a share in the violent abuse of Hunt and Hazlitt, probably the most outrageous and disgusting attacks in English literature. The notices of Shelley and Wordsworth were mingled praise and blame, and by Wilson. Yet Lockhart has written two classic English biographies, one on Burns, and the other on his father-in-law, Scott, and Wilson endeared himself by his work as professor of Moral Philosophy. The fact remains, however, that Wilson and Lockhart did some of the vilest things and exercised some of the most ridiculous judgment in all literature. Both later repented their early criticisms.

Gifford is usually accredited with the attacks on Hazlitt and Leigh Hunt, but as a matter of fact, he did not write much for the magazine. Gifford is also blamed for having permitted in his magazine the Keats and Shelley articles by John Wilson Croker and John Taylor Coleridge, respectively, two names that with that of Henry Brougham, who wrote the first Byron article in the *Edinburgh,* are anathema to all lovers of Keats, Shelley and Byron.

Yet these reviewers were very able and talented men.

Jeffrey erred when he wrote adversely of the poems of Scott and Wordsworth, and overestimated Rogers and Campbell, but he redeemed himself by his accepting some essays by Hazlitt and Carlyle (both of whom wrote sympathetic accounts of him), and by his admiration for Dickens. Jeffrey was also a generous friend financially to Hazlitt and Carlyle. Buchanan is known as the man who maligned Rossetti (and also Kipling) though he defended Whitman. The names of the authors of the attacks on those innocent novels *The Scarlet Letter* and *Jane Eyre*, now studied in girls' high schools, are almost unknown: they are A. C. Coxe and Miss Elizabeth Rigby (Lady Eastlake). Lord Morley and Andrew Lang made mistakes in their notices of Swinburne and Hardy, respectively. Time has, however, justified Henley for his views on Stevenson.

A brief account of the literary history and associations of each of the articles reprinted, follows.

I.   The article on William Hazlitt's *The Round Table* was attributed by Hazlitt to the editor, and appeared in the *Quarterly Review* for April, 1817.

It is the first of the three articles in the *Quarterly Review* which prompted Hazlitt to write his *Letter to William Gifford* (1819). As a matter of fact the abuse and substance of Gifford's three attacks are quoted and summarized in Hazlitt's letter. *The Round Table* (to which Hunt also contributed some essays) was singled out for attack, because it contained a reprint of an abusive Pitt article. Later Gifford's condemnation of the *Characters of Shakespeare's Plays* (January, 1818) is said to have stopped the sale of that work. The *Quarterly* returned to the attack on Hazlitt's *Lectures on English Poets* in July, 1818. Subsequent thrusts by Gifford evoked a parting shot from the Hazlitt gun in the essay on Gifford, in *The Spirit of the Age* (1825). Gifford is known now chiefly because of Hazlitt's letter and Hazlitt ranks to-day as the greatest critic and essayist of his time. Hazlitt had his own faults, and his unpardonable reviews of Coleridge's *Christabel* and the *Biographia Literaria* in the *Edinburgh Review* have never been forgiven him.

The *Letter to William Gifford* remains one of the most effective replies by an author to a critic in English literature. It was greatly admired by Keats. Gifford never replied to Hazlitt.

It is not necessary here to go into the attacks on Hazlitt in *Blackwood's Magazine,* which at first was favourable to him, and even reported his lectures. Suffice it to say that the *London Magazine* under the editorship of John Scott rushed to the defence of Hazlitt and Hunt from *Blackwood's* assaults and Scott was shot in a duel by J. H. Christie, the friend of Lockhart, one of the editors, February, 1821. Again Hazlitt had brought a suit against *Blackwood's* which was settled. The abuse stopped and then again commenced. Another suit was threatened. Hazlitt was even more severely branded by *Blackwood's* than by the *Quarterly.* P. P. Howe's *Life of Hazlitt* goes into his troubles with *Blackwood's* and gives a list of some of the vile names the Magazine called him.

The *Blackwood's* article that caused Hazlitt most concern appeared in the same issue as the famous article on Keats. It was called "Hazlitt Cross-Questioned" and consisted of eight questions and signed "An Old Friend With a New Face." In the same number there were two other vile references to him, one being the now notorious allusion "pimpled Hazlitt."

There was a defence of Hazlitt in an anonymous pamphlet *Hypocrisy Unveiled and Calumny Detected*, in a review of *Blackwood's Magazine*.* The author called attention to the fact that *Blackwood's* had recently had an article on Jeffrey and Hazlitt, praising both of them, and declared the *volte face* was made because Hazlitt had become a contributor to the *Edinburgh Magazine*. The author of the pamphlet was challenged to a duel by the editors, and thus the Lockhart-Wilson authorship got out.

II.   I have given the first of the eight series of articles called "On the Cockney School of Poetry." This appeared in that notorious issue of October, 1817, under the new régime of John Wilson and John Gibson Lockhart.

The articles on the Cockney School were devoted to Leigh Hunt, except the fourth, which is the famous attack on Keats' *Endymion*. Probably no critical articles in English ever achieved the notoriety that the early Hunt

---

*The copy in the New York Public Library has the name, James Graham as author, written in lead pencil, on the title-page.

articles did. Hunt is now known as a tame essayist, but his poetry, the subject of these articles, is not very highly rated.

Hunt was the most calumniated man of his day and attacks on him are sheer billingsgate. His poem *The Story of Rimini* which was the target of the second of the series is harmless enough. He was simply buried in abusive epithets, and he himself was accused of adultery. The authorship of the articles lies between Lockhart and Wilson; the first one was undoubtedly Lockhart's; they were all signed Z. In later years Wilson apologized and made his famous remark about the animosities being mortal while the humanities live forever. He offered Hunt the pages of the magazine for contributions, an offer which was declined. Lockhart later in life pleaded his youth in extenuation of his attacks and blamed Wilson. In alluding to the attacks in his *Autobiography*, Hunt did not chastise these enemies of those days.

In addition to the eight articles, the last of which appeared in 1825, there were published two letters to Hunt signed Z., the same signatures as appeared to the articles. These were even more scurrilous than the articles themselves. They were written in reply to Hunt's own defence of himself in the *Examiner* and to the other defences of him. The first two Cockney School articles appeared in October and November, 1817, respectively. In January and May, 1818, came the two letters to Hunt from Z. One of them, the second, says for example: "You, Leigh Hunt, are without exception, the weakest, wishy-washiest satirist whose pen ever dribbled. You are like a jack-ass that comes braying out of a pond in which he has been enclosed from Monday till Saturday." A verdict on *The Story of Rimini,* the famous innocuous poem of Hunt, in the first letter reads: "No woman who has not either lost her chastity, or is desirous of losing it, ever read the *Story of Rimini* without the flushings of shame and self-reproach. . . . There is not a single mother of a seduced daughter, or a single father of a profligate son, or a single repentant victim of a sophistical vice, that does not lavish the foulest of execrations on your devoted head."

This poem had the greatest influence in breaking down the fettered verse of Pope and influenced Shelley and Keats in their verse; it deals in a moral manner with a theme that has fascinated poets like Boker, Stephen Phillips and D'Annunzio. In his later editions, Hunt rewrote the poem, in the opinion of many not improving it.

Hunt was attacked thus by a man who became a Professor of Moral Philosophy (Wilson), and by another who became the son-in-law of Scott and got the Editorship of the *Quarterly* (Lockhart). They were young men at the time, Lockhart being only twenty-four.

Hunt's poems *The Story of Rimini* and *Foliage* were also bitterly attacked in two articles by Gifford, against whom he later wrote a satirical poem *Ultra-Crepidarius.* He never forgave Gifford and attacked him in his *Autobiography.* Hunt had in his early days been asked to become a contributor to the *Quarterly,* but refused, as he wanted to maintain his independence. The *Edinburgh Review* in an article (probably by Hazlitt) praised *The Story of Rimini.*

Hunt should be better known for his *Autobiography* which Carlyle put next to Lockhart's *Life of Scott*. It is one of the best in the language. In his essays he is a typical Mid-Victorian and he was the friend of Carlyle and Dickens. He was one of the few literary men Hawthorne cared to visit. As a critic, Hunt ranks high and he was the first to see the greatness of Keats and Shelley, as we see it to-day. He had his faults; his attack on his benefactor Byron, and his sponging on Shelley, are held against him.

He also gave first provocation by his early attacks on English writers, especially Scott, in *The Feast of the Poets*, and his libel on the Prince Regent which got him two years in jail. But he was never as vile as Wilson or Lockhart, whom his biographer, Andrew Lang, tried to whitewash.

III. The opening article in *Blackwood's* which contained the first Hunt article, was on Coleridge's *Biographia Literaria*. It was written by Wilson and brought up the old charge raised by Gifford about Coleridge's shabby treatment of his wife. Coleridge replied to this in a letter to Crabb Robinson and asked him about bringing suit, which, however, was never done. The letter defending his own conduct appears in Brandl's *Life of Coleridge*. The Coleridge article was prompted by the chapter in his book criticising *Bertram*, Maturin's play. Scott thought highly of this play, which he recommended for production and Wilson mistakenly thought he would please Scott thus.

There was a defence of Coleridge in a later issue of *Blackwood's* in a letter signed J. S.

Poverty later compelled Coleridge to do some work for *Blackwood's*. He got an advance and turned in two articles of no particular importance, for October, 1821 and January, 1822. Thus he wrote for the magazine that had ridiculed his poems and attacked his personal life. Hunt at least refused later to write for them.

Hazlitt also greeted the *Biographia Literaria* with a violent article in the *Edinburgh Review*. The review appears in his collected works. Thus was the reception of what Arthur Symons calls "the greatest book of criticism in English." Ironically enough, though in this book Coleridge complained of the attack upon him by his friend (Hazlitt) of *Christabel* in the *Edinburgh Review*, Hazlitt repeated the attack on the man who was his master. Coleridge was also hurt that the *Quarterly* did not notice his book any more than it did his other chief works; an article could have appeared through Southey, who wrote considerably for it.

IV. The article that figured most in Shelley's life is the *Quarterly Review* notice of *The Revolt of Islam*, in the April *Quarterly* for 1819. It is almost as famous in Shelley's life as the *Quarterly* notice of *Endymion* in Keats's life. I reprint it for the first time. Shelley's letters are full of allusions to it. Shelley first attributed the review to Southey; then to Milman. We know now that Shelley's classmate at Eton, Sir John Taylor Coleridge, wrote it. It is recorded that some one in a reading room in Florence saw Shelley reading the article and rush out laughing hysterically. Peacock called it one of the "most malignant effusions of the *odium theologicum* that ever appeared even in those days." Byron told Medwin how much the article angered him. In a letter to his publishers, Shelley wrote he was amused with the finale which compared him to the Egyptian King. It reminded him of the end of the first act of an opera, when everybody talks and sings at once after concordant discord sets up from the orchestra. He began a letter to the *Quarterly* calling upon it for proofs of the personal attack in it, but the letter was never sent. He wrote to Hunt thanking him for printing the defence of his private life in three numbers of the *Examiner*. He joked with his publishers about the reference to his chariot wheel being broken.

He inquired of Southey in a letter dated June, 1820, as to his authorship of the review. Southey replied he was not the author of it. Shelley also wrote a letter which he never sent, to the *Quarterly* when they attacked Keats, and began, saying he was not writing to defend himself; nevertheless he called the author of the article about himself "wretch" and "despicable writer," and pretended he was not disturbed by it. As a matter of fact, this was the one article that really annoyed him and he even intended stopping writing.

Of all magazines, *Blackwood's Magazine* came to Shelley's defence from the abuse of the *Quarterly*.

For once, Wilson joined hands with Hunt in the defence of Shelley. Shelley had been pleased by Wilson's notice of the *Revolt of Islam*, and wrote so. He was no

doubt greatly consoled when Wilson in the notice of
Alastor in the November, 1819 issue, rushed to arms in
his behalf and attacked the *Quarterly*. Yet *Blackwood's*
had in its peculiar inconsistency in an earlier number, in a
notice of *Rosalind and Helen*, lectured him sharply for
his views and in the notice of one of the few poems of his
which omitted promulgating such views, *Adonais*, denounced him violently.

Still, it is one of the curious paradoxes of book reviewing that the pioneer and defender of Shelley should
have been the most abusive enemy of Shelley's friends,
Hunt, Keats and Byron; that the mouthpiece of the church
and the state should have befriended its arch-foe.

It was DeQuincey's kind words to Wilson that had done
this service for Shelley.

The *Quarterly Review* did not reply to the defence of
Shelley's character, but it bided its time. When *Prometheus Unbound* appeared, it published the most demolish-
ing assault on Shelley as a poet, that had yet appeared.
His style, images, rhetoric, grammar, diction, were all
attacked. His incoherence, obscurity and absurdity were
emphasized. The reviewer said in effect: "See, you
complain we judge his work by his life. Here we consider him a poet *per se*." The reviewer concluded this
article (which it must be confessed contains some just
characterizations of Shelley's weakness as an artist, still
brought up) as follows: "Of Mr. Shelley himself we
know nothing, and desire to know nothing. Be his private
qualities what they may, his poems (and it is only with his
poems that we have any concern) are at war with reason,

with taste, with virtue, in short, with all that dignifies man, or that man reveres." (October, 1821.)

The other hostile reviews that appeared of Shelley's work in his lifetime are entertaining reading to-day. His elegy *Adonais* which is to-day read in schools and ranked with *Lycidas* and *In Memoriam*, was frightfully ridiculed, indecently so, in the *Literary Gazette*, an article which Dr. Haney reprints in his *Early Reviews Of The English Poets*. His *The Cenci* which some people consider the greatest English tragedy since the Shakespearean plays, was almost mercilessly damned. Haney reprints the notice from the *London Magazine*. But the notice of *The Cenci* in the *Literary Gazette*, of April 1, 1820, is simply terrible. It begins: "Of all the abominations which intellectual perversions and poetical atheism have produced in our times, this tragedy appears to us to be the most abominable." The article ends: "We now most gladly take leave of this work; and sincerely hope we shall never need again to look into one so stamped with pollution, impiousness and infamy."

Two other reviews of Shelley have been reprinted, the notice of *Alastor* from the *Monthly Review*, by Haney, and the mingled blame and praise in Wilson's article on the *Revolt of Islam* from *Blackwood's* by Stevenson in his *Early Reviews*.

V. Byron rarely noticed his reviewers after replying to the *Edinburgh Review* attack on his first volume, *The Hours of Idleness*, with the satire *English Bards and Scotch Reviewers*. There was a *Letter To The Editor*

Of My Grandmother's Review, signed by a fictitious name and published in Hunt's *Liberal,* in reply to the *British Review's* resentment of the jocular lines in *Don Juan* about bribing that periodical for a favourable review. There was the controversy with Southey.

However, the reply to *Blackwood's* attack, August, 1819, on the first two cantos of *Don Juan,* is one of the finest apologies of his views and his life. It is in the form of a letter to the elder D'Israeli and is dated March 15, 1820. It shows incidentally that the writer was a great prose writer and it should with his famous letters to Murray, about Bowles's attack on Pope, be better known. Byron in the reply makes a tirade against Southey, his quarrel with whom was later continued and constitutes one of the most interesting quarrels of authors. He also alludes to the fact that the same periodical, *Blackwood's,* had attacked his *Beppo.*

Byron's reply appeared after his death in Moore's *Life.* *Blackwood's* delivered a few more shots at *Don Juan,* but changed its tone after Byron's death. In 1869, it defended him from Mrs. Stowe's charge of incest.

The *Quarterly* to Southey's disgust did not attack or notice *Don Juan.*

The Byron Centenary (i. e., of his death) was celebrated in a few books about him, some unfortunately assuming to decide in the affirmative, on evidence that still leaves a reasonable doubt, that he had cohabited with his sister. In his letter to D'Israeli Byron repels the charge of Southey that he lived with the sister of Shelley's wife in a league of incest. He does not deny that Miss Clairmont was his mistress, but says she was related to Mrs. Shelley only by the marriage of their parents and not by blood.

However, it was conceded by all his enemies that Byron was a poet. Even in the middle of the nineteenth century, when the estimate of him as a poet was at a low ebb, no one questioned that he was still a poet; yet some critics of our day have asserted that Byron was not a poet.

VI.   We now leave the Georgian period and come to the Victorian age.

The attack on Carlyle's *French Revolution* (May 20, 1837) in *The Athenæum*, brought out a comment from him in the Appendix of his *Reminiscences* that he read it without pain, laid it down for a day or two, and then used the number containing the review as a tablecloth for the tea-kettle. He comments grimly upon the conclusion of the review which was: "Readers, have we made out our case?" Mill and Thackeray praised the book, and Southey thought highly of it.

Charles W. Dilke was at the time editor of *The Athenæum*.

VII.   The notice of Charlotte Brontë's novel *Jane Eyre* was sandwiched in between a favourable review in the *Quarterly*, December, 1848, of *Vanity Fair* and of a book of reports on governesses, the reviewer thinking this appropriate because the heroine of the novel was a governess. However, the least important part of the novel from a literary point of view, is the question of the treatment of the governess. The article is several times referred to by the novelist in her correspondence with W. S. Williams. She affects to believe that the lash of the *Quarterly* does not sting her, but the amount of correspondence devoted by her to the notices of reviewers of her books, makes us believe that their comments on her book meant much to her. She says she read the review without a pang; she concluded the author was a man, but no gentleman. The reviewer, however, was a woman, Miss Elizabeth Rigby, who later became Lady Eastlake. Her opinion that the author of the novel, if a woman, had forfeited the society of her sex, may seem strange to-day, when the novel is required reading for high school girls. It has also been shown on the screen.

Charlotte Brontë wrote a reply to it called "A Word to the *Quarterly*" and intended using it as a preface to her novel *Shirley*, but she cancelled the preface and used the one we now have. Lockhart, the editor, however, thought well of *Jane Eyre*.

In writing of the author of *Jane Eyre*, and referring to the *Quarterly*, Swinburne said: "We know that from the earlier days of Shelley onwards to the later day of Tennyson, 'whatsoever things are true, whatsoever things are honest, whatsoever things are just, whatsoever things are pure, whatsoever things are lovely, whatsoever things are of good report,' become untrue, dishonest, unjust, impure, unlovely and ill-famed when passed through the critical crucible of the *Quarterly Review*."

Yet over a quarter of a century later, Swinburne's signed article on Dickens appeared in the *Quarterly*.

The literary world brings together strange bedfellows.

VIII.   The ridiculously moral and patronizing article on *The Scarlet Letter* requires no comment.   It forms the concluding portion of an essay on Hawthorne's writing by A. C. Coxe, in the *Church Review* (January, 1851).

IX.   There can be no question that the most famous of the Tennyson reviews are those on the 1830 volume of poems by Christopher North (Wilson) in *Blackwood's* for February, 1832, and on the 1832 volume by Lockhart in the *Quarterly Review,* in the issue of April, 1833.

Lounsbury makes a thorough study of these reviews and Haney reprints the Lockhart article, the conclusion of which, making fun of Tennyson's verses in reply to Christopher North, is very clever.   Tennyson however, had friends among early reviewers, Hallam, Hunt, Bowring and Mill.

The article I reprint reviewing *Maud* is certainly antagonistic to the man who by that time had become poet laureate.   It is well written, and showed that the author was a man of independent judgment.   He probably was W. E. Aytoun, the poet, who had asked to review the poem.   For that matter most of the reviews of *The Princess* and *Maud* were unfavourable.

To-day there is a reaction against Tennyson and he ranks as the author of a few good poems and lyrics and some fine stanzas in *In Memoriam.*

X.   The article on Mr. Dickens, reprinted from the *Saturday Review* of May, 1858, was published on the occasion of the collected edition of his works.   It was reprinted in *Littell's Living Age*, for July 24, 1858, and some extracts from it appear in Fred G. Kitton's *Dickensiana* (London, 1886). We smile now at the reviewer's prophecy that Dickens would not live, and that forty years hence (i. e., 1898), Dickens's wit would not be understood. The editor of the magazine at that time was John D. Cook. The next year the *Saturday Review* returned to the attack with a virulent notice of a *Tale of Two Cities* (Dec. 17, 1859). It attacked the moral tone of the novel and said that the kind of work Dickens did would make one feel that devotion to literature would result in an incurable vulgarity of mind and taste, and intolerable arrogance of temper. A ridiculous rumour spread that as a result of this article Dickens was laid up in bed for several months and that warm applications and doctors were necessary to restore him. At his death, however, the *Saturday Review*, under a new editor since 1868, Philip Harwood, paid a very handsome tribute to him.

Bitter articles against Dickens appeared throughout his lifetime. His vulgarity, his making caricaturous characters, his bad English, his utilitarian attitude, his lack of culture or intellectual depth were referred to. Though the charges linger, most of these notices have been forgotten; Bagehot's essay of 1858 (half-praise, half-blame) however was collected in his *Literary Studies*. Summaries of these hostile articles appear in Kitton's *Dickensiana*. From October, 1837 (while *Pickwick* was still appearing), when the *Quarterly* of that date feared his reputation which went up like a rocket might go down like a stick, till the time of his death, the leading magazines took occasional flings at him.

In April, 1866, the *Westminster Review* said the more we looked at Dickens the more we detected the trickery of an artificer, that his whole art was founded upon false principles, his characters a bundle of deformities, his humour riotous extravagance, and that Pecksniff was chaff against Tartuffe. George Stott in the *Contemporary Review* (1869) found that no writer showed more than Dickens an uninstructed mind, lacking in judgment, breadth of view and critical acumen; he said a world of Dickens would become a vulgar Arcadia of virtuous artisans, gushing ladies and eccentric old gentlemen.

The one hostile notice that Dickens's biographer Forster answered, was Lewes's article in the *Fortnightly*, February, 1872, published after Dickens's death. Lewes said Dickens was a stagy sentimentalist and clever caricaturist. He tried to investigate why the novelist, with his faults, still had greatness. Forster found Lewes's studied depreciation especially odious.

Dickens had, however, practically all the literary men of England among his admirers.

In so far as is known Dickens ignored nearly all his critics. He did reply to the *Edinburgh Review* notice of *Little Dorrit*, but merely to correct the reviewer about some errors, and he was not concerned with setting forth his own merits as an artist. See *Household Words*, August 1, 1857, "Curious Misprint in the Edinburgh Review."

The strange thing is that while most of his reviewers

were in their general criticism often right, and their various accusations of artistic deficiencies in his work are still brought up against it, he has become a permanent literary world-figure with all his sins upon his head as admitted. The reviewers were wrong, chiefly in their prediction about the ultimate fate of his fame.

The biographers of Dickens have unwisely persisted in ignoring Dickens's hostile reviewers; they should have taken a lesson from the biographers of Wordsworth, Coleridge, Byron, Shelley, Keats and Tennyson, who have not shrunk from noticing these poets' adverse reviewers.

XI. The *Saturday Review* notice of Swinburne's *Poems and Ballads* (of August 4, 1866) was the most significant one. The periodical itself had great prestige, and its tone often set that of the other reviews. In the present case an advance copy of the book was reviewed before it was for sale. It started the campaign about the poet's sensuality and, as Gosse says, it created a prejudice from which he suffered the rest of his life. It set the leading papers against the poet and was really instrumental in fostering the notice that was to appear in the *Times,* fear of which led the publisher to withdraw the book from circulation. The book was admired by Lytton and did not even offend that moralist-critic Ruskin, and yet it shocked the reviewers. It brought out against Swinburne many who admired his preceding works. Finally, the clamour was so great that Swinburne wrote a general reply to his critics in his famous pamphlet *Notes On*

Poems and Ballads, written to protect the fortunes of his new publisher; his friend William Michael Rossetti also wrote in his defence.   In reviewing the latter publication, the tone of the *Saturday Review* turned slightly in Swinburne's favour.   The book of poems was published in America and created a furore there and a sheaf of press notices reprinted in an early edition of one of his books contains praises from obscure, now defunct, American papers.

It is singular that only a few years after the appearance of the review, a correspondence began between Swinburne and John Morley, author of the review, who had become editor of the *Fortnightly Review,* to which Swinburne submitted poems and essays which Morley published. Why Morley became an admirer of the man he so strongly condemned, I cannot see.   There is no reason except that the growing reputation of the poet influenced him.

And what a strange comment it is on Victorian reserve or cowardice that Morley never acknowledged publicly his authorship.   Of course, the review is not to his credit. In his *Recollections* published after Swinburne's death, he made no mention of it.   But the reserve still continued, for even after Morley's death, Gosse in his *Life of Swinburne* still kept the secret merely stating the reviewer was an Oxford man who also achieved prominence and became a friend of the poet.   Only later did Gosse give out Morley's name and the joke was, as we later learned, that Swinburne all along knew Morley had written that review and Morley did not know that Swinburne knew.

XII. I suppose there was more ink spilled about Buchanan's article *The Fleshly School of Poetry* than on any other hostile literary notice, with the exception of Griswold's attack on Poe. The results of the controversy by their partisan defenders have been summed up for Rossetti by his brother in the *Memoir,* and for Buchanan by Harriet Jay, his friend and biographer. It is a well known story of how the article appeared in the *Contemporary Review* for October, 1871, signed Thomas Maitland, how it was later republished enlarged in pamphlet form, how Rossetti himself replied to it in his "The Stealthy School of Poetry," in the *Athenæum,* an article now included among his collected works; how Swinburne rushed to the defence of his friend in a pamphlet *Under the Microscope;* how Rossetti became sick and took chloral; and how finally Buchanan dedicated a novel to Rossetti with a sonnet *An Old Enemy,* and wrote a favourable essay called *A Note on Dante Rossetti,* reprinted in his *Look Around Literature.* Buchanan made a number of public apologies though he never could see that the effect of the review should have been what it was. William Michael Rossetti retorts that he cannot understand why the man who formed the opinion of Rossetti in 1881, could not have had the same opinion in 1871, but he does not allow for the provocation Buchanan had. William Michael Rossetti claims that the feud was started by a parody, rumoured to have been written by Buchanan on Swinburne in the *Spectator* on the appearance of the *Poems and Ballads.* Buchanan admits also that he wrote the hostile review of Swinburne's *Poems and Bal-*

lads for the *Athenæum*. But Buchanan claims he had provocation for his article, because Swinburne in a note to one of his prose essays, not long before the *Contemporary* article, made a contemptuous allusion to David Gray, the poet who was a great friend of Buchanan and had died a premature death, and who figured in Buchanan's book *David Gray And Other Essays*, issued in 1868. Buchanan had still more provocation, for in the opening passage, in 1866, of William Michael Rossetti's brochure replying to Swinburne's critics, Buchanan was referred to as a poor and pretentious poetaster who stirs tempests in teapots, referring to the success of Buchanan's *London Poems* issued in the same year as the *Poems and Ballads*. William Michael Rossetti justified this contemptuous allusion because of the rumour of Buchanan's authorship of the parody *Sessions of Poets* in the *Spectator*.

Time has shown that Buchanan was not a sound literary critic in his attack on Swinburne and Rossetti. These men's poems were superior to his own. The laurels however rest with him; he apologised and he was never as brutal as the unforgiving Swinburne. Though he cast the first stone, his enemies attacked him out of undue proportion.

The matter also led to a lawsuit in which Buchanan was the victor against a paper which published a letter abusive of him. A poem *Jonas Fisher* (by the Earl of Southesk) was attributed to Buchanan in the *Examiner* review of it. Buchanan denied the authorship and a letter (now known to have been written by Swinburne) was published abusing him. Swinburne refused to help the paper with his testimony, because it attacked a favourite lady novelist of his.

Much was made in the Swinburne letter of Buchanan's defence of a sensual poet like Walt Whitman. While it is true that it was inconsistent on Buchanan's part to object to a trait found in one poet and not to the same trait found in another, he deserves credit for his championship of Whitman. He was also a champion of Herman Melville and mentions him in his poems. He was, however, an enemy of most of the modern writers, attacking bitterly Zola and Ibsen. He wrote a hostile article on Kipling called "The Voice of the Hooligan" for the *Contemporary Review*, which brought a reply by Besant.

He was an interesting man who could write free-thinking poems and a score of pot-boiler novels. It is fair to say that he is not the ogre that the notoriety of his essay brought him. It should also be remembered that the leading authorities regarded his attack just. Persecution followed Buchanan and he had even to publish a book of poems anonymously.

To-day Buchanan is less known as a poet, undeservedly in my opinion. Rossetti does not have the vogue he once had, but Swinburne survives even though his poems and ballads have gone down in public esteem because of the vogue of the free verse school.

XIII. The attacks that met *Leaves of Grass* have often been mentioned. Whitman has been a target for critics from the days of 1855 when mud was thrown at him by every outraged moralist and æsthete to the days of 1925, when Ernest Boyd, a very fine critic otherwise, in his justifiable fury against the affected poseurs in poetry, wrongly fathered Whitman upon them in the pages of the *American Mercury,* and repeated old charges against him.

Whitman himself gathered the reviews of the first edition of his poems, in the pages of the second edition in 1856; and in 1860 published his pamphlet *Leaves of Grass Imprints* which contained the reviews up to that time, including the three favourable ones he wrote himself. It is the impression of many people that the *Leaves of Grass* provoked only abuse or was ignored. On the contrary, the leading periodical of that time, the *North American Review,* and the leading newspaper, the *New York Tribune,* spoke at length and well of his book.

The best known articles against him are the attack by Swinburne, *Whitmania,* which is collected, and the famous very lengthy essay of Peter Bayne in the *Contemporary* for December, 1875. Swinburne had spoken highly of the poet in 1866 in his book on *Blake* and had written a poem to Whitman.

The one I give from the *Saturday Review* is especially brutal for the hatred felt for the poems would not permit the writer of the review to sanction the bestowing of any financial help on the poet. The period was when the poet's health and fame were at low ebb. It was not long after the Bayne article that Buchanan wrote a letter to the London *News* in behalf of the poet. The result was the hostile attack herein reprinted from the *Saturday Review,* March 18, 1876. Harwood was editor. Echoes of the battle were heard in America where Bayard Taylor in the *New York Tribune* wrote an editorial "In re Whitman," March 28, 1876. A few other hostile references to Whitman followed in later issues. The ever faithful John Burroughs and William D. O'Connor followed up by long defensive letters in the issues of April 13 and April 22, The *Tribune* continued an enemy and in a review of the 1881 volume had a hostile review, November 19, 1881, which is quoted by Bucke in his *Life of Whitman*. O'Connor continued defending the poet and devote much space to an attack in a review by Clarence Cooke in the early eighties in the *International Review*. The defence appears in the supplementary introduction he wrote to the reissue of his famous pamphlet *The Good Gray Poet* in Bucke's Life.

Buchanan did much service for Whitman's reputation. He, the avowed enemy of William Michael Rossetti and Swinburne, fought side by side with them for the American poet for many years. This fact should not be forgotten. In 1868 he had a magazine article on the poet in the *Broadway*, soon collected in his *David Gray* book. His letter to the *Daily News*, his account of his visit to the Socrates of Camden republished in *A Look Around Literature*, his biographer's report of his conversation with Robert Browning who attacked the poet, and his poems to the poet, constitute a monument to Buchanan.

The *Saturday Review* had published two earlier abusive articles on the poet, a very violent one on the occasion of Rossetti's selections, May 2, 1868, and a lengthy review of the first edition, March 15, 1856. The history of this review has not been recorded. The reviewer says some one had sent them (of course, it must have been the poet himself), a copy of Emerson's famous letter and three favourable reviews (which we now know Whitman wrote himself). Thus Whitman tried to win the English reviewer by the influence of his own favourable reviews. The review is made up of extracts from these and then from the preface of the book and the poems themselves. It recommended the throwing of the book into the fire.

XIV.   Lang's attack on *Tess of the D'Urbervilles*, is the second he made, he having previously criticised it in the *New Review.* The one I reprint is from *Longman's Magazine* (November, 1892), where he edited a monthly department called "At the Sign of the Ship." It was natural that the lover of Dumas, Scott and Stevenson, and the champion of romance against realism should write as he did. Stevenson also did not care for the novel because of the immoral tendencies. In our own day, George Moore has written an attack on some of Hardy's novels.

The article is interesting because it is really Lang's reply to Hardy's rejoinder in the Preface of *Tess* to Lang's first criticism of the novel.

XV.   It will be noticed that Henley's article from the *Pall Mall Magazine,* for December, 1901, is headed "R. L. S." These initials in quotation marks, ironically set there by Henley, were symbolic of the Stevenson myth that had grown up in only half a dozen years; for it was by his initials that Stevenson's friends, who wanted to overlook the truth about him, affectionately dubbed him.

Reading the article to-day, in the light of newly acquired facts about Stevenson's life, it seems rather tame. Instead of being a dastardly and unjust attack upon a friend's memory by one jealous of his success, the estimate is, as Stevenson's two latest biographers, Steuart and Hellman say, in the main right. In fact, one must admire Henley for having at the time told nothing derogatory of Stevenson, though he was in possession of many facts gleaned by these later biographers. How keen must have been the sensibilities of the critics in the last year of the Victorian reign, when they protested against this review of Graham Balfour's *Life* which really showed Stevenson as a "Seraph in Chocolate." Henley was justly incensed against Stevenson as a "Shorter Catechist," and from an intellectual point of view; though he may not have been fair when he doubted the sincerity of Stevenson. Henley was probably in the wrong when he wrote that now infamous letter marked private to Stevenson in the late eighties accusing Mrs. Stevenson of plagiarism even if she was guilty as charged.

The article is really not an attack on Stevenson, but upon the sugar-coated biography that deliberately concealed facts. Part of it tells of Henley's and Stevenson's collaboration at playwriting. Henley was right in refusing to go to Stevenson for morals, and refusing to place him with Dickens or Hazlitt.

The Henley article caused many protests among Stevenson's friends, notably Andrew Lang, who replied to it in *The Morning Post*.

ALBERT MORDELL

Philadelphia, January 25, 1926.

THE ROUND TABLE

By William Hazlitt

WHATEVER may have been the preponderating feelings with which we closed these volumes, we will not refuse our acknowledgments to Mr. Hazlitt for a few mirthful sensations which he has enabled us to mingle with the rest, by the hint that his Essays were meant to be "in the manner of the *Spectator* and *Tatler*." The passage in which this is conveyed happened to be nearly the last to which we turned; and we were about to rise from "the *Round Table*" heavily oppressed with a recollection of vulgar descriptions, silly paradoxes, flat truisms, misty sophistry, broken English, ill humour and rancorous abuse, when we were first informed of the modest pretensions of our host. Our thoughts then reverted with an eager impulse to the urbanity of Addison, his unassuming tone, and clear simplicity; to the ease and softness of his style, to the cheerful benevolence of his heart. The playful gaiety too, and the tender feelings of his coadjutor, poor Steele, came forcibly to our memory. The effect of the ludicrous contrast thus presented to us, it would be somewhat difficult to describe. We think that it was akin to what we have felt from the admirable nonchalance with which Liston, in the complex character of a weaver and an ass, seems to throw away all doubt of his being the most accomplished lover in the universe, and receives, as if they were merely his due, the caresses of the fairy Queen.

Amongst the objects which Mr. Hazlitt has thought it worth while, for the good of mankind, to take under his special superintendence, the "Manners" of the age have the first place. Nor are we surprised that this topic should have forced itself upon his attention: the circle in which he moves seems to be susceptible of great improvement, if an inference may be drawn from the account which he has given of its principal ornament. He informs us that one of his "most pleasant and least tiresome acquaintances is a humourist who has three or four quaint witticisms and proverbial phrases which he always repeats over and over." He appears also to have experienced some vile treatment from his intimate friends; as he is induced to protest that he "cannot help exclaiming against the gross and villainous trick which some people have when they wish to get rid of their company, of letting their fires go down and their candles run to seed."* That he has sufficient reasons therefore for directing his talents to the amelioration of manners, there can be no doubt:——the next point of importance is to ascertain the particular class of society upon which his habits of life have enabled him to make the most accurate observations, and to the improvement of which his labours are most likely to contribute. We are happy to have it in our power to state, that the objects of his most sedulous care are of the softer sex. It is not indeed the sex in general; but it is a highly interesting and amiable part of

* Vol. ii., p. 157.

it—that, namely, which passes under the denomination of "washerwoman." He professes more than once, with a laudable though unnecessary caution, that he is not used to "fashionable manners;" * and in perfect conformity with these protestations, he is sparing, even to abstemiousness, of all remarks upon gentlemen or gentlewomen: but, to make amends, when he gets amongst "the tub-tumbling viragoes," as he playfully calls them, he is quite at home: —his familiar acquaintance with all their ways makes him, in his own language, "over redundant;" and he dedicates one of his longest essays to a minute account of their appearance, their habits, and their conversation. To abridge this detail would, indeed, be to do it a gross injustice; the whole of it well deserves to be read, or at least, that highly finished part of it, which begins with—"How 'drat that Betty"—and ends with—"Him as has a niece and nevvy as they say eats him out of house and land."—We shall lay before our readers only one of the author's other pictures of social life, relying upon its being fully sufficient to convince them that this follower of the courtly Addison has opportunities, at least, which his "illustrious predecessor" never possessed; and that if he would but tell us all he has seen, we should be secure of obtaining many views of manners which have never yet appeared in print.

"Think," says he, "of a blooming girl who is condemned to open her mouth and shut her eyes, and see what heaven in the shape of a mischievous young fellow will send her!—up walks

* Vol. i., pp. 12, 125.

the aforesaid heaven or mischievous young fellow, (young Oura-nos, Hesiod would have called him,) and instead of a piece of paper, a thimble, or a cinder, claps into her mouth a peg of orange, or a long slice of citron."—v. ii. p. 125.

Let us pass from the subjects of Mr. Hazlitt's thoughts, to the style in which they are disclosed, and we shall find, in the first place, many convincing instances of the perfect success with which the freedom from affectation and para-dox, so characteristic of Addison, is imitated by his disciple.

Spleen is the soul of patriotism and of public good—v. ii. 79.
The definition of a true patriot is a good hater.—v. ii. 80.
He who speaks two languages has no country.—v. i. 238.
If the truth were known the most disagreeable people are the most amiable.—v. ii. 75.

Mr. Hazlitt, we should guess, is not quite disinterested in his endeavours to establish the truth of this last valuable apophthegm: and indeed there are many others of the same kind, in the enunciation of which he seems, clearly, to have been influenced by the benefit which he is likely to derive from them.

Few persons who have read the *Spectator* have ever afterwards forgotten the delightful papers on the *Paradise Lost*, or those on the Pleasures of the Imagination. In this department, as in others, Mr. Hazlitt is not willing to fall short of his "illustrious predecessor;" and accordingly we hear much of poetry, and of painting, and of music, and of *gusto*.* Of Hogarth, we are told that "he

* Here is one of the many definitions of this luminous writer, which possesses in an eminent degree the essential quality of being clearer than the word defined. Essay 29 "On Gusto," begins thus: "Gusto, in art, is power or passion defining any object!"

is too apt to perk morals and sentiments in your face, and is over redundant in his combinations." Of Titian, that "the *limbs* of his female figures have a luxurious softness and delicacy which appears *conscious* of the pleasure of the beholder." * Of Vandyke, that "the *impression slides* off from the eye, and does not, like the *tones* of Titian's *pencil, leave a sting* behind it in the mind of the spectator; †—and finally, that "the arts of painting and poetry flow from the sacred shrine of our own breasts, and are kindled at the living lamp of Nature." Addison and Steele never wrote anything so fine as this!

There is one merit which this author possesses besides that of successful imitation—he is a very eminent creator of words and phrases. Amongst a vast variety which have newly started into life we notice "firesider,"—"kitcheny," —"to smooth up,"—"to do off,"—and "to tiptoe down." To this we add a few of the author's newborn phrases, which bear sufficient marks of a kindred origin to entitle them to a place by their side. Such is the assertion that Spenser was "dipt in poetic luxury," the description of "a minute coil which clicks in the baking coal;" of "a numerousness scattering an individual gusto;" and of "curls that are ripe with sunshine."

Our readers are, perhaps, by this time as much acquainted with the style of this author as they have any desire to be; and their curiosity may have been a little excited to know what the man is. It may be told in two words:—he is a sour Jacobin: a fact which he is so good

---

* V. ii. 21.   † V. ii. 22.

as to disclose in the following pathetic lamentation over the failure of the French Revolution.

> The dawn of that day was overcast: that season of hope is past; it is fled with the other dreams of our youth which we cannot recall, but has left behind it traces which are not to be effaced by birthday and thanksgiving odes, or the chanting of Te Deums in all the churches of Christendom. To those hopes eternal regrets are due; to those who maliciously and wilfully blasted them, in the fear that they might be accomplished, we feel no less what we owe, hatred and scorn as lasting.

As we might expect from this confession of feeling, the waters of bitterness flow around this unhappy person unceasingly. There is nothing in the world which he seems to like, unless we except "washerwomen;" for whom he does appear to have some regard. He writes an essay in eager vituperation of "good nature" and good natured people: he abuses all poets, with the single exception of Milton: he, indeed, "was an honest man; he was Cromwell's secretary:" he abuses all country-people: he abuses the English: he abuses the Irish: he abuses the Scotch. Nor is it simply abuse; it is the language of Billingsgate, except that it is infinitely more rancorous than any thing which, we are willing to believe, he can have learnt in that school of natural civility. He seems to feel all the warmth of a private quarrel against whole nations; but against none so strongly as his own. Of poor John Bull his mildest expressions are that "he is silent because he has nothing to say and looks stupid because he is so:" that "if he has a red face and round belly he thinks himself a great man:" that "he has always been a surly, obstinate, meddlesome fellow:" that "he is but a dolt—beats his wife—quarrels with his neighbours —damns his servants, and gets drunk to kill the time." This rival of Pericles, in further eulogy of his countrymen, proceeds to state that "an Irishman who trusts to his principles, and a Scotchman who trusts to his impulses, are equally dangerous." Of the Irish he is moreover pleased to discover that "they are hypocrites in understanding—that there is something crude and discordant in all they do or say—that they are a wild people —that they betray principles, unite fierceness with levity, have an undercurrent of selfishness and cunning—and that their blood, if not heated by passion, turns to poison." All this is venomous enough. No abuse, however, which is directed against whole classes of men is of much importance: if undeserved it is utterly impotent and may well be utterly despised; but we shall be excused if stronger feelings have been roused by the foul and vulgar invective which is directed by such a thing as this against individuals who now rest in their graves, but who, in the bright career of their lives, were, perhaps, the chief sources of the glory which has been shed over our country in these latter times. Of Pitt it is said that he possessed "few talents and fewer virtues;" that his reputation was owing to "a negation (together with the common virtues) of the common vices of human nature, and by the complete negation of every other talent but an artful use of words and a certain dexterity of logical arrange-

ment;" that he had "no strong feelings, no distinct percep-
tions, no general principles, no comprehensive views of
things, no moral habits of thinking, no system of action,
no plan, no insight into human nature, no sympathy with
the passions of men or apprehension of their real designs,"
&c.—vol. ii. p. 164. Of Burke we have the following
character:

This man, who was a half poet and a half philosopher, has
done more mischief than perhaps any other person in the world.
His understanding was not competent to the discovery of any
truth, but it was sufficient to palliate a falsehood; his reasons,
of little weight in themselves, thrown into the scale of power,
were dreadful. Without genius to adorn the beautiful, he had
the art to throw a dazzling veil over the deformed and disgusting; and to strew the flowers of imagination over the rotten
carcass of corruption, not to prevent, but to communicate the
infection. His jealousy of Rousseau was one chief cause of his
opposition to the French Revolution. The writings of the one
had changed the institutions of a kingdom; while the speeches
of the other, with the intrigues of his whole party, had changed
nothing but the *turn-spit of the King's kitchen.* He would have
blotted out the broad pure light of Heaven, because it did not
first shine in at the little Gothic windows of St. Stephen's Chapel.
The genius of Rousseau had levelled the towers of the Bastile
with the dust; our zealous reformist, who would rather be doing
mischief than nothing, tried, therefore, to patch them up again,
by calling that loathsome dungeon the King's castle, and by
fulsome adulation of the virtues of a Court strumpet. This
man,—but enough of him here.—pp. 82, 83, note.

We are far from intending to write a single word in
answer to this loathsome trash; but we confess that these
passages chiefly excited us to take the trouble of noticing
the work. The author might have described washer-

women for ever; complimented himself unceasingly on his own "chivalrous eloquence;" prosed interminably about Chaucer; written, if possible, in a more affected, silly, confused, ungrammatical style, and believed, as he now believes, that he was surpassing Addison—we should not have meddled with him; but if the creature, in his endeavours to crawl into the light, must take his way over the tombs of illustrious men, disfiguring the records of their greatness with the slime and filth which marks his track, it is right to point him out that he may be flung back to the situation in which nature designed that he should grovel.

We learn from the Preface that a few of these essays were written by Mr. Hunt, the editor of the *Examiner* newspaper. We really have not time to discriminate between the productions of the two gentlemen, or to mete out to each his due portion of praise:—we beg that they will take the trouble to divide it themselves according to their respective claims. We can only mention here that Mr. Hunt sustains the part of the droll or merry fellow in the performance: it is he who entertains us with the account of his getting the nightmare by eating veal-pye, and who invents for that disorder the facetious name of Mnpvtglnau-auw-auww; who takes the trouble to inform us that he dislikes cats; to describe "the skillful spat of the finger nails which he gives his newspaper," and the mode in which he stirs his fire: it is he who devotes ten or twelve pages to the dissertation on "washerwomen," and who repeats, no doubt from faithful memory, the dialogues which pass between Betty and Molly, the maidservants, when they are first called in the morning, and describes, from actual observation, (or, it may be, experience,) the "conclusive digs in the side" with which Molly is accustomed to dispel the lingering slumbers of her bed-fellow.*

* *The Quarterly Review*, April 1817.   (William Gifford.)

ON THE COCKNEY SCHOOL OF POETRY

NO. I

Leigh Hunt

Our talk shall be (a theme we never tire on)
Of Chaucer, Spenser, Shakespeare, Milton,
    Byron,
(Our   England's   Dante)—Wordsworth—
    Hunt, and Keats,
The Muses' son of promise; and of what
    feats
He yet may do.

Cornelius Webb.

WHILE the whole critical world is occupied with balancing the merits, whether in theory or in execution, of what is commonly called The Lake School it is strange that no one seems to think it at all necessary to say a single word about another new school of poetry which has of late sprung up amongst us. This school has not, I believe, as yet received any name; but if I may be permitted to have the honour of christening it, it may henceforth be referred to by the designation of The Cockney School. Its chief Doctor and Professor is Mr. Leigh Hunt, a man certainly of some talents, of extravagant pretensions both in wit, poetry, and politics, and withal of exquisitely bad taste, and extremely vulgar modes of thinking and manners in all respects. He is a

man of little education. He knows absolutely nothing of
Greek, almost nothing of Latin, and his knowledge of
Italian literature is confined to a few of the most popular of Petrarch's sonnets, and an imperfect acquaintance
with Ariosto, through the medium of Mr. Hoole. As
to the French poets, he dismisses them in the mass as a
set of prim, precise, unnatural pretenders. The truth is,
he is in a state of happy ignorance about them and all
that they have done. He has never read *Zaire* nor
Phèdre. To those great German poets who have illuminated the last fifty years with a splendour to which this
country has, for a long time, seen nothing comparable,
Mr. Hunt is an absolute stranger. Of Spanish books he
has read *Don Quixote* (in the translation of Motteux),
and some poems of Lope de Vega in the imitations of my
Lord Holland. Of all the great critical writers, either of
ancient or of modern times, he is utterly ignorant, excepting only Mr. Jeffrey among ourselves.

With this stock of knowledge, Mr. Hunt presumes to
become the founder of a new school of poetry, and throws
away entirely the chance which he might have had of
gaining some true poetical fame, had he been less lofty
in his pretensions. *The Story of Rimini* is not wholly
undeserving of praise. It possesses some tolerable passages, which are all quoted in the *Edinburgh Reviewer's*
account of the poem, and not one of which is quoted in the
very illiberal attack upon it in the *Quarterly*. But such is
the wretched taste in which the greater part of the work is
executed, that most certainly no man who reads it once
will ever be able to prevail upon himself to read it again.

One feels the same disgust at the idea of opening *Rimini,* that impresses itself on the mind of a man of fashion, when he is invited to enter, for a second time, the gilded drawing-room of a little mincing boarding-school mistress, who would fain have an *At Home* in her house. Every thing is pretence, affectation, finery, and gaudiness. The beaux are attorneys' apprentices, with chapeau bras and Limerick gloves—fiddlers, harp teachers, and clerks of genius: the belles are faded fan-twinkling spinsters, prurient vulgar misses from school, and enormous citizens' wives. The company are entertained with lukewarm negus, and the sounds of a paltry piano forte.

All the great poets of our country have been men of some rank in society, and there is no vulgarity in any of their writings; but Mr. Hunt cannot utter a dedication, or even a note, without betraying the *Shibboleth* of low birth and low habits. He is the ideal of a Cockney Poet. He raves perpetually about "green fields," "jaunty streams," and "o'er-arching leafiness," exactly as a Cheapside shop-keeper does about the beauties of his box on the Camberwell road. Mr. Hunt is altogether unacquainted with the face of nature in her magnificent scenes; he has never seen any mountain higher than Highgate-hill, nor reclined by any stream more pastoral than the Serpentine River. But he is determined to be a poet eminently rural, and he rings the changes—till one is sick of him, on the beauties of the different "high views" which he has taken of God and nature, in the course of some Sunday dinner parties, at which he has assisted in the neighbourhood of London. His books are indeed not known in the country; his fame as a poet (and I might almost say, as a politician too) is entirely confined to the young attorneys and embryo-barristers about town. In the opinion of these competent judges, London is the world—and Hunt is a Homer.

Mr. Hunt is not disqualified by his ignorance and vulgarity alone, for being the founder of a respectable sect in poetry. He labours under the burden of a sin more deadly than either of these. The two great elements of all dignified poetry, religious feeling, and patriotic feeling, have no place in his writings. His religion is a poor tame dilution of the blasphemies of the *Encyclopædie*—his patriotism a crude, vague, ineffectual, and sour Jacobinism. His works exhibit no reverence either for God or man; neither altar nor throne have any dignity in his eyes. He speaks well of nobody but two or three great dead poets, and in so speaking of them he does well; but, alas! Mr. Hunt is no conjurer τεχνή 8 λανθανει. He pretends, indeed, to be an admirer of Spenser and Chaucer, but what he praises in them is never what is most deserving of praise—it is only that which he humbly conceives, bears some resemblance to the more perfect productions of Mr. Leigh Hunt; and we can always discover, in the midst of his most violent ravings about the court of Elizabeth, and the days of Sir Philip Sidney, and the Fairy Queen—that the real objects of his admiration are the Coterie of Hampstead and the Editor of the *Examiner*. When he talks about chivalry and King Arthur, he is always thinking of himself, and "*a small party of friends, who meet once a-week at a Round Table, to discuss the merits of a leg of mutton, and of the subjects upon which we are to write.*"—Mr. Leigh Hunt's ideas concerning the sublime, and concerning his own powers, bear a considerable resemblance to those of his friend Bottom, the weaver, on the same subjects; "I will roar, that it shall do any man's heart good to hear me"—"I will roar you an 'twere any nightingale."

The poetry of Mr. Hunt is such as might be expected from the personal character and habits of its author. As a vulgar man is perpetually labouring to be genteel—in like manner, the poetry of this man is always on the stretch to be grand. He has been allowed to look for a moment from the antechamber into the saloon, and mistaken the waving of feathers and the painted floor for the *sine qua non's* of elegant society. He would fain be always tripping and waltzing, and is sorry that he cannot be allowed to walk about in the morning with yellow breeches and flesh-coloured silk stockings. He sticks an artificial rosebud into his button hole in the midst of winter. He wears no neckcloth and cuts his hair in imitation of the Prints of Petrarch. In his verses he is always desirous of being airy, graceful, easy, courtly, and ITALIAN. If he had the smallest acquaintance with the great demi-gods of Italian poetry, he could never fancy that the style in which he writes, bears any, even the most remote resemblance to the severe and simple manner of Dante—the tender stillness of the lover of Laura—or the sprightly and good-natured unconscious elegance of the inimitable Ariosto. He has gone into a strange delusion about himself, and is just as absurd in supposing that he resembles the Italian Poets as a greater Quack still (Mr. Coleridge) is, in imagining that he is a Philosopher after the manner of Kant or Mendelssohn—and that "the eye of Lessing bears a remarkable likeness to MINE," i. e., the eye of Mr. Samuel Coleridge.*

The extreme moral depravity of the Cockney School is another thing which is for ever thrusting itself upon the public attention, and convincing every man of sense who looks into their productions, that they who sport such sentiments can never be great poets. How could any man of high original genius ever stoop publicly, at the present day, to dip his fingers in the least of those glittering and rancid obscenities which float on the surface of Mr. Hunt's Hippocrene? His poetry resembles that of a man who has kept company with kept-mistresses. His muse talks indelicately like a tea-sipping milliner girl. Some excuse for her there might have been, had she been hurried away by imagination or passion; but with her, indecency seems a disease, she appears to speak unclean things from perfect inanition. Surely they who are connected with Mr. Hunt by the tender relations of society, have good reason to complain that his muse should have been so prostituted. In *Rimini* a deadly wound is aimed at the dearest confidences of domestic bliss. The author has voluntarily chosen—a subject not of simple seduction alone—one in which his mind seems absolutely to gloat over all the details of adultery and incest.

---

* Mr. Wordsworth (meaning, we presume, to pay Mr. Coleridge a compliment,) makes him look very absurdly,
   "A noticeable man, with *large grey eyes.*"

The unhealthy and jaundiced medium through which the Founder of the Cockney School views every thing like moral truth, is apparent, not only from his obscenity, but also from his want of respect for all that numerous class of plain upright men, and unpretending women, in which the real worth and excellence of human society consists. Every man is, according to Mr. Hunt, a dull, potato-eating blockhead—of no greater value to God or man than any ox or dray-horse—who is not an admirer of Voltaire's *romans,* a worshipper of Lord Holland and Mr. Haydon, and a quoter of *John Buncle* and Chaucer's *Flower and Leaf.* Every woman is useful only as a breeding machine, unless she is fond of reading *Launcelot of the Lake,* in an antique summer-house.

How such an indelicate writer as Mr. Hunt can pretend to be an admirer of Mr. Wordsworth, is to us a thing altogether inexplicable. One great charm of Wordsworth's noble compositions consists in the dignified purity of thought, and the patriarchal simplicity of feeling, with which they are throughout penetrated and imbued. We can conceive a vicious man admiring with distant awe the spectacle of virtue and purity; but if he does so sincerely, he must also do so with the profoundest feeling of the error of his own ways, and the resolution to amend them. His admiration must be humble and silent, not pert and loquacious. Mr. Hunt praises the purity of Wordsworth as if he himself were pure, his dignity as if he also were dignified. He is always like the ball of Dung in the fable, pleasing himself, and amusing bye-standers with his "nos poma natamus." For the person who writes *Rimini,* to admire the *Excursion,* is just as impossible as it would be for a Chinese polisher of cherry-stones, or gilder of tea-cups, to burst into tears at the sight of the Theseus or the Torso.

The Founder of the Cockney School would fain claim poetical kindred with Lord Byron and Thomas Moore. Such a connection would be as unsuitable for them as for William Wordsworth. The days of Mr. Moore's follies are long since over; and, as he is a thorough gentleman, he must necessarily entertain the greatest contempt for such an under-bred person as Mr. Leigh Hunt. But Lord Byron! How must the haughty spirit of Lara and Harold contemn the subaltern sneaking of our modern tuft-hunter. The insult which he offered to Lord Byron in the dedication of *Rimini,*—in which he, a paltry cockney newspaper scribbler, had the assurance to address one of the most nobly-born of English Patricians, and one of the first geniuses whom the world ever produced, as "My dear Byron," although it may have been forgotten and despised by the illustrious person whom it most nearly concerned,—excited a feeling of utter loathing and disgust in the public mind, which will always be remembered whenever the name of Leigh Hunt is mentioned. We dare say Mr. Hunt has some fine dreams about the true nobility being the nobility of talent, and flatters himself, that with those who acknowledge only that sort of rank, he himself passes for being the *peer* of Byron. He is sadly mistaken. He is as completely a Plebeian in his mind as he is in his rank and station in society. To that highest and unalienable nobility which the great Roman satirist styles "sola atque unica," we fear his pretension would be equally unavailing.

The shallow and impotent pretensions, tenets, and attempts, of this man,—and the success with which his influence seems to be extending itself among a pretty numerous, though certainly a very paltry and pitiful, set of readers,—have for the last two or three years been considered by us with the most sickening aversion. The very culpable manner in which his chief poem was reviewed in the *Edinburgh Review* (we believe it is no secret, at his own impatient and feverish request, by his partner in the *Round Table*), was matter of concern to more readers than ourselves. The masterly pen which inflicted such signal chastisement on the early licentiousness of Moore, should not have been idle on that occasion. Mr. Jeffrey does ill when he delegates his important functions into such hands as those of Mr. Hazlitt. It was chiefly in consequence of that gentleman's allowing Leigh Hunt to pass unpunished through a scene of slaughter, which his execution might so highly have graced, that we came to the resolution of laying before our readers a series of essays on *the Cockney School*—of which here terminates the first.*

---

* *Blackwood's Magazine*, October, 1817.   (John G. Lockhart.)

SOME OBSERVATIONS ON THE *BIOGRAPHIA LITERARIA* OF S. T. COLERIDGE, ESQ.

WHEN a man looks back on his past existence, and endeavours to recall the incidents, events, thoughts, feelings, and passions of which it was composed, he sees something like a glimmering land of dreams, peopled with phantasms and realities undistinguishably confused and intermingled—here illuminated with dazzling splendour, there dim with melancholy mists,—or it may be shrouded in impenetrable darkness. To bring, visibly and distinctly, before our memory, on the one hand, all our hours of mirth and joy, and hope and exultation,—and, on the other, all our perplexities, and fears and sorrows, and despair and agony,—(and who has been so uniformly wretched as not to have been often blest?—who so uniformly blest as not to have been often wretched?)—would be as impossible as to awaken, into separate remembrance, all the changes and varieties which the seasons brought over the material world,—every gleam of sunshine that beautified the Spring,—every cloud and tempest that deformed the Winter. In truth, were this power and domination over the past given unto us, and were we able to read the history of our lives all faithfully and perspicuously recorded on the tablets of the inner spirit,—those

beings, whose existence had been most filled with important events and with energetic passions, would be the most
averse to such overwhelming survey—would recoil from
trains of thought which formerly agitated and disturbed,
and led them, as it were, in triumph beneath the yoke of
misery or happiness. The soul may be repelled from the
contemplation of the past as much by the brightness and
magnificence of scenes that shifted across the glorious
drama of youth, as by the storms that scattered the fair
array into disfigured fragments; and the melancholy that
breathes from vanished delight is, perhaps, in its utmost
intensity, as unendurable as the wretchedness left by the
visitation of calamity. There are spots of sunshine sleeping on the fields of past existence too beautiful, as there
are caves among its precipices too darksome, to be looked
on by the eyes of memory; and to carry on an image borrowed from the analogy between the moral and physical
world, the soul may turn away in sickness from the untroubled silence of a resplendent Lake, no less than from
the haunted gloom of the thundering Cataract. It is from
such thoughts, and dreams, and reveries, as these, that all
men feel how terrible it would be to live over again their
agonies and their transports; that the happiest would fear
to do so as much as the most miserable; and that to look
back to our cradle seems scarcely less awful than to look
forward to the grave.

But if this unwillingness to bring before our souls, in
distinct array, the more solemn and important events of
our lives, be a natural and perhaps a wise feeling, how
much more averse must every reflecting man be to the

ransacking of his inmost spirit for all its hidden emotions and passions, to the tearing away that shroud which oblivion may have kindly flung over his vices and his follies, or that fine and delicate veil which Christian humility draws over his virtues and acts of benevolence. To scrutinize and dissect the character of others is an idle and unprofitable task; and the most skilful anatomist will often be forced to withhold his hand when he unexpectedly meets with something he does not understand— some conformation of the character of his patient which is not explicable on his theory of human nature. To become operators on our own shrinking spirits is something worse; for by probing the wounds of the soul, what can ensue but callousness or irritability. And it may be remarked, that those persons who have busied themselves most with inquiries into the causes, and motives, and impulses of their actions, have exhibited, in their conduct, the most lamentable contrast to their theory, and have seemed blinder in their knowledge than others in their ignorance.

It will not be supposed that any thing we have now said in any way bears against the most important duty of self-examination. Many causes there are existing, both in the best and the worst parts of our nature, which must render nugatory and deceitful any continued diary of what passes through the human soul; and no such confessions could, we humbly conceive, be of use either to ourselves or to the world. But there are hours of solemn inquiry in which the soul reposes on itself; the true confessional is not the bar of the public, but it is the altar of religion;

there is a Being before whom we may humble ourselves
without being debased; and there are feelings for which
human language has no expression, and which, in the
silence of solitude and of nature, are known only unto the
Eternal.

The objections, however, which might thus be urged
against the writing and publishing accounts of all our
feelings,—all the changes of our moral constitution,—do
not seem to apply with equal force to the narration of our
mere speculative opinions. Their rise, progress, changes,
and maturity, may be pretty accurately ascertained; and as
the advance to truth is generally step by step, there seems
to be no great difficulty in recording the leading causes
that have formed the body of our opinions, and created,
modified, and coloured our intellectual character. Yet
this work would be alike useless to ourselves and others,
unless pursued with a true magnanimity. It requires, that
we should stand aloof from ourselves, and look down, as
from an eminence, on our souls toiling up the hill of
knowledge;—that we should faithfully record all the
assistance we received from guides or brother pilgrims;—
that we should mark the limit of our utmost ascent, and,
without exaggeration, state the value of our acquisitions.
When we consider how many temptations there are even
here to delude ourselves, and by a seeming air of truth
and candour to impose upon others, it will be allowed,
that, instead of composing memoirs of himself, a man of
genius and talent would be far better employed in general-
izing the observations and experiences of his life, and giving them to the world in the form of philosophic reflec-

tions, applicable not to himself alone, but to the universal
mind of Man.

What good to mankind has ever flowed from the confessions of Rousseau, or the autobiographical sketch of
Hume? From the first we rise with a confused and miserable sense of weakness and of power—of lofty aspirations
and degrading appetencies—of pride swelling into blasphemy, and humiliation pitiably grovelling in the dust—
of purity of spirit soaring on the wings of imagination,
and grossness of instinct brutally wallowing in "Epicurus'
stye,"—of lofty contempt for the opinion of mankind,
yet the most slavish subjection to their most fatal preju-
dices—of a sublime piety towards God, and a wild violation of his holiest laws. From the other we rise with
feelings of sincere compassion for the ignorance of the
most enlightened. All the prominent features of Hume's
character were invisible to his own eyes; and in that
meagre sketch which has been so much admired, what is
there to instruct, to rouse, or to elevate—what light
thrown over the duties of this life or the hopes of that
to come? We wish to speak with tenderness of a man
whose moral character was respectable, and whose talents
were of the first order. But most deeply injurious to
every thing lofty and high-toned in human Virtue, to
every thing cheering, and consoling, and sublime in that
Faith which sheds over this Earth a reflection of the
heavens, is that memoir of a worldly-wise Man; in which
he seems to contemplate with indifference the extinction
of his own immortal soul, and jibes and jokes on the dim
and awful verge of Eternity.

We hope that our readers will forgive these very imperfect reflections on a subject of deep interest, and accompany us now on our examination of Mr. Coleridge's *Literary Life,* the very singular work which caused our ideas to run in that channel. It does not contain an account of his opinions and literary exploits alone, but lays open, not infrequently, the character of the Man as well as of the Author; and we are compelled to think, that while it strengthens every argument against the composition of such Memoirs, it does, without benefitting the cause either of virtue, knowledge, or religion, exhibit many mournful sacrifices of personal dignity, after which it seems impossible that Mr. Coleridge can be greatly respected either by the Public or himself.

Considered merely in a literary point of view, the work is most execrable. He rambles from one subject to another in the most wayward and capricious manner; either from indolence, or ignorance, or weakness, he has never in one single instance finished a discussion; and while he darkens what was dark before into tenfold obscurity, he so treats the most ordinary common-places as to give them the air of mysteries, till we no longer know the faces of our old acquaintances beneath their cowl and hood, but witness plain flesh and blood matters of fact miraculously converted into a troop of phantoms. That he is a man of genius is certain; but he is not a man of a strong intellect nor of powerful talents. He has a great deal of fancy and imagination, but little or no real feeling, and certainly no judgment. He cannot form to himself any harmonious landscape such as it exists in nature, but beautified by

the serene light of the imagination. He cannot conceive
simple and majestic groups of human figures and characters acting on the theatre of real existence. But his
pictures of nature are fine only as imaging the dreami-
ness, and obscurity, and confusion of distempered sleep;
while all his agents pass before our eyes like shadows, and
only impress and affect us with a phantasmagorial splendour.

It is impossible to read many pages of this work without thinking that Mr. Coleridge conceives himself to be a
far greater man than the Public is likely to admit; and we
wish to waken him from what seems to us a most ludicrous
delusion. He seems to believe that every tongue is wag-
ging in his praise—that every ear is open to imbibe the
oracular breathings of his inspiration. Even when he
would fain convince us that his soul is wholly occupied
with some other illustrious character, he breaks out into
laudatory exclamations concerning himself; no sound is
so sweet to him as that of his own voice; the ground is
hallowed on which his footsteps tread; and there seems to
him something more than human in his very shadow. He
will read no books that other people read; his scorn is as
misplaced and extravagant as his admiration; opinions
that seem to tally with his own wild ravings are holy and
inspired; and, unless agreeable to his creed, the wisdom of
ages is folly; and wits, whom the world worship, dwarfed
when they approach his venerable side. His admiration
of nature or of man, we had almost said his religious feelings towards his God, are all narrowed, weakened, and
corrupted, and poisoned by inveterate and diseased ego-

tism; and instead of his mind reflecting the beauty and glory of nature, he seems to consider the mighty universe itself as nothing better than a mirror in which, with a grinning and idiot self-complacency, he may contemplate the Physiognomy of Samuel Taylor Coleridge. Though he has yet done nothing in any one department of human knowledge, yet he speaks of his theories, and plans, and views, and discoveries, as if he had produced some memorable revolution in Science. He at all times connects his own name in Poetry with Shakespeare, and Spenser, and Milton; in politics with Burke, and Fox, and Pitt; in metaphysics with Locke, and Hartley, and Berkely, and Kant—feeling himself not only to be the worthy compeer of those illustrious Spirits, but to unite, in his own mighty intellect, all the glorious powers and faculties by which they were separately distinguished, as if his soul were endowed with all human power, and was the depository of the aggregate, or rather the essence of all human knowledge. So deplorable a delusion as this, has only been equalled by that of Joanna Southcote, who mistook a complaint in the bowels for the divine afflatus; and believed herself about to give birth to the regenerator of the world, when sick unto death of an incurable and loathsome disease.

The truth is, that Mr. Coleridge is but an obscure name in English literature. In London he is well known in literary society, and justly admired for his extraordinary loquacity: he has his own little circle of devoted worshippers, and he mistakes their foolish babbling for the voice of the world. His name, too, has been often foisted into Reviews, and accordingly is known to many who never saw any of his works. In Scotland few know or care anything about him; and perhaps no man who has spoken and written so much, and occasionally with so much genius and ability, ever made so little impression on the public mind. Few people know how to spell or pronounce his name; and were he to drop from the clouds among any given number of well informed and intelligent men north of the Tweed, he would find it impossible to make any intelligible communication respecting himself; for of him and his writings there would prevail only a perplexing dream, or the most untroubled ignorance. We cannot see in what the state of literature would have been different, had he been cut off in childhood, or had he never been born; for except a few wild and fanciful ballads, he has produced nothing worthy remembrance. Yet, insignificant as he assuredly is, he cannot put pen to paper without a feeling that millions of eyes are fixed upon him and he scatters his *Sibylline Leaves* around him, with as majestical an air as if a crowd of enthusiastic admirers were rushing forward to grasp the divine promulgations, instead of their being, as in fact they are, coldly received by the accidental passenger, like a lying lottery puff or a quack advertisement.

This most miserable arrogance seems, in the present age, confined almost exclusively to the original members of the Lake School, and is, we think, worthy of especial notice, as one of the leading features of their character. It would be difficult to defend it either in Southey or Wordsworth; but in Coleridge it is altogether ridiculous.

Southey has undoubtedly written four noble Poems—
Thalaba, Madoc, Kehama, and *Roderick* and if the
Poets of this age are admitted, by the voice of posterity,
to take their places by the side of the Mighty of former
times in the Temple of Immortality, he will be one of
that sacred company. Wordsworth, too, with all his
manifold errors and defects, has, we think, won to himself a great name, and, in point of originality, will be
considered as second to no man of this age. They are
entitled to think highly of themselves, in comparison
with their most highly gifted contemporaries; and therefore, though their arrogance may be offensive, as it often
is, it is seldom or ever utterly ridiculous. But Mr. Coleridge stands on much lower ground, and will be known to
future times only as a man who overrated and abused his
talents—who saw glimpses of that glory which he could
not grasp—who presumptuously came forward to officiate
as High-Priest at mysteries beyond his ken—and who
carried himself as if he had been familiarly admitted into
the Penetralia of Nature, when in truth he kept perpetually stumbling at the very Threshold.

This absurd self-elevation forms a striking contrast with
the dignified deportment of all the other great living
Poets. Throughout all the works of Scott, the most orig-
inal-minded man of this generation of Poets, scarcely a
single allusion is made to himself; and then it is with a
truly delightful simplicity, as if he were not aware of
his immeasurable superiority to the ordinary run of mankind. From the rude songs of our forefathers he has
created a kind of Poetry, which at once brought over the

dull scenes of this our unimaginative life all the pomp, and glory, and magnificence of a chivalrous age. He speaks to us like some ancient Bard awakened from his tomb, and singing of visions not revealed in dreams, but contemplated in all the freshness and splendour of reality. Since he sung his bold, and wild, and romantic lays, a more religious solemnity breathes from our mouldering Abbeys, and a sterner grandeur frowns over our time-shattered Castles. He has peopled our hills with Heroes, even as Ossian peopled them; and, like a presiding spirit, his Image haunts the magnificent cliffs of our Lakes and Seas. And if he be, as every heart feels, the author of those noble Prose Works that continue to flash upon the world, to him exclusively belongs the glory of wedding Fiction and History in delighted union, and of embodying in imperishable records the manners, character, soul and spirit of Caledonia; so that, if all her annals were lost, her memory would in those Tales be immortal. His truly is a name that comes to the heart of every Briton with a start of exultation, whether it be heard in the hum of cities or in the solitude of nature. What has Campbell ever obtruded on the Public of his private history? Yet his is a name that will be hallowed for ever in the souls of pure, and aspiring, and devout youth, and to those lofty contemplations in which Poetry lends its aid to Religion, his immortal Muse will impart a more enthusiastic glow, while it blends in one majestic hymn all the noblest feelings which can spring from earth, with all the most glorious hopes that come from the silence of eternity. Byron indeed speaks of himself often, but his is like the voice of an angel heard crying in the storm or the whirl-wind; and we listen with a kind of mysterious dread to the tones of a Being whom we scarcely believe to be kindred to ourselves, while he sounds the depths of our nature, and illuminates them with the lightnings of his genius. And finally, who more gracefully unostentatious than Moore, a Poet who has shed delight, and joy, and rapture, and exultation, through the spirit of an enthusiastic People, and whose name is associated in his native Land with everything noble and glorious in the cause of Patriotism and Liberty. We could easily add to the illustrious list; but suffice it to say, that our Poets do in general bear their faculties meekly and manfully, trusting to their conscious powers, and the susceptibility of generous and enlightened natures, not yet extinct in Britain, whatever Mr. Cole-ridge may think; for certain it is, that a host of worship-pers will crowd into the Temple, when the Priest is in-spired, and the flame he kindles is from Heaven.

Such has been the character of great Poets in all coun-tries and in all times. Fame is dear to them as their vital existence—but they love it not with the perplexity of fear, but the calmness of certain possession. They know that the debt which nature owes them must be paid, and they hold in surety thereof the universal pas-sions of mankind. So Milton felt and spoke of himself, with an air of grandeur, and the voice as of an Archangel, distinctly hearing in his soul the music of after genera-tions, and the thunder of his mighty name rolling through the darkness of futurity. So divine Shakespeare felt and spoke; he cared not for the mere acclamations of his subjects; in all the gentleness of his heavenly spirit he felt himself to be their prophet and their king, and knew,

> When all the breathers of this world are dead,
> That he entombed in men's eyes would lie.

Indeed, who that knows anything of Poetry could for a moment suppose it otherwise? What ever made a great Poet but the inspiration of delight and love in himself, and an empassioned desire to communicate them to the wide spirit of kindred existence? Poetry, like Religion, must be free from all grovelling feelings; and above all, from jealousy, envy, and uncharitableness. And the true Poet, like the Preacher of the true religion, will seek to win unto himself and his Faith, a belief whose foundation is in the depths of love, and whose pillars are the noblest passions of humanity.

It would seem that in truly great souls all feeling of self-importance, in its narrower sense, must be incompatible with the consciousness of a mighty achievement. The idea of the mere faculty or power is absorbed as it were in the idea of the work performed. That work stands out in its glory from the mind of its Creator; and in the contemplation of it, he forgets that he himself was the cause of its existence, or feels only a dim but sublime association between himself and the object of his admiration; and when he does think of himself in conjunction with others, he feels towards the scoffer only a pitying sorrow for his blindness—being assured, that though at all times there will be weakness, and ignorance, and worthlessness, which can hold no communion with him or with his thoughts, so will there be at all times the pure, the noble, and the pious, whose delight it will be to love, to admire, and to imitate; and that never, at any point of time, past, present, or to come, can a true Poet be defrauded of his just fame.

But we need not speak of Poets alone (though we have done so at present to expose the miserable pretensions of Mr. Coleridge), but look through all the bright ranks of men distinguished by mental power, in whatever department of human science. It is our faith, that without moral there can be no intellectual grandeur; and surely the self-conceit and arrogance which we have been exposing, are altogether incompatible with lofty feelings and majestic principles. It is the Dwarf alone who endeavours to strut himself into the height of the surrounding company; but the man of princely stature seems unconscious of the strength in which nevertheless he rejoices, and only sees his superiority in the gaze of admiration which he commands. Look at the most inventive spirits of this country, —those whose intellects have achieved the most memorable triumphs. Take, for example, Leslie in physical science, and what airs of majesty does he ever assume? What is Samuel Coleridge compared to such a man? What is an ingenious and fanciful versifier to him who has, like a magician, gained command over the very elements of nature,—who has realized the fictions of Poetry, —and to whom Frost and Fire are ministering and obedient spirits? But of this enough.—It is a position that doubtless might require some modification, but in the main, it is and must be true, that real Greatness, whether in Intellect, Genius, or Virtue, is dignified and unostentatious; and that no potent spirit ever whimpered over the blindness of the age to his merits, and, like Mr. Coleridge, or a child blubbering for the moon, with clamorous outcries implored and imprecated reputation.

The very first sentence of this Literary Biography shows how incompetent Mr. Coleridge is for the task he has undertaken.

It has been my lot to have had my name introduced both in conversation and in print, more frequently than I find it easy to explain; *whether I consider the fewness, unimportance, and limited circulation of my writings, or the retirement and distance in which I have lived, both from the literary and political world.*

Now, it is obvious, that if his writings be few, and unimportant, and unknown, Mr. Coleridge can have no reason for composing his Literary Biography. Yet in singular contradiction to himself—

"If," says he, at page 217, vol. i., *"the composition which I have made public,* and that too in a form the most certain of an extensive circulation, though the least flattering to an author's self-love, had been published in books, they *would have filled a respectable number of volumes."*

He then adds,

Seldom have I written that in a day the acquisition or investigation of which had not cost me *the precious labour of a month!*

He then bursts out into this magnificent exclamation,

Would that the criterion of a scholar's ability were the number and moral value of the truths which he has been the means of throwing into general circulation!

And he sums up all by declaring,

By what I *have* effected am I to be judged by my fellow men.

The truth is, that Mr. Coleridge has lived, as much as any man of his time, in literary and political society, and that he has sought every opportunity of keeping himself in the eye of the public, as restlessly as any charlatan who ever exhibited on the stage. To use his own words, "In 1794, when I had barely passed the verge of manhood, I published a small volume of juvenile poems." These poems, by dint of puffing, reached a third edition; and though Mr. Coleridge pretends now to think but little of them, it is amusing to see how vehemently he defends them against criticism, and how pompously he speaks of such paltry trifles. "They were marked *by an ease and simplicity* which I have studied, *perhaps with inferior success,* to bestow on my later compositions." But he afterwards repents at this sneer at his later compositions, and tells us, that they have nearly reached his standard of perfection! Indeed, his vanity extends farther back than his juvenile poems; and he says, "For a school boy, I was *above par in English versification,* and had already produced two or three compositions, which I may venture to say, *without reference to my age, were somewhat above mediocrity.*" Happily he has preserved one of those wonderful productions of his precocious boyhood, and our readers will judge for themselves what a clever child it was.

> Underneath a huge oak-tree,
> There was of swine a huge company;
> That grunted as they crunch'd the mast,
> For that was ripe and fell full fast.
> Then they trotted away for the wind grew high,
> One acorn they left and no more might you spy.

It is a common remark, that wonderful children seldom perform the promises of their youth, and undoubtedly this fine effusion has not been followed in Mr. Coleridge's riper years by works of proportionate merit.

We see, then, that our author came very early into public notice; and from that time to this, he has not allowed one year to pass without endeavouring to extend his notoriety. His poems were soon followed (they may have been preceded) by a tragedy, entitled, the *Fall of Robespierre*, a meagre performance, but one which, from the nature of the subject, attracted considerable attention. He also wrote a whole book, utterly incomprehensible to Mr. Southey, we are sure, in that Poet's *Joan of Arc*; and became as celebrated for his metaphysical absurdities, as his friend had become for the bright promise of genius exhibited by that unequal, but spirited poem. He next published a Series of political essays, entitled, the *Watchman*, and *Conciones ad Populum*. He next started up, fresh from the schools of Germany, as the principal writer in the *Morning Post*, a *strong opposition paper*. He then published various outrageous political poems, some of them of a gross personal nature. He afterwards

assisted Mr. Wordsworth in planning his *Lyrical Ballads;*
and contributing several poems to that collection, he
shared in the notoriety of the Lake School.   He next published a mysterious periodical work, *The Friend,* in which
he declared it was his intention to settle at once, and for
ever, the principles of morality, religion, taste, manners,
and the fine arts, but which died of a galloping consumption in the twenty-eighth week of its age.   He then
published the tragedy of *Remorse,* which dragged out a
miserable existence of twenty nights, on the boards of
Drury-Lane, and then expired for ever, like the oil of the
orchestral lamps.   He then forsook the stage for the pulpit, and, by particular desire of his congregation, published
two *Lay Sermons.*   He then walked in broad day-light
into the shop of Mr. Murray, Albemarle Street, London,
with two ladies hanging on each arm, *Geraldine* and
Christabel,—a bold step for a person at all desirous of a
good reputation, and most of the trade have looked shy
at him since that exhibition.   Since that time, however, he
has contrived means of giving to the world a collected
edition of all his poems, and advanced to the front of the
stage with a thick octavo in each hand, all about himself
and other Incomprehensibilities.   We had forgot that he
was likewise a contributor to Mr. Southey's *Omniana,*
where the Editor of the *Edinburgh Review* is politely
denominated an "ass," and then *became himself a writer in
the said Review.*   And to sum up "the strange eventful
history" of this modest, and obscure, and retired person,
we must mention, that in his youth he held forth in a
vast number of Unitarian chapels—preached his way

through Bristol, and "Brummagem," and Manchester, in a "blue coat and white waistcoat;" and in after years, when he was not so much afraid of "the scarlet woman," did, in a full suit of sables, lecture on Poesy, to "crowded, and, need I add, highly respectable audiences," at the Royal Institution. After this slight and imperfect outline of his poetical, oratorical, metaphysical, political, and theological exploits, our readers will judge, when they hear him talking of "his retirement and distance from the literary and political world," what are his talents for autobiography, and how far he has penetrated into the mysterious nonentities of his own character.

Mr. Coleridge has written copiously on the Association of Ideas, but his own do not seem to be connected either by time, place, cause and effect, resemblance, or contrast, and accordingly it is no easy matter to follow him through all the vagaries of his Literary Life. We are told,

At school *I enjoyed the inestimable advantage* of a very sensible, though at the same time a very severe master. * * * I learnt from him that Poetry, even that of the loftiest and wildest odes, had a logic of its own as severe as that of science. * * * * * Lute, harp, and lyre; muse, muses, and inspirations; Pegasus, Parnassus, and Hippocrene; were all an abomination to him. In fancy I can almost hear him now exclaiming, '*Harp? Harp? Lyre? Pen and Ink! Boy you mean! Muse! boy! Muse! your Nurse's daughter you mean! Pierian Spring! O Aye! the cloister Pump!*' * * * * Our classical knowledge was the least of the good gifts which we derived from his zealous and conscientious tutorage.

With the then head-master of the grammar-school, Christ Hospital, we were not personally acquainted; but

we cannot help thinking that he has been singularly unfortunate in his Eulogist. He seems to have gone out of
his province, and far out of his depth, when he attempted
to teach boys the profoundest principles of Poetry. But
we must also add, that we cannot credit this account of
him; for this doctrine of poetry being at all times logical,
is that of which Wordsworth and Coleridge take so much
credit to themselves for the discovery; and verily it is
one too wilfully absurd and extravagant to have entered
into the head of an honest man, whose time must have
been wholly occupied with the instruction of children.
Indeed Mr. Coleridge's own poetical practices render this
story incredible; for, during many years of his authorship,
his diction was wholly at variance with such a rule, and the
strain of his poetry as illogical as can be well imagined.
When Mr. Bowyer prohibited his pupils from using, in
their themes, the above mentioned names, he did, we
humbly submit, prohibit them from using the best means
of purifying their taste and exalting their imagination.
Nothing could be so graceful, nothing so natural, as classical allusions, in the exercises of young minds, when first
admitted to the fountains of Greek and Latin Poetry;
and the Teacher who could seek to dissuade their in-
genuous souls from such delightful dreams, by coarse,
vulgar, and indecent ribaldry, instead of deserving the
name of "sensible," must have been a low-minded vulgar
fellow, fitter for the Porter than Master of such an Establishment. But the truth probably is, that all this is a
fiction of Mr. Coleridge, whose wit is at all times most
execrable and disgusting. Whatever the merits of his

Master were, Mr. Coleridge, even from his own account, seems to have derived little benefit from his instruction, and for the "inestimable advantage," of which he speaks, we look in vain through this Narrative. In spite of so excellent a teacher, we find Master Coleridge,

> Even before my fifteenth year, bewildered *in metaphysicks and in theological controversy.* Nothing else pleased me. *History and particular facts* lost all interest in my mind. Poetry itself, yea novels and romances, became insipid to me. This preposterous pursuit was beyond doubt *injurious, both to my natural powers and to the progress of my education.*

This deplorable condition of mind continued "even unto my seventeenth year." And now our readers must prepare themselves for a mighty and wonderful change, wrought, all on a sudden, on the moral and intellectual character of this metaphysical Greenhorn. *"Mr. Bowles' Sonnets, twenty in number, and just then published in a quarto volume* (a most important circumstance!) *were put into my hand!"* To those sonnets, next to the Schoolmaster's lectures on Poetry, Mr. Coleridge attributes the strength, vigour, and extension, of his own very original Genius.

> By those works, year after year, I was enthusiastically delighted and inspired. My earliest acquaintances will not have forgotten the undisciplined eagerness and impetuous zeal with which I labour'd to make proselytes, not only *of my companions, but of all with whom I conversed, of whatever rank, and in whatever place.* As my school finances did not permit me to purchase copies, I made, within less than a year and a half, *more than forty transcriptions, as the best presents I could make to those who had in any way won my regard.* My obligations to Mr. Bowles were indeed important, and for radical good!

There must be some grievous natural defect in that mind which, even at the age of seventeen, could act so insanely; and we cannot but think, that no real and healthy sensibility could have exaggerated to itself so grossly the merits of Bowles' Sonnets. They are undoubtedly most beautiful, and we willingly pay our tribute of admiration to the genius of the amiable writer; but they neither did nor could produce any such effects as are here described, except upon a mind singularly weak and helpless. We must, however, take the fact as we find it; and Mr. Coleridge's first step, after his worship of Bowles, was to see distinctly into the defects and deficiencies of Pope (a writer whom Bowles most especially admires, and has edited), and through all the false diction and borrowed plumage of Gray! * But here Mr. Coleridge drops the subject of Poetry for the present, and proceeds to other important matters.

> Fair laughs the Morn, and soft the Zephyr blows,
>   While proudly riding o'er the azure realm,
> In gallant trim the gilded Vessel goes,
>   Youth at the Prow, and Pleasure at the Helm!
> Regardless of the sweeping Whirlwind's sway,
> That, bush'd in grim repose, expects its evening **Prey.**
> <div align="right">GRAY's <i>Bard.</i></div>

---

* There is something very offensive in the high and contemptuous tone which Wordsworth and Coleridge assume, when speaking of this great Poet. They employ his immortal works as a text-book, from which they quote imaginary violations of logic and sound sense, and examples of vicious poetic diction. Mr. Coleridge informs us that Wordsworth "couched him," and that, from the moment of the operation, his eyes were startled with the deformities of the *Bard* and the *Elegy in*

On this beautiful and sublime passage Mr. Coleridge
has not one word of admiration to bestow, but tells us with
a sneer (for what reason we know not), that "realm" and
"sway" are rhymes dearly purchased. He then says, "that
it depended wholly in the compositor's putting or not
putting *a small capital*, both in this and in many other passages of the same Poet, whether the words should be per-
sonifications or mere abstracts." This vile absurdity is followed by a direct charge of Plagiarism from Shakespeare.

> How like a younker or a prodigal
> The skarfed bark puts from her native bay,
> Hugg'd and embraced by the strumpet wind!
> How like a prodigal doth she return,
> With over-weather'd ribs and ragged sails,
> Torn, rent, and beggar'd by the strumpet wind!
>   SHAKESPEARE.

Now we put it to our readers to decide between us and the
Critic. We maintain that here there is no plagiarism nor
imitation. Both Poets speak of a Ship, and there all likeness ends. As well might Falconer be accused of imitation in his glorious description of a vessel in full sail leaving harbour—or Scott, in his animated picture of Bruce's
galley beating through the Sound of Mull—or Byron, in
his magnificent sketch of the Corsair's war-ship—or
Wordsworth, in his fine simile of a vessel "that hath the
plain of Ocean for her own domain"—or Wilson, in his
vision of the moonlight vessel sailing to the Isle of Palms

---

the Country Church-yard! Such despicable fooleries are perhaps beneath notice; but we must not allow the feathers of a
Bird of Paradise to be pecked at by such a Daw as Coleridge.

—or the Ettrick Shepherd, in his wild dream of the Abbot's pinnace buried in the breakers of Staffa—or Mr. Coleridge himself, in his spectre-ship in the *Ancient Mariner*. For, in the first place, Shakespeare describes his ship by likening it *to something else, namely, a prodigal;* and upon that moral meaning depends the whole beauty of the passage. Of this there is nothing in Gray. Secondly, Shakespeare does not speak of any ship in particular, *but generally.* The beauty of the passage in Gray depends on its being *prophetic of a particular misfortune,* namely, the drowning of young Prince Henry. Thirdly, in Shakespeare, the vessel "puts from her native bay;" and upon that circumstance the whole description depends. In Gray we only behold her majestically sailing in the open sea. Fourthly, in Shakespeare "she returns;" but in Gray she is the prey of the evening whirlwind. Fifthly, in Shakespeare she returns "with over-weather'd ribs and ragged sails." In Gray she is sunk into the deep, "with all her bravery on." Sixthly, in Gray we behold a joyous company on her deck, "Youth at her prow, and Pleasure at her Helm;" but in Shakespeare we never think of her deck at all. Seventhly, in Shakespeare she is a "skarfed bark;" in Gray, a "gilded vessel." Eighthly, Shakespeare has, in the whole description, studiously employed the most plain, homely, familiar, and even unpoetical diction, and thereby produced the desired effect. Gray has laboured his description with all the resources of consummate art, and it is eminently distinguished for pomp, splendour, and magnificence. Lastly, except articles, prepositions, and conjunctions, there is not *a single word common*

to the two passages; so that they may indeed with pro-
priety be quoted, to shew how *differently* the same object
can appear to different poetical minds; but Mr. Coleridge
"has been couched," and Mr. Wordsworth having performed the operation unskilfully, the patient is blind.

We regret that Mr. Coleridge has passed over without
notice all the years which he spent "in the happy quiet
of ever-honoured Jesus College, Cambridge." That must
have been the most important period of his life, and was
surely more worthy of record than the metaphysical
dreams or the poetical extravagancies of his boyhood.
He tells us, that he was sent to the University "an excellent Greek and Latin scholar, and a tolerable
Hebraist;" and there might have been something rousing
and elevating to young minds of genius and power, in his
picture of himself, pursuits, visions, and attainments, during the bright and glorious morning of life, when he
inhabited a dwelling of surpassing magnificence, guarded,
and hallowed, and sublimed by the Shadows of the
Mighty. We should wish to know what progress he
made there in his own favourite studies; what place he
occupied, or supposed he occupied, among his numerous
contemporaries of talent; how much he was inspired by
the genius of the place; how far he "pierced the caves of
old Philosophy," or sounded the depths of the Physical
Sciences.* All this unfortunately is omitted, and he

---

* The fact is, that Mr. Coleridge made no figure at the
University. He never could master the simplest elements of the
mathematics. Yet in all his metaphysical, and indeed many of
his critical writings, there is an ostentatious display of a familiar

hurries on to details often trifling and uninfluential, sometimes low, vile, and vulgar, and, what is worse, occasionally inconsistent with any feeling of personal dignity and
self-respect.

After leaving College, instead of betaking himself to
some respectable calling, Mr. Coleridge, with his characteristic modesty, determined to set on foot a periodical
work called *The Watchman*, that through it *"all might
know the truth."* The price of this very useful article
was *"four-pence."* Off he set on a tour to the north to
procure subscribers, "preaching in most of the great towns
as a hireless Volunteer, in a blue coat and white waistcoat, that not a rag of the Woman of Babylon might be
seen on me." In preaching, his object was to shew that
our Saviour was the real son of Joseph, and that the Cruci-
fixion was a matter of small importance. Mr. Coleridge
is now a most zealous member of the Church of England
—devoutly believes every iota in the thirty-nine articles,
and that the Christian Religion is only to be found in its
purity in the homilies and liturgy of that Church. Yet,
on looking back to his Unitarian zeal, he exclaims,

---

and profound knowledge of the principles of that science. This
is dishonest quackery; for Mr. Coleridge knows that he could
not, if taken by surprise, demonstrate any one proposition in the
first book of Euclid. His classical knowledge was found at the
University to be equally superficial. He gained a prize there for
a Greek Ode, which for ever blasted his character as a scholar;
all the rules of that language being therein perpetually violated.
We were once present in a literary company, where Porson
offered to shew in it, to a gentleman who was praising this Ode,
134 examples of bad Greek.

O, never can I remember those days *with either shame or regret!* For I was *most sincere, most disinterested!* *.Wealth, rank, life itself,* then seem'd cheap to me, compared with the interests of truth, and the will of my Maker. I cannot even accuse myself of having been actuated by *vanity!* for in the expansion of my enthusiasm *I did not think of myself at all!*

This is delectable. What does he mean by saying that life seemed cheap? What danger could there be in the performance of his exploits, except that of being committed as a Vagrant? What indeed could rank appear to a person thus voluntarily degraded? Or who would expect vanity to be conscious of its own loathsomeness? During this tour he seems to have been constantly exposed to the insults of the vile and the vulgar, and to have associated with persons whose company must have been most odious to a Gentleman. Greasy Tallow-chandlers, and pursey Woollen-drapers, and grim-featured dealers in Hard-ware, were his associates at Manchester, Derby, Nottingham, and Sheffield; and among them the light of truth was to be shed from its cloudy tabernacle in Mr. Coleridge's Pericranium. At the house of a "Brummagem Patriot" he appears to have got dead drunk with strong ale and tobacco, and in that pitiable condition he was exposed to his disciples, lying upon a sofa, "with my face like a wall that is white-washing, *deathy* pale, and with the cold drops of perspiration running down it from my forehead." Some one having said, "Have you seen a paper to-day, Mr. Coleridge?" the wretched man replied, with all the staring stupidity of his lamentable condition, "Sir! I am far from convinced that a Christian is permitted to read either newspapers, or any other words of merely political and temporary interest." This witticism quite enchanted his enlightened auditors, and they prolonged their festivities to an "early hour next morning." Having returned to London with a thousand subscribers on his list, the *Watchman* appeared in all his glory; but, alas! not on the day fixed for the first burst of his effulgence; which foolish delay incensed many of his subscribers. The *Watchman*, on his second appearance, spoke blasphemously, and made indecent applications of Scriptural language; then, instead of abusing Government and Aristocrats, as Mr. Coleridge had pledged himself to his constituents to do, he attacked his own Party; so that in seven weeks, before the shoes were old in which he travelled to Sheffield, the *Watchman* went the way of all flesh, and his remains were scattered "through sundry old iron shops," where for one penny could be purchased each precious relic. To crown all, "his London Publisher was a——;" and Mr. Coleridge very narrowly escaped being thrown into gaol for his heroic attempt to shed over the manufacturing towns the illumination of knowledge. We refrain from making any comments on this deplorable story.

This Philosopher, and Theologian, and Patriot, now retired to a village in Somersetshire, and, after having sought to enlighten the whole world, discovered that he himself was in utter darkness.

Doubts rushed in, broke upon me from the fountains of the great deep, and fell from the windows of heaven. The fontal truths of natural Religion, and the book of Revelation, alike contributed to the flood; and it was long ere my Ark touched upon Ararat, and rested. My head was with Spinoza, though my heart was with Paul and John.

At this time, "by a gracious Providence, for which I can never be sufficiently grateful, the generous and munificent patronage of Mr. Josiah and Mr. Thomas Wedgewood enabled me to finish my education in Germany." All this is very well; but what Mr. Coleridge learnt in Germany we know not, and seek in vain to discover through these volumes. He tells us that the Antijacobin wits accused him of abandoning his wife and children, and implicated in that charge his friends Mr. Robert Southey and Mr. Charles Lamb. This was very unjust; for Mr. Southey is, and always was, a most exemplary Family-man, and Mr. Lamb, we believe, is still a Bachelor. But Mr. Coleridge assumes a higher tone than the nature of the case demands or justifies, and his language is not quite explicit. A man who abandons his wife and children is undoubtedly both a wicked and pernicious member of society; and Mr. Coleridge ought not to deal in general and vague terms of indignation, but boldly affirm, if he dare, that the charge was false then, and would be false now, if repeated against himself. Be this as it may, Mr. Coleridge has never received any apology from those by whom he was insulted and accused of disgraceful crime; and yet has he, with a humility most unmanly, joined their ranks, and become one of their most slavish Sycophants.

On his return from Germany, he became the principal writer of the political and literary departments of the

Morning Post. This, though unquestionably a useful, respectable, and laborious employment, does not appear to us at all sublime; but Mr. Coleridge thinks otherwise —compares himself, the Writer of the leading Article, to Edmund Burke—and, for the effect which his writings produced on Britain, refers us to the pages of the *Morning Chronicle.* In this situation, he tells us that "he wasted the prime and manhood of his intellect," but "added nothing to his reputation or fortune, the industry of the week supplying the necessities of the week." Yet the effects of his labours were wonderful and glorious. He seems to think that he was the cause of the late War; and that, in consequence of his Essays in the *Morning Post,* he was, during his subsequent residence in Italy, the specified object of Bonaparte's resentment. Of this he was warned by Baron Von Humboldt and Cardinal Fesch; and he was saved from arrest by a Noble Benedictine, and the "gracious connivance of that good old man the Pope!" We know of no parellel to such insane vanity as this, but the case of the celebrated John Dennis, who, when walking one day on the sea-beach, imagined a large ship sailing by to have been sent by Ministry to capture him; and who, on another occasion, waited on the Duke of Marlborough, when the congress for the peace of Utrecht was in agitation, to entreat his interest with the plenipotentiaries, that they should not consent to his being given up. The Duke replied, that he had not got himself excepted in the articles of peace, yet he could not help thinking that he had done the French almost as much damage as even Mr. Dennis.

We have no room here to expose, as it deserves to be exposed, the multitudinous political inconsistence of Mr. Coleridge, but we beg leave to state one single fact: He abhorred, hated, and despised Mr. Pitt,—and he now loves and reveres his memory. By far the most spirited and powerful of his poetical writings, is the *War Eclogue, Slaughter, Fire, and Famine;* and in that composition he loads the Minister with imprecations and curses, long, loud, and deep. But afterwards, when he has thought it prudent to change his Principles, he denies that he ever felt any indignation towards Mr. Pitt; and with the most unblushing falsehood declares, that at the very moment his muse was consigning him to infamy, death, and damnation, he would "have interposed his body between him and danger." We believe that all good men, of all parties, regard Mr. Coleridge with pity and contempt.

Of the latter days of his literary life, Mr. Coleridge gives us no satisfactory account. The whole of the second volume is interspersed with mysterious inuendoes. He complains of the loss of all his friends, not by death, but estrangement. He tries to account for the enmity of the world to him, a harmless and humane man, who wishes well to all created things, and "of his wondering finds no end." He upbraids himself with indolence, procrastination, neglect of his worldly concerns, and all other bad habits,—and then, with incredible inconsistency, vaunts loudly of his successful efforts in the cause of Literature, Philosophy, Morality, and Religion. Above all, he weeps and wails over the malignity of Reviewers, who have

persecuted him almost from his very cradle, and seem
resolved to bark him into the grave. He is haunted by
the Image of a Reviewer wherever he goes. They "push
him from his stool," and by his bedside they cry, "Sleep
no more." They may abuse whomsoever they think fit,
save himself and Mr. Wordsworth. All others are fair
game—and he chuckles to see them brought down. But
his sacred person must be inviolate, and rudely to touch
it, is not high treason, it is impiety. Yet his "ever-
honoured friend, the laurel-honouring Laureate," is a
Reviewer—his friend Mr. Thomas Moore is a Reviewer
—his friend Dr. Middleton, Bishop of Calcutta, was the
Editor of a Review—almost every friend he ever had is
a Reviewer;—and to crown all, he himself is a Reviewer.
Every person who laughs at his silly Poems—and his
incomprehensible metaphysics, is malignant—in which
case, there can be little benevolence in this world; and
while Mr. Francis Jeffrey is alive and merry, there can
be no happiness here below for Mr. Samuel Coleridge.

And here we come to speak of a matter, which, though
somewhat of a personal and private nature, is well deserving of mention in a Review of Mr. Coleridge's *Literary Life,* for sincerity is the first of virtues, and without
it no man can be respectable or useful. He has, in this
work, accused Mr. Jeffrey of meanness—hypocrisy—
falsehood—and breach of hospitality. That gentleman
is able to defend himself—and his defence is no business
of ours. But we now tell Mr. Coleridge, that instead
of humbling his adversary, he has heaped upon his own
head the ashes of disgrace—and with his own blundering

hands, so stained his character as a man of honour and high principles, that the mark can never be effaced. All the most offensive attacks on the writings of Wordsworth and Southey, had been made by Mr. Jeffrey before his visit to Keswick. Yet, does Coleridge receive him with open arms, according to his own account—listen, well-pleased, to all his compliments—talk to him for hours on his Literary Projects—dine with him as his guest at an Inn—tell him that he knew Mr. Wordsworth would be most happy to see him—and in all respects behave to him with a politeness bordering on servility. And after all this, merely because his own vile verses were crumpled up like so much waste paper, by the grasp of a powerful hand in the *Edinburgh Review*, he accuses Mr. Jeffrey of abusing hospitality which he never received, and forgets, that instead of being the host, he himself was the smiling and obsequious guest of the man he pretends to have despised. With all this miserable forgetfulness of dignity and self-respect, he mounts the high horse, from which he instantly is tumbled into the dirt; and in his angry ravings collects together all the foul trash of literary gossip to fling at his adversary, but which is blown stifling back upon himself with odium and infamy. But let him call to mind his own conduct, and talk not of Mr. Jeffrey. Many witnesses are yet living of his own egotism and malignity; and often has he heaped upon his "beloved Friend, the laurel-honouring Laureate," epithets of contempt, and pity, and disgust, though now it may suit his paltry purposes to worship and idolize. Of Mr. Southey we at all times think, and shall speak, with respect and admiration; but his open adversaries are, like Mr. Jeffrey, less formidable than his unprincipled friends. When Greek and Trojan meet on the plain, there is an interest in the combat; but it is hateful and painful to think, that a hero should be wounded behind his back, and by a poisoned stiletto in the hand of a false friend.*

The concluding chapter of this Biography is perhaps the most pitiful of the whole, and contains a most surprising mixture of the pathetic and the ludicrous.

"Strange," [says he] "as the delusion may appear, yet it is most true, that three years ago I did not know or believe that I had an enemy in the world; and now even my strongest consolations of gratitude are mingled with fear, and I reproach myself for being too often disposed to ask,—Have I one friend?"

We are thus prepared for the narration of some griev-ous cruelty, or ingratitude, or malice,—some violation

---

* In the *Examiner* of April 6th, 1817, there is a letter, signed "Vindex," from which the following extract is taken.

'The author of the "Friend" is troubled at times and seasons with a treacherous memory; but perhaps he *may* remember a visit to Bristol. He *may* remember—(I allude to no confidential whisperings—no unguarded private moments,—but to facts of open and ostentatious notoriety)—He may remember, *publicly*, before several strangers, and in the midst of a public library, turning into the most merciless ridicule "the dear Friend" whom he now calls Southey the Philologist, "Southey the Historian," Southey the Poet of Thalaba, the Madoc, and the Roderic. Mr. Coleridge recited an Ode of his dear Friend, in the hearing of these persons, with a tone and manner of the most contemptuous burlesque, and accused him of having stolen from Wordsworth images which he knew not how to use. Does he remember, that

of his peace, or robbery of his reputation; but our readers
will start when they are informed, that this melancholy
lament is occasioned solely by the cruel treatment which
his poem of *Christabel* received from the *Edinburgh Review* and other periodical Journals!   It was, he tells us,
universally admired in manuscript—he recited it many
hundred times to men, women and children, and always
with an electrical effect—it was bepraised by most of the
great Poets of the day—and for twenty years he was
urged to give it to the world.   But alas! no sooner had the
Lady Christabel "come out," than all the rules of good-
breeding and politeness were broken through, and the
loud laugh of scorn and ridicule from every quarter as-
sailed the ears of the fantastic Hoyden.   But let Mr.
Coleridge be consoled.   Mr. Scott and Lord Byron are
good-natured enough to admire Christabel, and the Public
have not forgotten that his Lordship handed her Ladyship
upon the stage.   It is indeed most strange, that Mr.
Coleridge is not satisfied with the praise of those he ad-

---

he also took down the *Joan of Arc,* and recited, in the same
ridiculous tone (I do not mean his *usual* tone, but one which he
meant should be ridiculous) more than a page of the poem, with
the ironical comment, "*This*, gentlemen, *is Poetry?*"   Does he
remember that he then recited, by way of contrast, some forty
lines of his cwn contribution to the same poem, in his usual
bombastic manner? and that after this disgusting display of
egotism and malignity, he observed, "Poor fellow, he may be a
Reviewer, but Heaven bless the man if he thinks himself a
Poet?"

Absentem qui rodit amicum
Hic *niger est:* hunc tu Romane caveto.'
                                        VINDEX.

mires,—but pines away for the commendation of those he contemns.

Having brought down his literary life to the great epoch of the publication of *Christabel*, he there stops short; and that the world may compare him as he appears at that era to his former self, when "he set sail from Yarmouth on the morning of the 10th September, 1798, in the Hamburg Packet," he has republished, from his periodical work the *Friend*, seventy pages of Satyrane's *Letters*. As a specimen of his wit in 1798, our readers may take the following:—

We were all on the deck, but in a short time I observed marks of dismay. The Lady retired to the cabin in some confusion; and many of the faces round me assumed a very doleful and frog-coloured appearance; and within an hour the number of those on deck was lessened by one half. I was giddy, but not sick; and the giddiness soon went away, but left a feverishness and want of appetite, which I attributed, in great measure, to the *"sæva mephitis"* of the bilge-water; and it was certainly not decreased by the *exportations from the cabin.* However, I was well enough to join the able-bodied passengers, one of whom observed, not inaptly, that Momus might have discovered an easier *way to see a man's inside* than by placing a window in his breast. He needed only have taken a salt-water trip in a packet-boat. I am inclined to believe, that a packet is far superior to a stage-coach as a means of making men *open out to each other!*

The importance of his observations during the voyage may be estimated by this one:—

At four o'clock I observed a wild duck swimming on the waves, *a single solitary wild duck!* It is not easy to conceive how interesting a thing it looked in that round objectless desert of waters!

At the house of Klopstock, brother of the Poet, he saw a portrait of Lessing, which he thus describes to the Public. "His eyes were uncommonly *like mine!* if any thing, rather larger and more prominent! But the lower part of his face! and his nose—O what an exquisite expression of elegance and sensibility!" He then gives a long account of his interview with Klopstock the Poet, in which he makes that great man talk in a very silly, weak, and ignorant manner. Mr. Coleridge not only sets him right in all his opinions on English literature, but also is kind enough to correct, in a very authoritative and dictatorial tone, his erroneous views of the characteristic merits and defects of the most celebrated German Writers. He has indeed the ball in his own hands throughout the whole game; and Klopstock, who, he says, "was seventy-four years old, with legs enormously swollen," is beaten to a standstill. We are likewise presented with an account of a conversation which his friend W. held with the German Poet, in which the author of the *Messiah* makes a still more paltry figure. We can conceive nothing more odious and brutal, than two young ignorant lads from Cambridge forcing themselves upon the retirement of this illustrious old man, and, instead of listening with love, admiration, and reverence, to his sentiments and opinions, insolently obtruding upon him their own crude and mistaken fancies,—contradicting imperiously everything he advances,—taking leave of him with a consciousness of their own superiority,—and, finally, talking of him and his genius in terms of indifference bordering on contempt. This Mr. W. had the folly and the insolence to say to

Klopstock, who was enthusiastically praising the *Oberon* of Wieland, that he never could see the smallest beauty in any part of that Poem.

We must now conclude our account of this "unaccountable" production. It has not been in our power to enter into any discussion with Mr. Coleridge on the various subjects of Poetry and Philosophy, which he has, we think, vainly endeavoured to elucidate. But we shall, on a future occasion, meet him on his own favourite ground. No less than 182 pages of the second volume are dedicated to the poetry of Mr. Wordsworth. He has endeavoured to define poetry—to explain the philosophy of metre—to settle the boundaries of poetic diction—and to show, finally, "what it is probable Mr. Wordsworth meant to say in his dissertation prefixed to his *Lyrical Ballads.*" As Mr. Coleridge has not only studied the laws of poetical composition, but is a Poet of considerable powers, there are, in this part of his Book, many acute, ingenious, and even sensible observations and remarks; but he never knows when to have done,—explains what requires no explanation,—often leaves untouched the very difficulty he starts,—and when he has poured before us a glimpse of light upon the shapeless form of some dark conception, he seems to take a wilful pleasure in its immediate extinction, and leads "us floundering on, and quite astray," through the deepening shadows of interminable night.

One instance there is of magnificent promise, and laughable non-performance, unequalled in the annals of literary History. Mr. Coleridge informs us, that he and Mr. Wordsworth (he is not certain which is entitled to the glory of the first discovery) have found out the difference between Fancy and Imagination. This discovery, it is prophesied, will have an incalculable influence on the progress of all the Fine Arts. He has written a long chapter purposely to prepare our minds for the great discussion. The audience is assembled—the curtain is drawn up—and there, in his gown, cap, and wig, is sitting Professor Coleridge. In comes a servant with a letter; the Professor gets up, and, with a solemn voice, reads it to the audience.—It is from an enlightened Friend; and its object is to shew, in no very courteous terms either to the Professor or his Spectators, that he may lecture, but that nobody will understand him. He accordingly makes his bow, and the curtain falls; but the worst of the joke is, that the Professor pockets the admittance-money,—for what reason, his outwitted audience are left, the best way they can, to "fancy or imagine."

But the greatest piece of Quackery in the Book is his pretended account of the Metaphysical System of Kant, of which he knows less than nothing. He will not allow that there is a single word of truth in any of the French Expositions of that celebrated System, nor yet in any of our British Reviews. We do not wish to speak of what we do not understand, and therefore say nothing of Mr. Coleridge's Metaphysics. But we beg leave to lay before our readers the following Thesis, for the amusement of a leisure hour.

This *principium commune essendi et cognoscendi*, as subsisting in a WILL, or primary ACT of self-duplication, is the mediate or indirect principle of every science; but it is the mediate and direct principle of the ultimate science alone, i. e. of transcendental philosophy alone. For it must be remembered, that all these Theses refer solely to one of the two Polar Sciences, namely, to that which commences with and rigidly confines itself within the subjective, leaving the objective (as far as it is exclusively objective) to natural philosophy, which is its opposite pole. In its very idea, therefore, as a systematic knowledge of our collective KNOWING (scientia scientiæ), it involves the necessity of some one highest principle of knowing, as at once the source and the accompanying form in all particular acts of intellect and perception. This, it has been shown, can be found only in the act and evolution of self-consciousness. We are not investigating an absolute principium essendi; for then, I admit, many valid objections might be started against our theory; but an absolute principium cognoscendi. The result of both the sciences, or their equatorial point, would be the principle of a total and undivided philosophy, as for prudential reasons, I have chosen to anticipate in the Scholium to Thesis VI. and the note subjoined.

We cannot take leave of Mr. Coleridge, without expressing our indignation at the gross injustice, and, we fear, envious persecution of his Criticism on Mr. Maturin's *Bertram*. He has thought it worth his while to analyse and criticise that Tragedy in a diatribe of fifty pages. He contends evidently against his own conviction, that it is utterly destitute of poetical and dramatic merit, and disgraceful, not to Mr. Maturin alone, but to the audiences who admired it when acted, and the reading Public, who admired it no less when printed. There is more malignity, and envy, and jealousy, and misrepresentation, and bad wit, in this Critical Essay, than in all the Reviews now existing, from the *Edinburgh* down to the *Lady's Magazine*. Mr. Coleridge ought to have behaved otherwise to an ingenious man like Mr. Maturin, struggling into reputation, and against narrow circumstances. He speaks with sufficient feeling of his own pecuniary embarrassments, and of the evil which Reviewers have done to his worldly concerns—but all his feeling is for himself, and he has done all in his power to pluck and blast the laurels of a man of decided Poetical Genius. This is not the behaviour which one Poet ought to shew to another; and if Mr. Coleridge saw faults and defects in *Bertram*, he should have exposed them in dignified manner, giving all due praise, at the same time, to the vigour, and even originality of that celebrated Drama. Mr. Coleridge knows that *Bertram* has become a stock play at the London Theatres, while his own *Remorse* is for ever withdrawn. Has this stung him? Far be it from us to impute mean motives to any man. But there is a bitterness—an anger—a scorn—we had almost said, a savage and revengeful fierceness in the tone of Mr. Coleridge, when speaking of Mr. Maturin, which it is, we confess, impossible to explain, and which, we fear, proceeds (perhaps unknown to his metaphysical self) from private pique and hostility, occasioned by superior merit and greater success. As a proof that our opinion is at least plausible, we quote Mr. Coleridge's description of *Bertram*.

This superfetation of blasphemy upon nonsense—this felo de se and thief captain—this loathsome and leprous confluence of robbery, adultery, murder, and cowardly assassination—this monster, whose best deed is, the having saved his betters from the degradation of hanging him, by turning Jack Ketch to himself.

What a wretched contrast does Mr. Coleridge here afford to Mr. Walter Scott. That gentleman, it is known,
encouraged Mr. Maturin, before he was known to the
public, by his advice and commendation; and along with
Lord Byron, was the principal means of bringing *Ber-*
tram on the stage. Such conduct was worthy of the
"Mighty Minstrel," and consistent with that true nobility
of mind by which he is characterized, and which makes
him rejoice in the glory of contemporary genius. Mr.
Coleridge speaks with delight of the success of his own
Tragedy—of his enlightened audience, and the smiling
faces of those he recollected to have attended his Lectures
on Poetry at the Royal Institution. How does he account
for the same audience admiring *Bertram?* Let him either
henceforth blush for his own fame, or admit Mr.
Maturin's claims to a like distinction.*

We have done. We have felt it our duty to speak with
severity of this book and its author—and we have given
our readers ample opportunities to judge of the justice
of our strictures. We have not been speaking in the cause
of Literature only, but, we conceive, in the cause of Morality and Religion. For it is not fitting that he should
be held up as an example to the rising generation (but, on
the contrary, it is most fitting that he should be exposed
as a most dangerous model), who has alternately em-

---

*We may here make mention of an admirable essay on this
Drama, read before the Royal Society of Edinburgh, by Mr.
McKenzie, the illustrious Author of the *Man of Feeling*. The
knowledge that high praise was bestowed on him by such a man,
may well comfort Mr. Maturin under the mean abuses of
an envious Rival.

braced, defended, and thrown aside all systems of Philosophy—and all creeds of Religion,—who seems to have no power of retaining an opinion,—no trust in the principles which he defends,—but who fluctuates from theory to theory, according as he is impelled by vanity, envy, or diseased desire of change,—and who, while he would subvert and scatter into dust those structures of knowledge, reared by the wise men of this and other generations, has nothing to erect in their room but the baseless and air-built fabrics of a dreaming Imagination.*

* *Blackwood's Magazine,* October, 1817. (John Wilson.)

THE REVOLT OF ISLAM

By Percy Bysshe Shelley

THIS is one of that industrious knot of authors, the tendency of whose works we have in our late Numbers exposed to the caution of our readers—novel, poem, romance, letters, tours, critique, lecture and essay follow one another, framed to the same measure, and in subjection to the same key-note, while the sweet undersong of the weekly journal, filling up all pauses, strengthening all weaknesses, smoothing all abruptnesses, harmonizes the whole strain. Of all his brethren Mr. Shelley carries to the greatest length the doctrines of the sect. He is, for this and other reasons, by far the least pernicious of them; indeed there is a naiveté and openness in his manner of laying down the most extravagant positions, which in some measure deprives them of their venom; and when he enlarges on what certainly are but necessary results of opinions more guardedly delivered by others, he might almost be mistaken for some artful advocate of civil order and religious institutions. This benefit indeed may be drawn from his book, for there is scarcely any more persuasive argument for truth than to carry out to all their legitimate consequences, the doctrines of error. But this is not Mr. Shelley's intention; he is, we are sorry to say, in sober earnest:—with perfect deliberation and the steadiest perseverance he perverts all the gifts of his nature, and does all the injury, both public and private, which his faculties enable him to perpetrate.

Laon and Cythna is the same poem with the *Revolt of Islam*—under the first name it exhibited some features which made "the experiment on the temper of the public mind," as the author calls it, somewhat too bold and hazardous. This knight-errant in the cause of "a liberal and comprehensive morality" had already sustained some "perilous handling" in his encounters with Prejudice and Error, and acquired in consequence of it a small portion of *the better part of valour.* Accordingly *Laon and Cythna* withdrew from circulation; and happy had it been for Mr. Shelley if he had been contented with his failure, and closed his experiments. But with minds of a certain class, notoriety, infamy, anything is better than obscurity; baffled in a thousand attempts after fame, they will still make one more at whatever risk,—and they end commonly like an awkward chemist who perseveres in tampering with his ingredients, till, in an unlucky moment, they take fire, and he is blown up by the explosion.

Laon and Cythna has accordingly re-appeared with a new name, and a few slight alterations. If we could trace in these any signs of an altered spirit, we should have hailed with the sincerest pleasure the return of one whom nature intended for better things, to the ranks of virtue and religion. But Mr. Shelley is no penitent; he has reproduced the same poison, a little, and but a little, more cautiously disguised, and as it is thus intended only to do the more mischief at less personal risk to the author, our duty requires us to use his own evidence against himself, to interpret him where he is obscure now, by himself where he was plain before, and to exhibit the "fearful consequences" to which he would bring us, as he drew them in the boldness of his first conception.

Before, however, we do this, we will discharge our duty to Mr. Shelley as poetical critics—in a case like the present, indeed, where the freight is so pernicious, it is but a secondary duty to consider the "build" of the vessel which bears it: but it is a duty too peculiarly our own to be wholly neglected. Though we should be sorry to see the *Revolt of Islam* in our readers' hands, we are bound to say that it is not without beautiful passages, that the language is in general free from errors of taste, and the versification smooth and harmonious. In these respects it resembles the latter productions of Mr. Southey, though the tone is less subdued, and the copy altogether more luxuriant and ornate than the original. Mr. Shelley indeed is an unsparing imitator; and he draws largely on the rich stores of another mountain poet, to whose religious mind it must be matter, we think, of perpetual sorrow to see the philosophy which comes pure and holy from his pen, degraded and perverted, as it continually is, by this miserable crew of atheists or pantheists, who have just sense enough to abuse its terms, but neither heart nor principle to comprehend its import, or follow its application. We shall cite one of the passages to which we alluded above, in support of our opinion: perhaps it is that

which has pleased us more than any other in the whole
poem.

> An orphan with my parents lived, whose eyes
> Were loadstars of delight, which drew me home
> When I might wander forth, nor did I prize
> *Aught* (any) human thing beneath Heaven's mighty dome
> Beyond this child; so when sad hours were come,
> And baffled hope like ice still clung to me;
> Since kin were cold, and friends had now become
> Heartless and false, I turned from all, to be,
> Cythna, the only source of tears and smiles to thee.
>
> What wert thou then? a child most infantine,
> Yet wandering far beyond that innocent age
> In all but its sweet looks, and mien divine;
> Even then, methought, with the world's tyrant rage
> A patient warfare thy young heart did wage,
> When those soft eyes of scarcely conscious thought
> Some tale or thine own fancies would engage
> To overflow with tears, or converse fraught
> With passion o'er their depths its fleeting light had wrought.
>
> She moved upon this earth, a shape of brightness,
> A power, that from its object scarcely drew
> One impulse of her being—in her lightness
> Most like some radiant cloud of morning dew
> Which wanders through the waste air's pathless blue
> To nourish some far desert; she did seem
> Beside me, gathering beauty as she grew
> Like the bright shade of some immortal dream
> Which walks, when tempest sleeps, the waves of life's dark
>   stream.
>
> As mine own shadow was this child to me,
> A second self—far dearer and more fair,
> *Which* clothed in undissolving radiancy
> All those steep paths, which languor and despair
> Of human things had made so dark and bare,

But which I trod alone—nor, till bereft
Of friends and overcome by lonely care,
Knew I what solace for that loss was left,
Though by a bitter wound my trusting heart was cleft.
—p. 42.

These, with all their imperfections, are beautiful stanzas; they are, however, of rare occurrence:—had the poem
many more such, it could never, we are persuaded, become
popular. Its merits and its faults equally conspire against
it; it has not much ribaldry or voluptuousness for prurient
imaginations, and no personal scandal for the malicious;
and even those on whom it might be expected to act most
dangerously by its semblance of enthusiasm, will have
stout hearts to proceed beyond the first canto. As a whole,
it is insupportably dull, and laboriously obscure; its
absurdities are not of the kind which provoke laughter;
the story is almost wholly devoid of interest, and very
meagre; nor can we admire Mr. Shelley's mode of making up for this defect;—as he has but one incident where
he should have ten, he tells that one so intricately, that
it takes the time of ten to comprehend it.

Mr. Shelley is a philosopher by the courtesy of the age,
and has a theory of course respecting the government of
the world; we will state in as few words as we can the
general outlines of that theory, the manner in which he
demonstrates it, and the practical consequences which he
proposes to deduce from it. It is to the second of these
divisions that we would beg his attention; we despair of
convincing him directly that he has taken up false and
pernicious notions; but if he pays any deference to the

common laws of reasoning, we hope to show him that, let the goodness of his cause be what it may, his manner of advocating it is false and unsound. This may be mortifying to a teacher of mankind; but a philosopher seeks the truth, and has no vanity to be mortified.

The existence of evil, physical and moral, is the grand problem of all philosophy; the humble find it a trial, the proud make it a stumbling-block; Mr. Shelley refers it to the faults of those civil institutions and religious creeds which are designed to regulate the conduct of man here, and his hopes in a hereafter. In these he seems to make no distinction, but considers them all as bottomed upon principles pernicious to man and unworthy of God, carried into details the most cruel, and upheld only by the stupidity of the many on the one hand, and the selfish conspiracy of the few on the other. According to him the earth is a boon garden needing little care or cultivation, but pouring forth spontaneously and inexhaustibly all innocent delights and luxuries to her innumerable children; the seasons have no inclemencies, the air no pestilences for man in his proper state of wisdom and liberty; his business here is to enjoy himself, to abstain from no gratification, to repent of no sin, hate no crime, but be wise, happy and free, with plenty of "lawless love." This is man's natural state, the state to which Mr. Shelley will bring us, if we will but break up the "crust of our outworn opinions," as he calls them, and put them into his magic chaldron. But kings have introduced war, legislators crime, priests sin; the dreadful consequences have been that the earth has lost her fertility, the seasons their mild-

ness, the air its salubrity, man his freedom and happiness.
We have become a foul-feeding carnivorous race, are
foolish enough to feel uncomfortable after the commission
of sin; some of us even go so far as to consider vice
odious; and we all groan under a multiplied burden of
crimes, *merely conventional;* among which Mr. Shelley
specifies with great *sang froid* the commission of *incest!*

We said that our philosopher makes no distinction in
his condemnation of creeds; we should rather have said,
that he makes no exception; distinction he does make, and
it is to the prejudice of that which we hold. In one place
indeed he assembles a number of names of the founders
of religions, to treat them all with equal disrespect.

> And through the host contention wild befell,
> As each of his own God the wonderous works did tell;
> * And Oromaze and Christ and Mahomet,
> Moses and Buddh, Zerdusht, and Brahm and Foh,
> A tumult of strange names, &c.—p. 227.

But in many other places he manifests a dislike to
Christianity which is frantic, and would be, if in such a case
any thing could be, ridiculous. When the votaries of all
religions are assembled with one accord (this unanimity
by the bye is in a vision of the *nineteenth* century) to
stifle the first breathings of liberty, and execute the revenge of a ruthless tyrant, he selects a Christian priest to
be the organ of sentiments outrageously and pre-emi-

---

* "And Oromaze, Joshua and Mahomet." p. 227. *Revolt
of Islam.* This is a very fair specimen of Mr. Shelley's alterations, which we see are wholly prudential, and artfully so, as the
blasphemy is still preserved entire.

nently cruel. The two characteristic principles upon
which Christianity may be said to be built are repentance
and faith. Of repentance he speaks thus:—

> Reproach not thine own soul, but know thyself;
> *Nor hate another's crime, nor loathe thine own.*
> It is the dark idolatry of self
> Which, when our thoughts and actions once are gone,
> Demands that we should weep and bleed and groan;
> O vacant expiation! be at rest—
> The past is death's—the future is thine own;
> And love and joy can make the *foulest* breast
> A paradise of flowers where peace might build her nest.
> —p. 188.

Repentance then is selfishness in an extreme which
amounts to idolatry! but what is Faith? our readers can
hardly be prepared for the odious accumulation of sin
and sorrow which Mr. Shelley conceives under his word.
"Faith is the Python, the Ogress, the Evil Genius, the
Wicked Fairy, the Giantess of our children's tales;" whenever any thing bad is to be accounted for, any hard name
to be used, this convenient monosyllable fills up the blank.

> Beneath his feet, 'mong ghastliest forms, represt
> Lay Faith, *an obscene worm.*—p. 118.

> ————————sleeping there
> With lidless eyes lie Faith, and Plague, and Slaughter,
> A ghastly brood conceived of Lethe's sullen water.—p. 220.

> And underneath thy feet writhe Faith and Folly,
> Custom and Hell, and mortal Melancholy.—p. 119.

> Smiled on the flowery grave, in which were lain
> Fear, Faith and Slavery.—p. 172.

Enough of Mr. Shelley's theory.—We proceed to examine the manner in which the argument is conducted, and this we cannot do better than by putting a case.

Let us suppose a man entertaining Mr. Shelley's opinions as to the causes of existing evil, and convinced of the necessity of a change in all the institutions of society, of his own ability to produce and conduct it, and of the excellence of that system which he would substitute in their place. These indeed are bold convictions for a young and inexperienced man, imperfectly educated, irregular in his application, and shamefully dissolute in his conduct; but let us suppose them to be sincere;—the change, if brought about at all, must be effected by a concurrent will, and that, Mr. Shelley will of course tell us, must be produced by an enlightened conviction. How then would a skilful reasoner, assured of the strength of his own ground, have proceeded in composing a tale of fiction for this purpose? Undoubtedly he would have taken the best laws, the best constitution, and the best religion in the known world; such at least as they most loved and venerated whom he was addressing; when he had put all these together, and developed their principles candidly, he would have shown that under all favourable circumstances, and with all the best propensities of our nature to boot, still the natural effect of this combination would be to corrupt and degrade the human race. He would then have drawn a probable inference, that if the most approved systems and creeds under circumstances more advantageous than could ever be expected to concur in reality, still produced only vice and misery, the fault lay in them, or at least mankind could lose nothing by adventuring on a change. We say with confidence that a skilful combatant would and must have acted thus; not merely to make victory final, but to gain it in any shape. For if he reasons from what we acknowledge to be bad against what we believe to be good; if he puts a government confessedly despotic, a religion monstrous and false, if he places on the throne a cruel tyrant, and at the altar a bigoted and corrupt priesthood, how can his argument have any weight with those who think they live under a paternal government and a pure faith, who look up with love and gratitude to a beneficent monarch, and reverence a zealous and upright priesthood? The laws and government on which Mr. Shelley's reasoning proceeds, are the Turkish, administered by a lawless despot; his religion is the Mahommedan, maintained by servile hypocrites; and his scene for their joint operation, Greece, the land full beyond all others of recollections of former glory and independence, now covered with shame and sunk in slavery. We are Englishmen, Christians, free, and independent; we ask Mr. Shelley how his case applies to *us?* or what *we* learn from it to the prejudice of our own institutions?

His residence at Oxford was a short one, and, if we mistake not, rather *abruptly* terminated; yet we should have thought that even in a freshman's term he might have learned from Aldrick not to reason from a particular to an universal; and any one of our fair readers we imagine who never heard of Aldrick, would see the absurdity of inferring that all of her own sex were the victims of the lust and tyranny of the other, from the fact, if it be a fact, that young women of Greece were carried off by force to the seraglio of Constantinople. This, however, is the sum and substance of the argument, as far as it attempts to prove the causes of existing evil. Mr. Shelley is neither a dull, nor, considering all his disadvantages, a very ignorant man; we will frankly confess, that with every disposition to judge him charitably, we find it hard to convince ourselves of his belief in his own conclusions.

We have seen how Mr. Shelley argues for the necessity of a change; we must bestow a word or two upon the manner in which he brings the change about, before we come to the consequences which he derives from it. Laon and Cythna, his hero and heroine, are the principal, indeed, almost the sole agents. The latter by her eloquence rouses all of her own sex to assert their liberty and independence; this perhaps was no difficult task; a female tongue in such a cause may be supposed to have spoken fluently at least, and to have found a willing audience; by the same instrument, however, she disarms the soldiers who are sent to seize and destroy her,—

> even the torturer who had bound
> Her meek calm frame, ere yet it was impaled
> Loosened her weeping then, nor could be found
> One human hand to harm her.—p. 84.

The influence of her voice is not confined to the Golden City, it travels over the land, stirring and swaying all hearts to its purpose:—

in hamlets and in towns
The multitudes collect tumultuously,—
Blood soon, although unwillingly, to shed.—p. 85.

These peaceable and tender advocates for "Universal
Suffrage and *no* representation" assemble in battle-array
under the walls of the Golden City, keeping night and
day strict blockade (which Mr. Shelley calls "a watch of
love,") around the desperate bands who still adhere to the
maintenance of the iron-hearted monarch on the throne.
Why the eloquence of Cythna had no power over *them*,
or how the monarch himself, who had been a slave to her
beauty, and to whom this model of purity and virtue, *had
borne a child*, was able to resist the spell of her voice, Mr.
Shelley leaves his readers to find out for themselves. In
this pause of affairs Laon makes his appearance to complete the revolution; Cythna's voice had done wonders,
but Laon's was still more powerful; the "sanguine slaves"
of page 96, who stabbed ten thousand in their sleep, are
turned in page 99 to fraternal bands; the power of the
throne crumbles into dust and the united hosts enter the
city in triumph. A good deal of mummery follows, of
national fêtes, reasonable rites, altars of federation, &c.
borrowed from that store-house of cast-off mummeries
and abominations, the French revolution. In the mean
time all the kings of the earth, pagan and Christian, send
more sanguine slaves, who slaughter the sons of freedom
in the midst of their merry-making; Plague and Famine
come to slaughter them in return; and Laon and Cythna,
who had chosen this auspicious moment in a ruined tower

for the commencement of their "reign of love," surrender
themselves to the monarch and are burnt alive.

Such is Mr. Shelley's victory, such its security, and such
the means of obtaining it! These last, we confess, are
calculated to throw a damp upon our spirits, for if the
hopes of mankind must depend upon the exertion of
super-eminent eloquence, we have the authority of one
who had well considered the subject, for believing that
they could scarcely depend upon anything of more rare
occurrence. *Plures in omnibus rebus, quàm in dicendo
admirabiles,* was the remark of Cicero a great many ages
ago, and the experience of all those ages has served but
to confirm the truth of it.

Mr. Shelley, however, is not a man to propose a difficult
remedy without suggesting the means of procuring it. If
we mistake not, Laon and Cythna, and even the sage, (for
there is a sort of good stupid Archimago in the poem)
are already provided, and intent to begin their mission
if we will but give them hearing. In short Mr. Shelley
is his own Laon: this is clear from many passages of the
preface and dedication. The lady to whom the poem is
addressed is certainly the original of Cythna: we have
more consideration for her than she has had for herself,
and will either mortify her vanity, or spare her feelings,
by not producing her before the public; it is enough for
the philanthropist to know that when the season arrives,
she will be forthcoming. Mr. Shelley says of himself and
her, in a simile picturesque in itself, but laughable in its
application,—

> thou and I,
> Sweet friend, can look from our tranquillity,
> Like lamps, into the world's tempestuous night—
> Two tranquil stars, while clouds are passing by
> Which wrap them from the foundering seaman's sight,
> That burn from year to year with unextinguished
> light.—p. xxxii.

Neither will the reader be much at a loss to discover what sapient personage is dimly shadowed out in Archimago; but a clue is afforded even to the uninitiate by a note in the preface, in which we are told that Mr. Malthus by his last edition has reduced the *Essay on Population* to a commentary illustrative of the unanswerableness of *Political Justice.*

With such instruments doubtless the glorious task will be speedily accomplished—and what will be the issue? This indeed is a serious question, but, as in most schemes of reform, it is easier to say what is to be removed, and destroyed, than what is to be put in its place. Mr. Shelley would abrogate our laws—this would put an end to felonies and misdemeanours at a blow; he would abolish the rights of property, of course there could thenceforward be no violations of them, no heart-burnings between the poor and the rich, no disputed wills, no litigated inheritances, no food in short for sophistical judges, or hireling lawyers; he would overthrow the constitution, and then we should have no expensive court, no pensions or sinecures, no silken lords or corrupt commoners, no slavish and enslaving army or navy; he would pull down our churches, level our Establishment, and burn our bibles— then we should pay no tithes, be enslaved by no supersti-

tions, abused by no priestly artifices: marriage he cannot
endure, and there would at once be a stop put to the
lamented increase of adulterous connections amongst us,
whilst by repealing the canon of heaven against incest, he
would add to the purity, and heighten the ardour of those
feelings with which brother and sister now regard each
other; finally, as the basis of the whole scheme, he would
have us renounce our belief in our religion, extinguish,
if we can, the light of conscience within us, which em-
bitters our joys here, and drown in oblivion the hopes
and fears that hang over our hereafter.   This is at least
intelligible; but it is not so easy to describe the structure,
which Mr. Shelley would build upon this vast heap of
ruins.   "Love," he says, "is to be the sole law which
shall govern the moral world;" but Love is a wide word
with many significations, and we are at a loss as to which
of them he would have it now bear.   We are loath to understand it in its lowest sense, though we believe that as
to the issue this would be the correctest mode of inter-
preting it; but this at least is clear, that Mr. Shelley does
not mean it in its highest sense: he does not mean that
love, which is the fulfilling of the law, and which walks
after the commandments, for he would erase the Decalogue, and every other code of laws; not the love which
is said to be of God, and which is beautifully coupled
with "joy, peace, long suffering, gentleness, goodness,
faith, meekness, temperance," for he pre-eminently ab-
hors that religion, which is built on that love and incul-
cates it as the essence of all duties, and its own ful-
filment.

It is time to draw to an end.—We have examined Mr. Shelley's system slightly, but, we hope, dispassionately; there will be those, who will say that we have done so coldly. He has indeed, to the best of his ability, wounded us in the tenderest part.—As far as in him lay, he has loosened the hold of our protecting laws, and sapped the principles of our venerable polity; he has invaded the purity and chilled the unsuspecting ardour of our fireside intimacies; he has slandered, ridiculed and blasphemed our holy religion; yet these are all too sacred objects to be defended bitterly or unfairly. We have learned, too, though not in Mr. Shelley's school, to discriminate between a man and his opinions, and while we shew no mercy to the sin, we can regard the sinner with allowance and pity. It is in this spirit, that we conclude with a few lines, which may serve for a warning to others, and for reproof, admonition, and even if he so pleases of encouragement to himself. We have already said what we think of his powers as a poet, and doubtless, with those powers, he might have risen to respectability in any honourable path, which he had chosen to pursue, if to his talents he had added industry, subordination, and good principles. But of Mr. Shelley much may be said with truth, which we not long since said of his friend and leader Mr. Hunt: he has not, indeed, all that is odious and contemptible in the character of that person; so far as we have seen he has never exhibited the bustling vulgarity, the ludicrous affectation, the factious flippancy, or the selfish heartlessness, which it is hard for our feelings to treat with the mere contempt they merit. Like him, however, Mr. Shelley is

a very vain man; and like most very vain men, he is but
half instructed in knowledge, and less than half-dis-
ciplined in his reasoning powers; his vanity, wanting the
control of the faith which he derides, has been his ruin;
it has made him too impatient of applause and distinction
to earn them in the fair course of labour; like a speculator
in trade, he would be rich without capital and without
delay, and, as might have been anticipated, his speculations
have ended only in disappointments. They both began,
his speculations and his disappointments, in early childhood, and even from that period he has carried about with
him a soured and discontented spirit—unteachable in boyhood, unamiable in youth, querulous and unmanly in
manhood,—singularly unhappy in all three. He speaks
of his school as "a world of woes," of his masters "as ty-
rants," of his school-fellows as "enemies,"—alas! what is
this, but to bear evidence against himself? every one who
knows what a public school ordinarily must be, will only
trace in these lines the language of an insubordinate, a
vain, a mortified spirit.

We would venture to hope that the past may suffice for
the speculations in which Mr. Shelley has hitherto engaged; they have brought him neither honour abroad nor
peace at home, and after so fair a trial it seems but common prudence to change them for some new venture.
He is still a young man, and though his account be assuredly black and heavy, he may yet hope to redeem his
time, and wipe it out. He may and he should retain all
the love for his fellow-creatures, all the zeal for their
improvement in virtue and happiness which he now pro-

fesses, but let that zeal be armed with knowledge and regulated by judgment. Let him not be offended at our freedom, but he is really too young, too ignorant, too inexperienced, and too vicious to undertake the task of reforming any world, but the little world within his own breast; that task will be a good preparation for the difficulties which he is more anxious at once to encounter. There is a book which will help him to this preparation, which has more poetry in it than Lucretius, more interest than Godwin, and far more philosophy than both. But it is a sealed book to a proud spirit; if he would read it with effect, he must be humble where he is now vain, he must examine and doubt himself where now he boldly condemns others, and instead of relying on his own powers, he must feel and acknowledge his weakness, and pray for strength from above.

We had closed our remarks on *Laon and Cythna*, when *Rosalind and Helen* was put into our hands: after having devoted so much more space to the former than its own importance merited, a single sentence will suffice for the latter. Though not without some marks of the same ability, which is occasionally manifested in Mr. Shelley's earlier production, the present poem is very inferior to it in positive merit, and far more abundant in faults: it is less interesting, less vigorous and chaste in language, less harmonious in versification, and less pure in thought; more rambling and diffuse, more palpably and consciously sophistical, more offensive and vulgar, more unintelligible. So it ever is and must be in the downward course of infidelity and immorality;—we can no more blot out the noblest objects of contemplation, and the most heart-stirring sources of gratitude from the creation without injury to our intellectual and moral nature, than we can refuse to walk by the light of the sun without impairing our ocular vision. Scarcely any man ever set himself in array against the cause of social order and religion, but from a proud and rebel mind, or a corrupt and undisciplined heart: where these are, true knowledge cannot grow. In the enthusiasm of youth, indeed, a man like Mr. Shelley may cheat himself with the imagined loftiness and independence of his theory, and it is easy to invent a thousand sophisms, to reconcile his conscience to the impurity of his practice: but this lasts only long enough to lead him on beyond the power of return; he ceases to be the dupe, but with desperate malignity he becomes the deceiver of others. Like the Egyptian of old, the wheels of his chariot are broken, the path of "mighty waters" closes in upon him behind, and a still deepening ocean is before him:—for a short time, are seen his impotent struggles against a resistless power, his blasphemous execrations are heard, his despair but poorly assumes the tone of triumph and defiance, and he calls ineffectually on others to follow him to the same ruin— finally, he sinks "like lead" to the bottom, and is forgotten. So it is now in part, so shortly will it be entirely with Mr. Shelley: if we might withdraw the veil of private life, and tell what we *now* know about him, it would be indeed a disgusting picture that we should exhibit, but it would be an unanswerable comment on our text; it is not easy for those who *read only*, to conceive how much low pride, how much cold selfishness, how much unmanly cruelty are consistent with the laws of this "universal" and "lawless love."   But we must only use our knowledge to check the groundless hopes which we were once prone to entertain of him.*

* The *Quarterly Review,* April, 1819. (John Taylor Coleridge.)

REMARKS ON *DON JUAN* *

By Lord Byron

IT has not been without much reflection and overcoming many reluctancies, that we have at last resolved to say a few words more to our readers concerning this very extraordinary poem. The nature and causes of our difficulties will be easily understood by those of them who have read any part of *Don Juan*—but we despair of standing justified as to the conclusion at which we have arrived, in the opinion of any but those who have read and understood the whole of a work, in the composition of which there is unquestionably a more thorough and intense infusion of genius and vice—power and profligacy —than in any poem which had ever before been written in the English, or indeed in any other modern language. Had the wickedness been less inextricably mingled with the beauty and the grace, and the strength of a most inimitable and incomprehensible muse, our task would have been easy: But SILENCE would be a very poor and a very useless chastisement to be inflicted by us, or by any one, on a production, whose corruptions have been so effectually embalmed—which, in spite of all that critics can do or refrain from doing, nothing can possibly prevent from taking a high place in the literature of our

---

* Over fifty stanzas are quoted, but omitted in this reprint. (The Editor.)

country, and remaining to all ages a perpetual monument of the exalted intellect, and the depraved heart, of one of the most remarkable men to whom that country has had the honour and the disgrace of giving birth.

That Lord Byron has never written any thing more decisively and triumphantly expressive of the greatness of his genius, will be allowed by all who have read this poem. That (laying all its manifold and grievous offences for a moment out of our view) it is by far the most admirable specimen of the mixture of ease, strength, gaiety, and seriousness extant in the whole body of English poetry, is a proposition to which, we are almost as well persuaded, very few of them will refuse their assent. With sorrow and humiliation do we speak it—the poet has devoted his powers to the worst of purposes and passions; and it increases his guilt and our sorrow, that he has devoted them entire. What the immediate effect of the poem may be on contemporary literature, we cannot pretend to guess—too happy could we hope that its lessons of boldness and vigour in language, and versification, and conception, might be attended to, as they deserve to be— without any stain being suffered to fall on the purity of those who minister to the general shape and culture of the public mind, from the mischievous insults against all good principle and all good feeling, which have been unworthily embodied in so many elements of fascination.

The moral strain of the whole poem is pitched in the lowest key—and if the genius of the author lifts him now and then out of his pollution, it seems as if he regretted the elevation, and made all haste to descend again. To

particularize the offences committed in its pages would
be worse than vain—because the great genius of the man
seems to have been throughout exerted to its utmost
strength, in devising every possible method of pouring
scorn upon every element of good or noble nature in the
hearts of his readers. Love—honour—patriotism—religion, are mentioned only to be scoffed at and derided, as
if their sole resting-place were, or ought to be, in the
bosoms of fools. It appears, in short, as if this miserable
man, having exhausted every species of sensual gratification—having drained the cup of sin even to its bitterest
dregs, were resolved to shew us that he is no longer a
human being, even in his frailties;—but a cool uncon-
cerned fiend, laughing with a detestable glee over the
whole of the better and worse elements of which human
life is composed—treating well nigh with equal derision
the most pure of virtues, and the most odious of vices—
dead alike to the beauty of the one, and the deformity
of the other—a mere heartless despiser of that frail but
noble humanity, whose type was never exhibited in a
shape of more deplorable degradation than in his own
contemptuously distinct delineation of himself. To confess in secret to his Maker, and weep over in secret agonies
the wildest and most phantastic transgressions of heart and
mind, is the part of a conscious sinner, in whom sin has
not become the sole principle of life and action—of a
soul for which there is yet hope. But to lay bare to the
eye of man and of *woman* all the hidden convulsions of
a wicked spirit—thoughts too abominable, we would hope,
to have been imagined by any but him that has expressed

them—and to do all this without one symptom of pain, contrition, remorse, or hesitation, with a calm careless ferociousness of contented and satisfied depravity—this was an insult which no wicked man of genius had ever before dared to put upon his Creator or his Species. This highest of all possible exhibitions of self-abandonment has been set forth in mirth and gladness, by one whose name was once pronounced with pride and veneration by every English voice. This atrocious consummation was reserved for Byron.

It has long been sufficiently manifest, that this man is devoid of religion. At times, indeed, the power and presence of the Deity, as speaking in the sterner workings of the elements, seems to force some momentary consciousness of their existence into his labouring breast;— a spirit in which there breathes so much of the divine, cannot always resist the majesty of its Maker. But of true religion terror is a small part—and of all religion, that founded on mere terror is the least worthy of such a man as Byron. We may look in vain through all his works for the slightest evidence that his soul had ever listened to the *gentle voice* of the oracles. His understanding has been subdued into conviction by some passing cloud; but his heart has never been touched. He has never written one line that savours of the spirit of meekness. His faith is but for a moment—"he believes and trembles," and relapses again into his gloom of unbelief— a gloom in which he is at least as devoid of HOPE and CHARITY as he is of FAITH.—The same proud hardness of heart which makes the author of *Don Juan* a despiser of the Faith for which his fathers bled, has rendered him a scorner of the better part of woman; and therefore it is that his love poetry is a continual insult to the beauty that inspires it. The earthy part of the passion is all that has found a resting place within his breast—His idol is all of clay—and he dashes her to pieces almost in the moment of his worship. Impiously railing against his God—madly and meanly disloyal to his Sovereign and his country,—and brutally outraging all the best feelings of female honour, affection, and confidence—How small a part of chivalry is that which remains to the descendant of the Byrons—a gloomy vizor, and a deadly weapon!

Of these offences, however, or of such as these, Lord Byron had been guilty abundantly before, and for such he has before been rebuked in our own, and in other more authoritative pages. There are other and newer sins with which the author of *Don Juan* has stained himself—sins of a class, if possible, even more despicable than any he had before committed; and in regard to which it is matter of regret to us, that as yet our periodical critics have not appeared to express themselves with any seemly measure of manly and candid indignation.

Those who are acquainted, (as who is not?) with the main incidents in the private life of Lord Byron;—and who have not seen this production, (and we are aware, that very few of our Northern readers have seen it)—will scarcely believe, that the odious malignity of this man's bosom should have carried him so far, as to make him commence a filthy and impious poem, with an elaborate satire on the character and manners of his wife—from

whom, even by his own confession, he has been separated
only in consequence of his own cruel and heartless mis-
conduct.   It is in vain for Lord Byron to attempt in
any way to justify his own behaviour in that affair; and,
now that he has so openly and audaciously invited inquiry
and reproach, we do not see any good reason why he
should not be plainly told so by the general voice of his
countrymen.   It would not be an easy matter to persuade
any Man who has any knowledge of the nature of
Woman, that a female such as Lord Byron has himself
described his wife to be, would rashly, or hastily, or
lightly separate herself, from the love with which she had
once been inspired for such a man as he is, or was.   Had
he not heaped insult upon insult, and scorn upon scorn—
had he not forced the iron of his contempt into her very
soul—there is no woman of delicacy and virtue, as he
admitted Lady Byron to be, who would not have hoped
all things and suffered all things from one, her love of
whom must have been inwoven with so many exalting
elements of delicious pride, and more delicious humility.
To offend the love of such a woman was wrong—but it
might be forgiven; to desert her was unmanly—but he
might have returned and wiped for ever from her eyes
the tears of her desertion;—but to injure, and to desert,
and then to turn back and wound her widowed privacy
with unhallowed strains of cold-blooded mockery—was
brutally, fiendishly, inexpiably mean.   For impurities
there might be some possibility of pardon, were they
supposed to spring only from the reckless buoyancy of
young blood and fiery passions,—for impiety there might

at least be pity, were it visible that the misery of the impious soul were as great as its darkness;—but for offences such as this, which cannot proceed either from the madness of sudden impulse, or the bewildered agonies of self-perplexing and self-despairing doubt—but which speak the wilful and determined spite of an unrepenting, unsoftened, smiling, sarcastic, joyous sinner—for such diabolical, such slavish vice, there can be neither pity nor pardon. Our knowledge that it is committed by one of the most powerful intellects our island ever has produced, lends intensity a thousand fold to the bitterness of our indignation. Every high thought that was ever kindled in our breasts by the muse of Byron—every pure and lofty feeling that ever responded from within us to the sweep of his majestic inspirations—every remembered moment of admiration and enthusiasm is up in arms against him. We look back with a mixture of wrath and scorn to the delight with which we suffered ourselves to be filled by one who, all the while he was furnishing us with delight, must, we cannot doubt it, have been mocking us with a cruel mockery—less cruel only, because less peculiar, than that with which he has now turned him from the lurking-place of his selfish and polluted exile, to pour the pitiful chalice of his contumely on the surrendered devotion of a virgin-bosom, and the holy hopes of the mother of his child. The consciousness of the insulting deceit which has been practised upon us, mingles with the nobler pain arising from the contemplation of perverted and degraded genius—to make us wish that no such being as Byron ever had existed. It is indeed a sad and an humiliating thing to know, that in the same year there proceeded from the same pen two productions, in all things so different, as the Fourth Canto of *Childe Harold* and this loathsome *Don Juan*.

Lady Byron, however, has one consolation still remaining, and yet we fear she will think it but a poor one. She shares the scornful satire of her husband, not only with all that is good, and pure, and high, in human nature, —its principles and its feelings; but with every individual also, in whose character the predominance of these blessed elements has been sufficient to excite the envy, or exacerbate the despair of this guilty man. We shall not needlessly widen the wound by detailing its cruelty; we have mentioned one, and, all will admit, the worst instance of the private malignity which has been embodied in so many passages of *Don Juan;* and we are quite sure, the lofty-minded and virtuous men whom Lord Byron has debased himself by insulting, will close the volume which contains their own injuries, with no feelings save those of pity for Him that has inflicted them, and for Her who partakes so largely in the same injuries; and whose hard destiny has deprived her for ever of that proud and pure privilege, which enables themselves to despise them. As to the rest of the world, we know not that Lord Byron could have invented any more certain means of bringing down contempt inexpiable on his own head, than by turning the weapons of his spleen against men whose virtues few indeed can equal, but still fewer are so lost and unworthy as not to love and admire.

The mode in which we have now expressed ourselves,

might be a sufficient apology for making no extracts from this poem itself. But our indignation, in regard to the morality of the poem, has not blinded us to its manifold beauties; and we are the more willing to quote a few of the passages which can be read without a blush, because the comparative rarity of such passages will, in all probability, operate to the complete exclusion of the work itself, from the libraries of the greater part of our readers. As it is out of the question for us to think of analysing the story, we must quote at the hazard of some of our quotations being very imperfectly understood.

* * * * *

The conclusion of the history of *this* passion is, that Don Juan is detected in the lady's chamber at midnight by her husband. Thinking her lover effectually concealed, Donna Julia rates her Lord in a style of volubility in which, it must be granted, there is abundance of the true *vis comica.*—The detection which follows almost immediately after the conclusion of the speech, gives much additional absurdity to the amazing confidence of the lady.

* * * * *

In consequence of this intrigue, Don Juan is sent on his travels; and the lady, who is shut up in a convent, takes leave of him in a beautiful letter.

* * * * *

Perhaps there are not a few women who may profit from seeing in what a style of contemptuous coldness the sufferings to which licentious love exposes them are talked of by such people as the author of *Don Juan.* The many fine eyes that have wept dangerous tears over his descriptions of the Gulnares and Medoras cannot be the worse for seeing the true side of *his* picture.

*   *   *   *   *

The amour with this Spanish lady is succeeded by a shipwreck, in which Juan alone escapes. He is dashed on the shore of the Cyclades, where he is found by a beautiful and innocent girl, the daughter of an old Greek pirate,—with whom, as might be supposed, the same game of guilt and abandonment is played over again. There is, however, a very superior kind of poetry in the conception of this amour—the desolate isle—the utter loneliness of the maiden, who is as ignorant as she is innocent—the helpless condition of the youth—every thing conspires to render it a true romance. How easy for Lord Byron to have kept it free from any stain of pollution! What cruel barbarity, in creating so much of beauty only to mar and ruin it! This is really the very suicide of genius.

*   *   *   *   *

But the best and the worst part of the whole is without doubt the description of the shipwreck. As a piece of terrible painting, it is as much superior as can be to every description of the kind—not even excepting that in the *Æneid*—that ever was created. In comparison with the fearful and intense reality of its horrors, every thing that any former poet had thrown together to depict the agonies of that awful scene, appears chill and tame.

*   *   *   *   *

But even here the demon of his depravity does not desert him. We dare not stain our pages with quoting any specimens of the disgusting merriment with which he has interspersed his picture of human suffering. He paints it well, only to shew that he scorns it the more effectually; and of all the fearful sounds which ring in the ears of the dying, the most horrible is the demoniacal laugh with which this unpitying brother exults over the contemplation of their despair. Will our readers believe that the most innocent of all his odious sarcasms is contained in these two lines?*

> They grieved for those that perished in the cutter.
> And also for the biscuit, casks, and butter.

* *Blackwood's Magazine,* August, 1819.

THE FRENCH REVOLUTION

By Thomas Carlyle

ORIGINALITY of thought is unquestionably the best excuse for writing a book; originality of style is a rare and a refreshing merit; but it is paying rather dear for one's whistle, to qualify for obtaining it in the university of Bedlam. Originality, without justness of thought, is but novelty of error: and originality of style, without sound taste and discretion, is sheer affectation. Thus, as ever, the *corruptio optimi* turns out to be *pessima;* the abortive attempt to be more than nature has made us, and to add a cubit to our stature, ends by placing us below what we might be, if contented with being simply and unaffectedly ourselves. There is not, perhaps, a more decided mark of the decadence of literature, than the frequency of such extravagance; especially, if it eventually becomes popular. The youth of literature is distinguished by a progressive approach to simplicity and to good taste; but the culminating point once attained, the good and the beautiful, as the Italian poet sings, become commonplace and tiresome,—"caviare to the general;" and the sound canons of criticism and of logic are capriciously deserted, to produce no matter what, provided it be new. Let it not, however, be thought that we advocate the theory of a permanent Augustan age, and "giving our days and nights to Addison." Language is a natural fluent; and to arrest its course is as undesirable as it is difficult. Style, to be good, must bear a certain relation to the mind from which it emanates; and when new ideas and new sciences change the national character, the modes of national expression must change also. Our received ideas, therefore, of classical styles are narrow and unphilosophic; and are derived from the fact, that as far as regards the dead languages, the classical era was followed, not by an increasing, but a decreasing civilization; and that the silver and brazen ages of the Greek and Latin tongues were produced by a deterioration of mind as well as of language. When, however, great changes arrive suddenly and unprepared, they produce, not reforms merely, but revolutions; and in revolutions, literary as well as political, there occurs between the overthrow of the old and the creation of the new, an epoch of transition in which all monstrous and misshapen things are produced in the unguided search of an unknown and unimagined beauty. In such an epoch of transition we believe a large portion of the literature of Germany still to exist; in such an epoch is the literature of *la jeune France;* but when an English writer is found to adopt the crudities and extravagancies of these nascent schools of thought, and to copy their mannerisms without rhyme, reason, taste, or selection, we can only set it down to an imperfection of intellect, to an incapacity for feeling, truth, and beauty, or to a hopeless determination to be singular, at any cost or sacrifice.

The applicability of these remarks to the *History of the French Revolution* now before us, will be understood by such of our readers as are familiar with Mr. Carlyle's contributions to our periodical literature. But it is one thing to put forth a few pages of quaintness, neologism, and a whimsical coxcombry; and another, to carry such questionable qualities through three long volumes of misplaced persiflage and flippant pseudo-philosophy. To such a pitch of extravagance and absurdity are these peculiarities exalted in the volumes before us, that we should pass them over in silence, as altogether unworthy of criticism, if we did not know that the rage for German literature may bring such writing into fashion with the ardent and unreflecting; at least, in cases where the faults we deprecate are not pushed, as in the present instance, to a transcendental excess. Under that impression, however, we must take occasion to protest against all and sundry attempts to engraft the idiom of Germany into the king's English, or to transfuse the vague verbiage and affected sentimentality of a sect of Germans into our simple and intelligible philosophy. As yet, the barriers which separate prose from verse, in our language, are firm and unbroken; as yet, our morals and metaphysics are not quite Pindaric; and our narrative may be understood by any plain man who has learned to read. We are not habitually in the clouds, rapt and inspired; and we can read the great majority of our native authors without thinking of a strait waistcoat.

With respect to languages, in particular, every nation must be permitted to "speak for itself;" and the pedantry of engrafting on any language foreign modes of expression, is unmitigated folly. Words may successfully be naturalized when they express new ideas; but foreign grammatical idioms are ever ill-assorted patches, which disfigure, and cannot adorn, the cloth to which they are appended. The German compound substantive, for instance, will always appear ludicrous in our simple monosyllabic tongue; and when introduced into prose, is worse than ludicrous,—it is mischievous. It is often sufficiently difficult to detect a confusion of idea, even when that idea is expressed at full, in a sentence of many words; but a compound substantive is merely the sign of such a sentence, the sign of a sign; and its full and precise meaning can only be obtained by intense and laborious study. Such words are misleading and dangerous; and the proper raw material for the construction of *galimatias*. By their use, an author may fancy himself sublime, when he is only ridiculous; he may conceit himself original, when he is only uttering a commonplace truism in a new way.

This last remark brings us at once to the matter of the book. What need have we of a new History of the French Revolution? We have the contemporary history of that gigantic event in superabundance; and the time is not yet arrived for christening ourselves Posterity. We have looked carefully through these volumes; and, their peculiarity of style and the looseness of their reasoning apart, we have not found a fact in them that is not better told in Mignet, and twenty other unpretending historians. There is, moreover, in them the deadly *crambe repetita* of referring the faults and the failures of the Revolution to the speculative opinions, or "philosophism," as the author calls it, of the eighteenth century. "Faith," he says, "is gone out; scepticism is come in. Evil abounds and accumulates; no one has faith to withstand it, to amend it, to begin by amending himself." Now, faith and scepticism had nothing directly to do with the affair; it was want, and misery, and oppression in the lower classes, utter corruption and incapacity in the higher, that made the revolt. Or if the faith in a state religion must be admitted to be necessary to ensure a tame submission to wrong, the leaders in that infidelity were the church dignitaries, who polluted their own altars. Society has subsisted under all modifications of popular belief; but the faith necessary to its prosperity, is a faith in truth, in honour, honesty, patriotism, and public virtue; and this had, in revolutionary France, been choked in the highest classes by the precepts and the examples of the hierarchy, while it lived and flamed in the confiding masses that trusted too implicitly to any knave who affected the garb of patriotism. Had the people possessed a little less faith in the virtues of the Church and State authorities, they would have prevented the revolution, by nipping its causes in the bud. Louis XIV., the Regent, and Louis XV., would never have existed such as they were; and events would have taken another direction.

The faults which we have been compelled thus to denounce, are the more provoking, as they are not unmingled with many finely conceived passages, and many just and vigorous reflections. The author's mind is so little accustomed to weigh carefully its own philosophy, and is so thoroughly inconsistent with itself, that the grossest absurdity in speculation does not prevent his perceiving and adopting truths in the closest relation of opposition to it.

Thus, while he attributes evils innumerable to infidelity and philosophism, and openly preaches passive obedience, religious and political, he does not the less wisely sum up the material causes of the revolt, and put forth many just views of men and things, and of the multiplied errors committed both "within and without the walls of Troy." So, too, as to style, amidst an all-prevailing absurdity of mannerism, there are passages of great power, and occasionally of splendid, though impure eloquence. Had the author been bred in another school, we should say that he might have written well and usefully; if we did not think that his admiration of that school must be in some way connected with defects in the native constitution of his mind. Having, however, expressed our unfavourable opinion thus freely, it becomes a duty to back our assertions by proof, and to give extracts as well of excellencies as of defects. In the following passage we have inconsistency of thought, vagueness of expression, and quaintness of style, all mixed together:—

Meanwhile it is singular how long the rotten will hold together, provided you do not handle it roughly. For whole generations it continues standing, "with a ghastly affectation of life," after all life and truth has fled out of it: so loath are men to quit their old ways; and, conquering indolence and inertia, venture on new. Great truly is the Actual; is the Thing that has rescued itself from bottomless deeps of theory and possibility, and stands there as a definite indisputable Fact, whereby men do work and live, or once did so. Wisely shall men cleave to that, while it will endure; and quit it with regret, when it gives way under them. Rash enthusiast of Change, beware! Hast thou well considered all that Habit does in this life of ours; how all Knowledge and all Practice hang wondrous over infinite abysses of the Unknown, Impracticable; and our whole being is an infinite abyss, *overarched* by Habit as by a thin Earth-rind, laboriously built together?

If things naturally hold together when they are rotten, the inference is in favour and not against a voluntary effect of change, and then, what are "realities rescued from the bottomless depths of theory," but downright jargon and no meaning?

(More than an entire *Athenæum* page of quotations follows. These are omitted here.) Readers, have we made out our case?—(The Editor.)

---

* *The Athenaeum,* May 20, 1837.

JANE EYRE

By Charlotte Bronte

JANE EYRE,* as a work, and one of equal popularity,
is, in almost every respect, a total contrast to *Vanity
Fair*. The characters and events, though some of them
masterly in conception, are coined expressly for the purpose of bringing out great effects. The hero and heroine
are beings both so singularly unattractive that the reader
feels they can have no vocation in the novel but to be
brought together; and they do things which, though not
impossible, lie utterly beyond the bounds of probability.
On this account a short sketch of the plan seems requisite;
not but what it is a plan familiar enough to all readers of
novels—especially those of the old school and those of
the lowest school of our own day. For Jane Eyre is
merely another Pamela, who, by the force of her character and the strength of her principles, is carried victor-
iously through great trials and temptations from the man
she loves. Nor is she even a Pamela adapted and refined
to modern notions; for though the story is conducted
without those derelictions of decorum which we are to
believe had their excuse in the manners of Richardson's
time, yet it is stamped with a coarseness of language and
laxity of tone which have certainly no excuse in ours. It

* Two lengthy quotations are omitted in reprinting this
article.—(The Editor.)

is a very remarkable book: we have no remembrance of another combining such genuine power with such horrid taste. Both together have equally assisted to gain the great popularity it has enjoyed; for in these days of extravagant adoration of all that bears the stamp of novelty and originality, sheer rudeness and vulgarity have come in for a most mistaken worship.

The story is written in the first person. Jane begins with her earliest recollections, and at once takes possession of the reader's intensest interest by the masterly picture of a strange and oppressed child she raises up in a few strokes before him. She is an orphan, and a dependant in the house of a selfish, hard-hearted aunt, against whom the disposition of the little Jane chafes itself in natural antipathy, till she contrives to make the unequal struggle as intolerable to her oppressor as it is to herself. She is therefore, at eight years of age, got rid of to a sort of Dothegirls Hall, where she continues to enlist our sympathies for a time with her little pinched fingers, cropped hair, and empty stomach. But things improve: the abuses of the institution are looked into. The Puritan patron, who holds that young orphan girls are only safely brought up upon the rules of La Trappe, is superseded by an enlightened committee—the school assumes a sound English character—Jane progresses duly from scholar to teacher, and passes ten profitable and not unhappy years at Lowood. Then she advertises for a situation as governess, and obtains one immediately in one of the midland counties. We see her, therefore, as she leaves Lowood, to enter upon a new life—a small, plain, odd creature, who has been brought up dry upon school learning, and somewhat stunted accordingly in mind and body, and who is now thrown upon the world as ignorant of its ways, and as destitute of its friendships, as a shipwrecked mariner upon a strange coast.

Thornfield Hall is the property of Mr. Rochester— a bachelor addicted to travelling. She finds it at first in all the peaceful prestige of an English gentleman's seat when "nobody is at the hall." The companions are an old decayed gentlewoman housekeeper—a far away cousin of the squire's—and a young French child, Jane's pupil, Mr. Rochester's ward and reputed daughter. There is a pleasing monotony in the summer solitude of the old country house, with its comfort, respectability, and dulness, which Jane paints to the life; but there is one circumstance which varies the sameness and casts a mysterious feeling over the scene. A strange laugh is heard from time to time in a distant part of the house—a laugh which grates discordantly upon Jane's ear. She listens, watches, and inquires, but can discover nothing but a plain matter of fact woman, who sits sewing somewhere in the attics, and goes up and down stairs peaceably to and from her dinner with the servants. But a mystery there is, though nothing betrays it, and it comes in with marvellous effect from the monotonous reality of all around. After awhile Mr. Rochester comes to Thornfield, and sends for the child and her governess occasionally to bear him company. He is a dark, strange-looking man—strong and large— of the brigand stamp, with fine eyes and lowering brows —blunt and sarcastic in his manners, with a kind of misanthropical frankness, which seems based upon utter contempt for his fellow-creatures, and a surly truthfulness which is more rudeness than honesty. With his arrival disappears all the prestige of country innocence that had invested Thornfield Hall. He brings the taint of the world upon him, and none of its illusions. The queer little governess is something new to him. He talks to her at one time imperiously as to a servant, and at another recklessly as to a man. He pours into her ears disgraceful tales of his past life, connected with the birth of little Adèle, which any man with common respect for a woman, and that a mere girl of eighteen, would have spared her; but which eighteen in this case listens to as if it were nothing new, and certainly nothing distasteful. He is captious and Turk-like—she is one day his confidant, and another his unnoticed dependant. In short, by her account, Mr. Rochester is a strange brute, somewhat in the Squire Western style of absolute and capricious eccentricity, though redeemed in him by signs of a cultivated intellect, and gleams of a certain fierce justice of heart. He has a *mind*, and when he opens it at all, he opens it freely to her. Jane becomes attached to her "master," as Pamela-like she calls him, and it is not difficult to see that solitude and propinquity are taking effect upon him also. An odd circumstance heightens the dawning romance. Jane is awoke one night by that strange discordant laugh close to her ear—then a noise as if hands feeling along the wall. She rises—opens her door, finds the passage full of smoke, is guided by it to her master's room, whose bed she discovers enveloped in flames, and by her timely aid saves his life. After this they meet no more for ten days, when Mr. Rochester returns from a visit to a neighbouring family, bringing with him a houseful of distinguished guests; at the head of whom is Miss Blanche Ingram, a haughty beauty of high birth, and evidently the especial object of the Squire's attentions— upon which tumultuous irruption Miss Eyre slips back into her naturally humble position.

Our little governess is now summoned away to attend her aunt's death-bed, who is visited by some compunctions towards her, and she is absent a month. When she returns Thornfield Hall is quit of all its guests, and Mr. Rochester and she resume their former life of captious cordiality on the one side, and diplomatic humility on the other. At the same time the bugbear of Miss Ingram and of Mr. Rochester's engagement with her is kept up, though it is easy to see that this and all concerning that lady is only a stratagem to try Jane's character and affection upon the most approved Griselda precedent. Accordingly an opportunity for explanation ere long offers itself, where Mr. Rochester has only to take it. Miss Eyre is desired to walk with him in shady alleys, and to sit with him on the roots of an old chestnut-tree towards the close of evening, and of course she cannot disobey her "master"—whereupon there ensues a scene which, as far as we remember, is new equally in art or nature; in which Miss Eyre confesses her love—whereupon Mr. Rochester drops not only his cigar (which she seems to be in the habit of lighting for him) but his mask, and finally offers not only heart, but hand. The wedding-day is soon fixed, but strange misgivings and presentiments haunt the young lady's mind. The night but one before, her bed-room is entered by a horrid phantom, who tries on the wedding veil, sends Jane into a swoon of terror, and defeats all the favourite refuge of a bad dream by leaving the veil in two pieces. But all is ready. The bride has no friends to assist—the couple walk to church—only the clergyman and the clerk are there—but Jane's quick eye has seen two figures lingering among the tombstones, and these two follow them into church. The ceremony commences, when at the due charge which summons any man to come forward and show just cause why they should not be joined together, a voice interposes to forbid the marriage. There is an impediment, and a serious one. The bridegroom has a wife not only living, but living under the very roof of Thornfield Hall. Hers was that discordant laugh which had so often caught Jane's ear; she it was who in her malice had tried to burn Mr. Rochester in his bed—who had visited Jane by night and torn her veil, and whose attendant was that same pretended sewwoman who had so strongly excited Jane's curiosity. For Mr. Rochester's wife is a creature, half fiend, half maniac, whom he had married in a distant part of the world, and whom now, in his self-constituted code of morality, he had thought it his right, and even his duty, to supersede by a more agreeable companion. Now follow scenes of a truly tragic power. This is the grand crisis in Jane's life. Her whole soul is wrapt up in Mr. Rochester. He has broken her trust, but not diminished her love. He entreats her to accept all that he still can give, his heart and his home; he pleads with the agony not only of a man who has never known what it was to conquer a passion, but of one who, by that same self-constituted code, now burns to atone for a disappointed crime. There is no one to help her against him or against herself. Jane had no friends to stand by her at the altar, and she has none to support her now she is plucked away from it. There is no one to be offended or disgraced at her following him to the sunny land of Italy, as he proposes, till the maniac should die. There is no duty to any one but to herself, and this feeble reed quivers and trembles beneath the overwhelming weight of love and sophistry opposed to it. But Jane triumphs; in the middle of the night she rises—glides out of her room—takes off her shoes as she passes Mr. Rochester's chamber;—leaves the house, and casts herself upon a world more desert than ever to her—

"Without a shilling and without a friend."

Thus the great deed of self-conquest is accomplished; Jane has passed through the fire of temptation from without and from within; her character is stamped from that day; we need therefore follow her no further into wanderings and sufferings which, though not unmixed with plunder from Minerva-lane, occupy some of, on the whole, the most striking chapters in the book. Virtue of course finds her reward. The maniac wife sets fire to Thornfield Hall, and perishes herself in the flames. Mr. Rochester, in endeavouring to save her, loses the sight of his eyes. Jane rejoins her blind master; they are married, after which of course the happy man recovers his sight.

Such is the outline of a tale in which, combined with great materials for power and feeling, the reader may trace gross inconsistencies and improbabilities, and chief and foremost that highest moral offence a novel writer can commit, that of making an unworthy character interesting in the eyes of the reader. Mr. Rochester is a man who deliberately and secretly seeks to violate the laws both of God and man, and yet we will be bound half our lady readers are enchanted with him for a model of generosity and honour. We would have thought that such a hero had had no chance, in the purer taste of the present day; but the popularity of *Jane Eyre* is a proof how deeply the love for illegitimate romance is implanted in our nature. Not that the author is strictly responsible for this. Mr. Rochester's character is tolerably consistent. He is made as coarse and as brutal as can in all conscience be required to keep our sympathies at a distance. In point of literary consistency the hero is at all events impugnable, though we cannot say as much for the heroine.

As to Jane's character—there is none of that harmonious unity about it which made little Becky so grateful a subject of analysis—nor are the discrepancies of that kind which have their excuse and their response in our nature. The inconsistencies of Jane's character lie mainly not in her own imperfections, though of course she has her share, but in the author's. There is that confusion in the relations between cause and effect, which is not so much

untrue to human nature as to human art. The error in
Jane Eyre is, not that her character is this or that, but
that she is made one thing in the eyes of her imaginary
companions, and another in that of the actual reader.
There is a perpetual disparity between the account she
herself gives of the effect she produces, and the means
shown us by which she brings that effect about. We hear
nothing but self-eulogiums on the perfect tact and wondrous penetration with which she is gifted, and yet almost
every word she utters offends us, not only with the
absence of these qualities, but with the positive contrasts
of them, in either her pedantry, stupidity, or gross vulgarity. She is one of those ladies who put us in the
unpleasant predicament of undervaluing their very virtues
for dislike of the person in whom they are represented.
One feels provoked as Jane Eyre stands before us—for in
the wonderful reality of her thoughts and descriptions,
she seems accountable for all done in her name—with
principles you must approve in the main, and yet with
language and manners that offend you in every particular.
Even in that *chef-d'œuvre* of brilliant retrospective
sketching, the description of her early life, it is the childhood and not the child that interests you. The little
Jane, with her sharp eyes and dogmatic speeches, is a
being you neither could fondle nor love. There is a
hardness in her infantine earnestness, and a spiteful pre-
cocity in her reasoning, which repulses all our sympathy.
One sees that she is of a nature to dwell upon and treasure
up every slight and unkindness, real or fancied, and such

natures we know are surer than any others to meet with
plenty of this sort of thing. As the child, so also the
woman—an uninteresting, sententious, pedantic thing;
with no experience of the world, and yet with no simplicity
or freshness in its stead. What are her first answers to
Mr. Rochester but such as would have quenched all
interest, even for a prettier woman, in any man of common
knowledge of what was nature—and especially in a *blasé*
monster like him? A more affected governessy effusion
we never read. The question is à propos of *cadeaux*.

"Who talks of cadeaux?" said he gruffly: "did you expect a
present, Miss Eyre? Are you fond of presents?" and he
searched my face with eyes that I saw were dark, irate, and
piercing.

"I hardly know, Sir; I have little experience of them; they
are generally thought pleasant things."

"Generally thought! But what do *you* think?"

"I should be obliged to take time, Sir, before I could give you
an answer worthy of your acceptance: a present has many faces
to it, has it not? and one should consider all before pronouncing
an opinion as to its nature."

"Miss Eyre, you are not so unsophisticated as Adèle: she demands a cadeau clamorously the moment she sees me; you beat
about the bush."

"Because I have less confidence in my deserts than Adèle has;
she can prefer the right of old acquaintance and the right too of
custom; for she says you have always been in the habit of giving
her playthings; but if I had to make out a case I should be
puzzled since I am a stranger, and have done nothing to entitle
me to an acknowledgment."

"Oh! don't fall back on over modesty! I have examined
Adèle, and find you have taken great pains with her: she is not
bright—she has no talent, yet in a short time she has made much
improvement."

"Sir, you have now given me my cadeau; I am obliged to you: it is the meed teachers most covet; praise of their pupil's progress."

"Humph!" said Mr. Rochester.—vol. i., p. 234.

Let us take a specimen of her again when Mr. Rochester brings home his guests to Thornfield. The fine ladies of this world are a new study to Jane, and capitally she describes her first impression of them as they leave the dinner table and return to the drawing-room—nothing can be more gracefully graphic than this.

There were but eight of them, yet somehow as they flocked in, they gave the impression of a much larger number. Some of them were very tall, and all had a sweeping amplitude of array that seemed to magnify their persons as a mist magnifies the moon. I rose and curtseyed to them: one or two bent their heads in return; the others only stared at me.

They dispersed about the room, reminding me, by the lightness and buoyancy of their movements, of a flock of white plumy birds. Some of them threw themselves in half-reclining positions on the sofas and ottomans; some bent over the tables and examined the flowers and books; the rest gathered in a group round the fire: all talked in a low but clear tone which seemed habitual to them.—vol. ii. p. 38.

But now for the reverse. The moment Jane Eyre sets these graceful creatures conversing, she falls into mistakes which display not so much a total ignorance of the habits of society, as a vulgarity of mind inherent in herself. They talked together by her account like *parvenues* trying to show off. They discuss the subject of governesses before her very face, in what Jane affects to consider the exact tone of fashionable contempt. They bully the servants in language no lady would dream of using to her own—far less to those of her host and entertainer—though certainly the "Sam" of Jane Eyre's is not precisely the head servant one is accustomed to meet with in houses of the Thornfield class. For instance, this is a conversation which occurs in her hearing. An old gypsy has come to the Hall, and the servants can't get rid of her.

*   *   *   *   *

The old gypsy woman, by the way, turns out to be Mr. Rochester—whom Jane of course alone recognizes—as silly an incident as can well be contrived. But the crowning scene is the offer—governesses are said to be sly on such occasions, but Jane out-governesses them all—little Becky would have blushed for her. They are sitting together at the foot of the old chestnut tree, as we have already mentioned, towards the close of evening, and Mr. Rochester is informing her, with his usual delicacy of language, that he is engaged to Miss Ingram—"a strapper! Jane, a real strapper!"—and that as soon as he brings home his bride to Thornfield, she, the governess, must "trot forthwith"—but that he shall make it his duty to look out for employment and an asylum for her—indeed, that he has already heard of a charming situation in the depths of Ireland—all with a brutal jocoseness which most women of spirit, unless grievously despairing of any other lover, would have resented, and any woman of sense would have seen through. But Jane, that profound reader of the human heart, and especially of Mr.

Rochester's, does neither. She meekly hopes she may be allowed to stay where she is till she has found another shelter to betake herself to—she does not fancy going to Ireland—Why?

"It is a long way off, Sir." "No matter—a girl of your sense will not object to the voyage or the distance." "Not the voyage, but the distance, Sir; and then the sea is a barrier——" "From what, Jane?" "From England and from Thornfield; and——" "Well?" "From *you*, Sir."—vol. ii., p. 205.

and then the lady bursts into tears in the most approved fashion.

Although so clever in giving hints, how wonderfully slow she is in taking them! Even when, tired of his cat's play, Mr. Rochester proceeds to rather indubitable demonstrations of affection—"enclosing me in his arms, gathering me to his breast, pressing his lips on my lips"—Jane has no idea what he can mean. Some ladies would have thought it high time to leave the Squire alone with his chestnut tree; or, at all events, unnecessary to keep up that tone of high-souled feminine obtusity which they are quite justified in adopting if gentlemen will not speak out—but Jane again does neither. Not that we say she was wrong, but quite the reverse, considering the circumstances of the case—Mr. Rochester was her master, and "Duchess or nothing" was her first duty—only she was not quite so artless as the author would have us suppose.

But if the manner in which she secures the prize be not inadmissible according to the rules of the art, that in which she manages it when caught, is quite without authority or precedent, except perhaps in the servants' hall. Most lover's play is wearisome and nonsensical to the lookers on—but the part Jane assumes is one which could only be efficiently sustained by the substitution of Sam for her master. Coarse as Mr. Rochester is, one winces for him under the infliction of this housemaid *beau idéal* of the arts of coquetry. A little more, and we should have flung the book aside to lie for ever among the trumpery with which such scenes ally it; but it were a pity to have halted here, for wonderful things lie beyond— scenes of suppressed feeling, more fearful to witness than the most violent tornadoes of passion—struggles with such intense sorrow and suffering as it is sufficient misery to know that any one should have conceived, far less passed through; and yet with that stamp of truth which takes precedence in the human heart before actual experience. The flippant, fifth-rate, plebeian actress has vanished, and only a noble, high-souled woman, bound to us by the reality of her sorrow, and yet raised above us by the strength of her will, stands in actual life before us. If this be Jane Eyre, the author has done her injustice hitherto, not we. Let us look at her in the first recognition of her sorrow after the discomfiture of the marriage. True, it is not the attitude of a Christian, who knows that all things work together for good to those who love God, but it is a splendidly drawn picture of a natural heart, of high power, intense feeling, and fine religious instinct, falling prostrate, but not grovelling, before the tremendous blast of sudden affliction. The house is cleared of those who had come between her and a disgraceful happiness.

* * * * *

We have said that this was the picture of a natural heart. This, to our view, is the great and crying mischief of the book. Jane Eyre is throughout the personification of an unregenerate and undisciplined spirit, the more dangerous to exhibit from that prestige of principle and self-control which is liable to dazzle the eye too much for it to observe the inefficient and unsound foundation on which it rests. It is true Jane does right, and exerts great moral strength, but it is the strength of a mere heathen mind which is a law unto itself. No Christian grace is perceptible upon her. She has inherited in fullest measure the worst sin of our fallen nature—the sin of pride. Jane Eyre is proud, and therefore she is ungrateful too. It pleased God to make her an orphan, friendless, and penniless—yet she thanks nobody, and least of all Him, for the food and raiment, the friends, companions, and instructors of her helpless youth—for the care and education vouchsafed to her till she was capable in mind as fitted in years to provide for herself. On the contrary, she looks upon all that has been done for her not only as her undoubted right, but as falling far short of it. The doctrine of humility is not more foreign to her mind than it is repudiated by her heart. It is by her own talents, virtues, and courage that she is made to attain the summit of human happiness, and, as far as Jane Eyre's own statement is concerned, no one would think that she owed anything either to God above or to man below. She flees from Mr. Rochester, and has not a being to turn to. Why was this? The excellence of the present institution at Casterton, which succeeded that of Cowan Bridge near Kirkby Lonsdale—these being distinctly, as we hear, the original and the reformed Lowoods of the book—is pretty generally known. Jane had lived there for eight years with 110 girls and 15 teachers. Why had she formed no friendships among them? Other orphans have left the same and similar institutions, furnished with friends for life, and puzzled with homes to choose from. How comes it that Jane had acquired neither? Among that number of associates there were surely some exceptions to what she so presumptuously stigmatizes as "the society of inferior minds." Of course it suited the author's end to represent the heroine as utterly destitute of the common means of assistance, in order to exhibit both her trials and her powers of self-support—the whole book rests on this assumption—but it is one which, under the circumstances, is very unnatural and very unjust.

Altogether the autobiography of Jane Eyre is pre-eminently an anti-Christian composition. There is throughout it a murmuring against the comforts of the rich and against the privations of the poor, which, as far as each individual is concerned, is a murmuring against God's appointment—there is a proud and perpetual assertion of the rights of man, for which we find no authority either in God's word or in God's providence—there is that pervading tone of ungodly discontent which is at once the most prominent and the most subtle evil

which the law and the pulpit, which all civilized
society in fact has at the present day to contend with.
We do not hesitate to say that the tone of mind and
thought which has overthrown authority and violated
every code human and divine abroad, and fostered Char-
tism and rebellion at home, is the same which has also
written *Jane Eyre*.

Still we say again this is a very remarkable book. We
are painfully alive to the moral, religious, and literary
deficiencies of the picture, and such passages of beauty
and power as we have quoted cannot redeem it, but it is
impossible not to be spellbound with the freedom of the
touch. It would be mere hackneyed courtesy to call it
"fine writing." It bears no impress of being written at all,
but is poured out rather in the heat and hurry of an
instinct, which flows ungovernably on to its object, indifferent by what means it reaches it, and unconscious too.
As regards the author's chief object, however, it is a
failure—that, namely, of making a plain, odd woman,
destitute of all the conventional features of feminine
attraction, interesting in our sight. We deny that he has
succeeded in this. Jane Eyre, in spite of some grand
things about her, is a being totally uncongenial to our feelings from beginning to end. We acknowledge her firm-
ness—we respect her determination—we feel for her
struggles; but, for all that, and setting aside higher con-
siderations, the impression she leaves on our mind is that
of a decidedly vulgar-minded woman—one whom we
should not care for as an acquaintance, whom we should
not seek as a friend, whom we should not desire for a

relation, and whom we should scrupulously avoid for a governess.

There seem to have arisen in the novel-reading world some doubts as to who really wrote this book; and various rumours, more or less romantic, have been current in Mayfair, the metropolis of gossip, as to the authorship. For example, *Jane Eyre* is sentimentally assumed to have proceeded from the pen of Mr. Thackeray's governess, whom he had himself chosen as his model of Becky, and who, in mingled love and revenge, personified him in return as Mr. Rochester. In this case, it is evident that the author of *Vanity Fair*, whose own pencil makes him grey-haired, has had the best of it, though his children may have had the worst, having, at all events, succeeded in hitting that vulnerable point in the Becky bosom, which it is our firm belief no man born of woman, from her Soho to her Ostend days, had ever so much as grazed. To this ingenious rumour the coincidence of the second edition of *Jane Eyre* being dedicated to Mr. Thackeray has probably given rise. For our parts, we see no great interest in the question at all. The first edition of *Jane Eyre* purports to be edited by Currer Bell, one of a trio of brothers, or sisters, or cousins, by names Currer, Acton, and Ellis Bell, already known as the joint-authors of a volume of poems. The second edition the same—dedicated, however, "by the author," to Mr. Thackeray; and the dedication (itself an indubitable *chip* of *Jane Eyre*) signed Currer Bell. Author and editor therefore are one, and we are as much satisfied to accept this double individual under the name of "Currer

Bell," as under any other, more or less euphonious. Whoever it be, it is a person who, with great mental powers, combines a total ignorance of the habits of society, a great coarseness of taste, and a heathenish doctrine of religion. And as these characteristics appear more or less in the writings of all three, Currer, Acton, and Ellis alike, for their poems differ less in degree of power than in kind, we are ready to accept the fact of their identity or of their relationship with equal satisfaction. At all events there can be no interest attached to the writer of *Wuthering Heights*—a novel succeeding *Jane Eyre* and purporting to be written by Ellis Bell—unless it were for the sake of more individual reprobation. For though there is a decided family likeness between the two, yet the aspect of the Jane and Rochester animals in their native state, as Catherine and Heathfield, is too odiously and abominably pagan to be palatable even to the most vitiated class of English readers. With all the unscrupulousness of the French school of novels it combines that repulsive vulgarity in the choice of its vice which supplies its own antidote. The question of authorship, therefore, can deserve a moment's curiosity only as far as *Jane Eyre* is concerned, and though we cannot pronounce that it appertains to a real Mr. Currer Bell and to no other, yet that it appertains to a man, and not, as many assert, to a woman, we are strongly inclined to affirm. Without entering into the question whether the power of the writing be above her, or the vulgarity below her, there are, we believe, minutiæ of circumstantial evidence which at once acquit the feminine hand. No woman—a lady

friend, whom we are always happy to consult, assures
us—makes mistakes in her own *métier*—no woman *trusses
game* and garnishes dessert-dishes with the same hands, or
talks of so doing in the same breath. Above all, no
woman attires another in such fancy dresses as Jane's
ladies assume—Miss Ingram coming down, irresistible,
"in a *morning* robe of sky-blue crape, a gauze azure scarf
twisted in her hair!" No lady, we understand, when
suddenly roused in the night, would think of hurrying on
"*a frock*." They have garments more convenient for such
occasions, and more becoming too. This evidence seems
incontrovertible. Even granting that these incongruities
were purposely assumed, for the sake of disguising the
female pen, there is nothing gained; for if we ascribe
the book to a woman at all, we have no alternative but
to ascribe it to one who has, for some sufficient reason,
long forfeited the society of her own sex.

And if by no woman, it is certainly also by no artist.
The Thackeray eye has had no part there. There is not
more disparity between the art of drawing Jane assumes
and her evident total ignorance of its first principles, than
between the report she gives of her own character and the
conclusions we form for ourselves. Not but what, in
another sense, the author may be classed as an artist of
very high grade. Let him describe the simplest things
in nature—a rainy landscape, a cloudy sky, or a bare
moorside, and he shows the hand of a master; but the
moment he talks of the art itself, it is obvious that he is a
complete ignoramus.

We cannot help feeling that this work must be far

from beneficial to that class of ladies whose cause it affects to advocate. *Jane Eyre* is not precisely the mouthpiece one would select to plead the cause of governesses, and it is therefore the greater pity that she has chosen it: for there is none we are convinced which at the present time, more deserves and demands an earnest and judicious befriending.*

* *The Quarterly Review*, December, 1848. (Elizabeth Rigby, later Lady Eastlake.)

THE SCARLET LETTER

By Nathaniel Hawthorne

AS yet our literature, however humble, is undefiled, and as such is a just cause for national pride, nor, much as we long to see it elevated in style, would we thank the Boccaccio who should give it the classic stamp, at the expense of its purity. Of course we cannot expect to see it realize that splendid ideal which a thoughtful Churchman would sketch for it, as equally chaste in morals, lofty in sentiment, uncorrupt in diction, and in all points conformable to truth; but surely we may demand that it shall keep itself from becoming an offence to faith, and a scandal to virtue. Not that we expect the literary pimp to cease from his disgusting trade, but that we hope to keep writers of that class out of the pale of Letters, and to effect the forcible expulsion of any one of a higher class, who, gaining upon our confidence by dealing at first in a sterling article, afterwards debases his credit, by issuing with the same stamp a vile, but marketable, alloy. In a word, we protest against any toleration to a popular and gifted writer, when he perpetrates bad morals. Let this brokerage of lust be put down at the very beginning. Already, among the million, we have imitations enough of George Sand and Eugene Sue; and if as yet there be no reputable name, involved in the manufacture of a Brothel Library, we congratulate the country that we are yet in time to save such a reputation as that of Hawthorne. Let him stop where he has begun, lest we should be forced to select an epitaph from *Hudibras*, for his future memorial:

> "Quoth he—for many years he drove
> A kind of broking trade in love,
> Employed in all th' intrigues and trust
> Of feeble, speculative lust;
> Procurer to th' extravaganzy
> And crazy ribaldry of fancy."

It is chiefly, in hopes, to save our author from embarking largely into this business of Fescennine romance, that we enter upon a brief examination of his latest and most ambitious production, *The Scarlet Letter.*

The success which seems to have attended this bold advance of Hawthorne, and the encouragement which has been dealt out by some professed critics,* to its worst symptoms of malice prepense, may very naturally lead, if unbalanced by a moderate dissent, to his further compromise of his literary character. We are glad, therefore, that *The Scarlet Letter* is, after all, little more than an experiment, and need not be regarded as a step necessarily fatal. It is an attempt to rise from the composition of petty tales, to the historical novel; and we use the expression *an attempt,* with no disparaging significance, for it is confessedly a trial of strength only just beyond some former efforts, and was designed as part of a series. It may properly be called a novel, because it has all the ground-work, and might have been very easily elaborated

* See a later article in the *Massachusetts Quarterly.*

into the details, usually included in the term; and we call
it *historical*, because its scene-painting is in a great degree
true to a period of our Colonial history, which ought to
be more fully delineated. We wish Mr. Hawthorne
would devote the powers which he only partly discloses
in this book, to a large and truthful portraiture of that
period, with the patriotic purpose of making us better
acquainted with the stern old worthies, and all the *dra-
matis personæ* of those times, with their yet surviving
habits, recollections, and yearnings, derived from maternal
England. Here is, in fact, a rich and even yet an un-
explored field for historic imagination; and touches are
given in *The Scarlet Letter*, to secret springs of romantic
thought, which opened unexpected and delightful epi-
sodes to our fancy, as we were borne along by the tale.
Here a maiden reminiscence, and here a grave ecclesiastical
retrospection, clouding the brow of the Puritan colonists,
as they still remembered home, in their wilderness of
lasting exile! Now a lingering relic of Elizabethan
fashion in dress, and now a turn of expression, betraying
the deep traces of education under influences renounced
and foresworn, but still instinctively prevalent!

Time has just enough mellowed the facts, and genea-
logical research has made them just enough familiar, for
their employment as material for descriptive fiction; and
the New England colonies might now be made as pictur-
esquely real to our perception, as the Knickerbocker tales
have made the Dutch settlements of the Hudson. This,
however, can never be done by the polemical pen of a
blind partisan of the Puritans; it demands Irving's humor-

ously insinuating gravity and all his benevolent satire, with a large share of honest sympathy for at least the earnestness of wrong-headed enthusiasm. We are stimulated to this suggestion by the very lifelike and striking manner in which the days of Governor Winthrop are sketched in the book before us, by the beautiful picture the author has given us of the venerable old pastor Wilson, and by the outline portraits he has thrown in, of several of their contemporaries. We like him, all the better for his tenderness of the less exceptionable features of the Puritan character; but we are hardly sure that we like his flings at their failings. If it should provoke a smile to find us sensitive in this matter, our consistency may be very briefly demonstrated. True, we have our own fun with the follies of the Puritans; it is our inseparable privilege as Churchmen, thus to compensate ourselves for many a scar which their frolics have left on our comeliness. But when a degenerate Puritan, whose Socinian conscience is but the skimmed-milk of their creamy fanaticism, allows such a conscience to curdle within him, in dyspeptic acidulation, and then belches forth derision at the sour piety of his forefathers—we snuff at him, with an honest scorn, knowing very well that he likes the Puritans for their worst enormities, and hates them only for their redeeming merits.

The Puritan rebelling against the wholesome discipline of that Ecclesiastical Law, which Hooker has demonstrated, with Newtonian evidence, to be but a moral system of central light with its dependent order and illumination; the Puritan with his rough heel and tough heart, mounted upon altars, and hacking down crosses, and sepulchres, and memorials of the dead; the Puritan with his axe on an Archbishop's neck, or holding up in his hand the bleeding head of a martyred king; the Puritan in all this guilt, has his warmest praise, and his prompt witness that he allows the deeds of his fathers, and is ready to fill up the measure of their iniquity; but the Puritans, with a blessed inconsistency, repeating liturgic doxologies to the triune GOD, or, by the domestic hearth, bowing down with momentary conformity, to invoke the name of Jesus, whom the Church had taught him to adore as an atoning Saviour—these are the Puritans at whom the driveller wags his head, and shoots out his tongue!   We would not laugh in that man's company. No—no! we heartily dislike the Puritans, so far as they were Puritan; but even in them we recognize many good old English virtues, which Puritanism could not kill. They were in part our ancestors, and though we would not accept the bequest of their enthusiasm, we are not ashamed of many things to which they clung, with principle quite as characteristic.   We see no harm in a reverent joke now and then, at an abstract Puritan, in spite of our duty to our progenitors, and *Hudibras* shall still be our companion, when, at times, the mental bow requires fresh elasticity, and bids us relax its string.   There is, after all, something of human kindness, in taking out an old grudge in the comfort of a hearty, side-shaking laugh, and we think we are never freer from bitterness of spirit, than when we contemplate the Banbury zealot hanging his cat on Monday, and reflect that Strafford and Montrose fell victims to the same mania that destroyed poor puss. But there is another view of the same Puritan, which even a Churchman may charitably allow himself to respect, and when precisely that view is chosen by his degenerate offspring for unfilial derision, we own to a sympathy for the grim old Genevan features, at which their seventh reproduction turns up a repugnant nose; for sure we are that the young Ham is gloating over his father's nakedness, with far less of sorrow for the ebriety of a parent, than of satisfaction in the degradation of an orthodox patriarch. Now without asserting that it is so, we are not quite so sure, as we would like to be, that our author is not venting something of this spirit against the Puritans, in his rich delineation of "godly Master Dimmesdale," and the sorely abused confidence of his flock. There is a provoking concealment of the author's motive, from the beginning to the end of the story; we wonder what he would be at; whether he is making fun of all religion, or only giving a fair hint of the essential sensualism of enthusiasm. But, in short, we are astonished at the kind of incident which he has selected for romance. It may be such incidents were too common, to be wholly out of the question, in a history of the times, but it seems to us that good taste might be pardoned for not giving them prominence in fiction. In deference to the assertions of a very acute analyst, who has written ably on the subject of colonization, we are inclined to think, as we have said before, that barbarism was indeed "the first danger" of the pilgrim settlers. Of a period nearly cotemporary with that of Mr. Hawthorne's narrative, an habitual eulogist has recorded that "on going to its Church and court records, we discover mournful evidences of incontinence, even in the respectable families; as if, being cut off from the more refined pleasures of society, their baser passions had burnt away the restraints of delicacy, and their growing coarseness of manners had allowed them finally to seek, in these baser passions, the spring of their enjoyments." We are sorry to be told so, by so unexceptionable a witness.* We had supposed, with the Roman satirist, that purity might at least be credited to those primitive days, when a Saturnian simplicity was necessarily revived in primeval forests, by the New England colonists:

> Quippe aliter tunc orbe novo, cœloque recenti
> Vivebant homines:

but a Puritan doctor in divinity publishes the contrary, and a Salemite novelist selects the intrigue of an adulterous minister, as the groundwork of his ideal of those times! We may acknowledge, with reluctance, the historical fidelity of the picture, which retailers of fact and fiction thus concur in framing, but we cannot but wonder that a novelist should select, of all features of the period, that which reflects most discredit upon the cradle of his country, and which is in itself so revolting, and so incapable of receiving decoration from narrative genius.

And this brings inquiry to its point. Why has our author selected such a theme? Why, amid all the suggestive incidents of life in a wilderness; of a retreat from civilization to which, in every individual case, a thousand

---

* *Barbarism the first Danger*, by H. Bushnell, D.D.

circumstances must have concurred to reconcile human nature with estrangement from home and country; or amid the historical connections of our history with Jesuit adventure, savage invasion, regicide outlawry, and French aggression, should the taste of Mr. Hawthorne have preferred as the proper material for romance, the nauseous amour of a Puritan pastor, with a frail creature of his charge, whose mind is represented as far more debauched than her body? Is it, in short, because a running undertide of filth has become as requisite to a romance, as death in the fifth act to a tragedy? Is the French era actually begun in our literature? And is the flesh, as well as the world and the devil, to be henceforth dished up in fashionable novels, and discussed at parties, by spinsters and their beaux, with as unconcealed a relish as they give to the vanilla in their ice cream? We would be slow to believe it, and we hope our author would not willingly have it so, yet we honestly believe that *The Scarlet Letter* has already done not a little to degrade our literature, and to encourage social licentiousness: it has started other pens on like enterprises, and has loosed the restraint of many tongues, that have made it an apology for "the evil communications which corrupt good manners." We are painfully tempted to believe that it is a book made for the market, and that the market has made it merchantable, as they do game, by letting everybody understand that the commodity is in high condition, and smells strongly of incipient putrefaction.

We shall entirely mislead our reader if we give him to suppose that *The Scarlet Letter* is coarse in its details, or indecent in its phraseology. This very article of our own, is far less suited to ears polite, than any page of the romance before us; and the reason is, we call things by their right names, while the romance never hints the shocking words that belong to its things, but, like Mephistopheles, insinuates that the arch-fiend himself is a very tolerable sort of person, if nobody would call him Mr. Devil. We have heard of persons who could not bear the reading of some Old Testament Lessons in the service of the Church: such persons would be delighted with our author's story; and damsels who shrink at the reading of the Decalogue, would probably luxuriate in bathing their imagination in the crystal of its delicate sensuality. The language of our author, like patent blacking, "would not soil the whitest linen," and yet the composition itself, would suffice, if well laid on, to Ethiopize the snowiest conscience that ever sat like a swan upon that mirror of heaven, a Christian maiden's imagination. We are not sure we speak quite strong enough, when we say, that we would much rather listen to the coarsest scene of Goldsmith's *Vicar*, read aloud by a sister or daughter, than to hear from such lips, the perfectly chaste language of a scene in *The Scarlet Letter*, in which a married wife and her reverend paramour, with their unfortunate offspring, are introduced as the actors, and in which the whole tendency of the conversation is to suggest a sympathy for their sin, and an anxiety that they may be able to accomplish a successful escape beyond the seas, to some country where their shameful commerce may be perpetuated. Now, in Goldsmith's story there are very coarse words, but we do not remember anything that saps the foundations of the moral sense, or that goes to create unavoidable sympathy with unrepenting sorrow, and deliberate, premeditated sin. The *Vicar of Wakefield* is sometimes coarsely virtuous, but *The Scarlet Letter* is delicately immoral.

There is no better proof of the bad tendency of a work, than some unintentional betrayal on the part of a young female reader, of an instinctive consciousness against it, to which she has done violence, by reading it through. In a beautiful region of New England, where stage-coaches are not yet among things that were, we found ourselves, last summer, one of a travelling party, to which we were entirely a stranger, consisting of young ladies fresh from boarding-school, with the proverbial bread-and-butter look of innocence in their faces, and a nursery thickness about their tongues. Their benevolent uncle sat outside upon the driver's box, and ours was a seat next to a worshipful old dowager, who seemed to bear some matronly relation to the whole coach-load, with the single exception of ourselves. In such a situation it was ours to keep silence, and we soon relapsed into nothingness and a semi-slumberous doze. Meanwhile our young friends were animated and talkative, and as we were approaching the seat of a College, their literature soon began to expose itself. They were evidently familiar with the Milliners' Magazines in general, and even with Graham's and Harper's. They had read James, and they had read Dickens; and at last their criticisms rose to Irving and Walter Scott, whose various merits they discussed with an artless anxiety to settle for ever the question whether the one was not "a

charming composer," and the other "a truly beautiful
writer." Poor girls! had they imagined how much harmless amusement they were furnishing to their drowsy,
dusty, and very unentertaining fellow traveller, they
might, quite possibly, have escaped both his praise and his
censure! They came at last to Longfellow and Bryant,
and rhythmically regaled us with the "muffled drum" of
the one, and the somewhat familiar opinion of the other,
that

> "Truth crushed to earth will rise again."

And so they came to Hawthorne, of whose *Scarlet Letter*
we then knew very little, and that little was favourable,
as we had seen several high encomiums of its style. We
expected a quotation from the *Celestial Railroad*, for we
were travelling at a rate which naturally raised the era of
railroads in one's estimation, by rule of contrary; but no—
the girls went straight to *The Scarlet Letter.* We soon
discovered that one Hester Prynne was the heroine, and
that she had been made to stand in the pillory, as, indeed,
her surname might have led one to anticipate. We discovered that there was a mysterious little child in the question, that she was a sweet little darling, and that her
"sweet, pretty little name," was "Pearl." We discovered
that mother and child had a meeting, in a wood, with a
very fascinating young preacher, and that there was a
hateful creature named Chillingworth, who persecuted
the said preacher, very perseveringly. Finally, it appeared
that Hester Prynne was, in fact, Mrs. Hester Chillingworth, and that the hateful old creature aforesaid had a

very natural dislike to the degradation of his spouse, and quite as natural a hatred of the wolf in sheep's clothing who had wrought her ruin. All this leaked out in conversation, little by little, on the hypothesis of our protracted somnolency. There was a very gradual approximation to the point, till one inquired—"didn't you think, from the first, that he was the one?" A modest looking creature, who evidently had not read the story, artlessly inquired—"what one?"—and then there was a titter at the child's simplicity, in the midst of which we ventured to be quite awake, and to discover by the scarlet blush that began to circulate, that the young ladies were not unconscious to themselves that reading *The Scarlet Letter* was a thing to be ashamed of. These school-girls had, in fact, done injury to their young sense of delicacy, by devouring such a dirty story; and after talking about it before folk, inadvertently, they had enough of mother Eve in them, to know that they were ridiculous, and that shame was their best retreat.

Now it would not have been so if they had merely exhibited a familiarity with *The Heart of Mid-Lothian*, and yet there is more mention of the foul sin in its pages, than there is in *The Scarlet Letter*. Where then is the difference? It consists in this—that the holy innocence of Jeanie Deans, and not the shame of Effie, is the burthen of that story, and that neither Effie's fall is made to look like virtue, nor the truly honourable agony of her stern old father, in bewailing his daughter's ruin, made a joke, by the insinuation that it was quite gratuitous. But in Hawthorne's tale, the lady's frailty is philosophized into a natural and necessary result of the Scriptural law of marriage, which, by holding her irrevocably to her vows, as plighted to a dried up old book-worm, in her silly girlhood, is viewed as making her heart an easy victim to the adulterer. The sin of her seducer too, seems to be considered as lying not so much in the deed itself, as in his long concealment of it, and, in fact, the whole moral of the tale is given in the words—"Be true—be true," as if sincerity in sin were virtue, and as if "Be clean—be clean," were not the more fitting conclusion. "The untrue man" is, in short, the hang-dog of the narrative, and the unclean one is made a very interesting sort of a person, and as the two qualities are united in the hero, their composition creates the interest of his character. Shelley himself never imagined a more dissolute conversation than that in which the polluted minister comforts himself with the thought, that the revenge of the injured husband is worse than his own sin in instigating it. "Thou and I never did so, Hester"—he suggests: and she responds—"never, never! What we did had *a consecration of its own,* we felt it so—we said so to each other!" This is a little too much—it carries the Bay-theory a little too far for our stomach! "Hush, Hester!" is the sickish rejoinder; and fie, Mr. Hawthorne! is the weakest token of our disgust that we can utter. The poor bemired hero and heroine of the story should not have been seen wallowing in their filth, at such a rate as this.

We suppose this sort of sentiment must be charged to the doctrines enforced at "Brook-farm," although "Brook-farm" itself could never have been Mr. Hawthorne's home, had not other influences prepared him for such a Bedlam. At all events, this is no mere slip of the pen; it is the essential morality of the work. If types, and letters, and words can convey an author's idea, he has given us the key to the whole, in a very plain intimation that the Gospel has not set the relations of man and woman where they should be, and that a new Gospel is needed to supersede the seventh commandment, and the bond of Matrimony. Here it is, in full: our readers shall see what the world may expect from Hawthorne, if he is not stopped short, in such brothelry. Look at this conclusion:—

Women—in the continually recurring trials of wounded, wasted, wronged, misplaced, or erring and sinful passion, or with the dreary burden of a heart unyielded, because unvalued and unsought—came to Hester's cottage, demanding why they were so wretched, and what the remedy! Hester comforted and counselled them as best she might. She assured them too *of her firm belief*, that, at some brighter period, when the world should have grown ripe for it, in Heaven's own time, *a new truth would be revealed, in order to establish the whole relation between man and woman on a surer ground of mutual happiness.*

This is intelligible English; but are Americans content that such should be the English of their literature? This is the question on which we have endeavoured to deliver our own earnest convictions, and on which we hope to unite the suffrages of all virtuous persons in sympathy with the abhorrence we so unhesitatingly express. To think of making such speculations the amusement of the daughters of America! The late Convention of females at Boston, to assert the "rights of woman," may show us that there are already some, who think the world is even now *ripe for it;* and safe as we may suppose our own fair relatives to be above such a low contagion, we must remember that to a woman, the very suggestion of a mode of life for her, as preferable to that which the Gospel has made the glorious sphere of her duties and her joys, is an insult and a degradation, to which no one that loves her would allow her to be exposed.

We assure Mr. Hawthorne, in conclusion, that nothing less than an earnest wish that his future career may redeem this misstep, and prove a blessing to his country, has tempted us to enter upon a criticism so little suited to our tastes, as that of his late production. We commend to his attention the remarks of Mr. Alison, on cotemporary popularity, to be found in the review of Bossuet. We would see him, too, rising to a place amongst those immortal authors who have "clothed the lessons of religion in the burning words of genius;" and let him be assured, that, however great his momentary success, there is no lasting reputation for such an one as he is, except as it is founded on real worth, and fidelity to the morals of the Gospel. The time is past, when mere authorship provokes posthumous attention; there are too many who write with ease, and too many who publish books, in our times, for an author to be considered anything extraordinary. Poems perish in newspapers nowadays, which, at one time, would have made, at least, a name for biographical dictionaries; and stories lie dead in the pages of magazines, which would once have secured their author a mention with posterity. Hereafter those only will be thought

of, who have embalmed their writings in the hearts and
lives of a few, at least, who learned from them to love
truth and follow virtue. The age of "mute inglorious
Milton," is as dead as the age of chivalry. Everybody
can write, and everybody can publish. But still, the wise
are few; and it is only the wise, who can attain, in any
worthy sense, to shine as the stars for ever.*

* *Church Review*, January, 1851. (A. C. Coxe.)

MAUD *

By Alfred Tennyson

W E are old enough to remember the time when the bare announcement of a new poem from the pen of Byron, or of a new romance from that of Scott, was sufficient to send a thrill of curiosity and expectation through the whole body of the public. No ingenious newspaper puffs, containing hints as to the nature and tone of the forthcoming production, were then required to stimulate the jaded appetite and prepare it for the enjoyment of the promised feast. Gluttons all of us, we had hardly devoured one dish fit for a banquet of the gods, before we were ready for another; and it needed not the note of lute or psaltery, sackbut or dulcimer, to induce us to pounce, ravenous as eagles, upon the coming prey. Some selfishness undoubtedly there was; for we have known desperate, and even demoniacal, struggles take place for the possession of an early copy. The mail-coach, which was supposed to carry one or more of these precious parcels a week or so before the general delivery, was in much greater danger of being stopped and plundered than if the boot had been stuffed with boxes contain-

---

* *Maud, and other Poems.* By Alfred Tennyson, D.C.L., Poet Laureate. London, 1855.

Five extracts are omitted. The rest are retained on account of the exigencies of the text. (The editor.)

ing the laminous issue of the Bank of England. One
ancient guard, well known to travellers on the north road
for his civility to passengers and his admiration of rum
and milk, used to exhibit a lump behind his ear, about the
size of a *magnum bonum* plum, arising from an injury
caused by the pistol of a literary footpad, who attacked
the mail near Alnwick for the purpose of obtaining forcible possession of a proof copy of *Rob Roy*. Judges were
known to have absented themselves from the bench
for the undisturbed engorgement, and for weeks afterwards the legal opinions which they delivered were
strangely studded with mediæval terms. As for the poetical apprentices, Byron was, indeed, the very prince of the
flat-caps. No sooner was a fresh work of his announced,
than opium and prussic acid rose rapidly in the market;
and the joyous tidings of some new harlotry by Mr.
Thomas Moore created a fluttering as of besmirched doves
among the delicate damsels of Drury Lane.

All that, however, is matter of history, for the world
since then has become, if not wiser, much more callous
and indifferent. We have been fed for a long time upon
adulterated viands, and have grown mightily suspicious of
the sauce. Since the literary caterers, with very few exceptions, betook themselves to puffing, and to the dubious
task of representing garbage only fit for cat's-meat, as
pieces of the primest quality, men have grown shy through
frequent disappointment, and will not allow themselves
to be seduced into anticipatory ecstasies even by the most
tempting bill of fare. When every possible kind of publication—from the lumbering journals and salacious court-

gossip of some antiquated patrician pantaloon, edited by
his senseless son, down to the last History of the High-
way, with sketches of eminent burglars—from the play
after the perusal of which in manuscript Mr. Macready
was attacked by British cholera, down to the poem so
very spasmodic that it reminds you of the writhing of a
knot of worms—from audacious, though most contemptible, forgeries on the dead, down to the autobiography of
a rogue and a swindler—is represented as "a work of surpassing interest, full of genius, calculated to make a lasting impression on the public mind," and so forth, can it
be wondered at if the public has long ago lost faith
in such announcements? It would be as easy to induce a
pack of fox-hounds to follow a trail through the town of
Wick in the herring season, as to allure purchasers by dint
of this indiscriminate system of laudation.

Yet we deny not that at times we feel a recurrence
of the old fever-fit of expectation. The advertisement of
a forthcoming novel by Sir E. B. Lytton would excite in
the bosoms of many of us sensations similar to those which
agitate a Junior Lord of the Treasury at the near approach
of quarter-day. If we could only be assured of the exact
time when Mr. Macaulay's new volumes are to appear, we
might, even now, forgive him for having kept us so long
upon the tenter-hooks. Let Lord Palmerston fix a precise day for the issue of his Life and Political Reminiscences, and we gage our credit that, before dawn, the
doors of his publisher will be besieged; and, to come to
the immediate subject of this article, we have been waiting
for a long time, with deep anxiety, for the promised new

volume of poems by Alfred Tennyson. The young cormorant, whom from our study window we see sitting upon a rock in the voe, was an egg on a ledge of the cliff when we first heard whisper that the Laureate was again preparing to sing. The early daisies were then starring the sward, and the primroses blooming on the bank; and now the poppies are red amongst the corn, and the corn itself yellowing into harvest. Post after post arrived, and yet they brought not *Maud*—a sore disappointment to us, for we are dwelling in the land of the Niebelungen, where, Providence be praised, there are no railways, and cheap literature is deliciously scarce—so we fell back upon Tennyson's earlier poems, solaced ourselves with the glorious rhythm of "Locksley Hall" and the "Morte D'Arthur," lay among the purple heather, and read "Ulysses" and the "Lotos-eaters," and dreamed luxuriously of the "Sleeping Beauty." These, and one or two others, such as "Dora," and the "Gardener's Daughter," are poems of which we never tire, so exquisite is their expression, and so delicate their music; and for their sake we are content to pass over a good deal that is indifferent in quality, and much that is affected in manner. For— the truth must be said, notwithstanding the chirping of numerous indiscreet admirers who are incapable of distinguishing one note from another—Alfred Tennyson is singularly unequal in composition. Some of the poems upon which he appears to have bestowed the greatest amount of labour, and on which we suspect he particularly plumes himself, are his worst, and we never could join in the admiration which we have heard expressed for

In Memoriam. | It is simply a dirge, with countless variations, calculated, no doubt, to show the skill of the musician, but conveying no impression of reality or truthfulness to the mind. Grief may be so drawled out and protracted as to lose its primary character, and to assume that very modified form which the older poets used to denominate the luxury of woe. One epitaph, in prose or verse, is enough for even the best of our race, and the briefer it can be made, the better. To sit down deliberately and elaborate several scores in memory of the same individual, is a waste of ingenuity on the part of the writer, and a sore trial of temper to the reader. Nor can we aver that we are at all partial to this kind of funereal commemoration when carried to an extreme. Poets may be excused for fabricating, in their hours of melancholy, an occasional dirge or so, which may serve as a safety-valve to their excited feelings; but their voices were given them for something better than to keep wheezing all day long like a chorus of consumptive sextons. Therefore we have never included *In Memoriam* in the list of our travelling library, but have left it at home on the same shelf with Blair's *Grave*, and the *Oraisons Funèbres*.

We confess to have been disappointed with *The Princess*. The idea of the poem, though somewhat bizarre, was novel and ingenious, and allowed scope for great variety, but it necessarily implied the possession of more humorous power than Mr. Tennyson has yet displayed. In it, however, are to be found some most beautiful lines and passages—so beautiful, indeed, that they almost seem out of place in a poem which, as a whole, leaves so faint and vague an impression on the mind of the reader. We ought, however, to accept *The Princess, a Medley,* for what it probably was intended to be—a freak of fancy; and in that view it would be unfair to apply to it any stringent rules of criticism.

Even those who esteemed his later volumes more highly than we were able to do—who protested that they had wept over portions of *In Memoriam,* and that they were able to extract deep lessons of philosophy from divers dark sayings in *The Princess,* which, to uninitiated eyes, seemed rather devoid of meaning—even they were constrained to admit that something better might have been expected from Alfred. And now, when, after a breathing-time, he had taken the field afresh, we entertained a sincere and earnest hope that his new poem would be equal, if not superior, to any of his former productions.

We have at last received *Maud,* and we have risen from its perusal dispirited and sorrowful. It is not a light thing nor a trivial annoyance to a sincere lover of literature to have it forced upon his conviction that the man, who has unquestionably occupied for years the first place among the living British poets, is losing ground with each successive effort. During the earlier part of the present century, when poetry as an especial art was more cultivated if not more prized than now, there were many competitors for the laurels; and when the song of one minstrel ceased or grew faint, another was emulous with his strain. It is not so now. We have, indeed, much piping, but little real melody; and knowing that we have but a very slight poetical reserve to fall back upon, we watch with more than ordinary vigilance and anxiety the career of those who have already won a reputation. It is singular, but true, that the high burst of poetry which many years ago was simultaneously exhibited both in Germany and Great Britain, has suddenly declined in either country— that no adequate successors should be found to Schiller, Goethe, Tieck, and Uhland, in the one—or to Scott, Byron, Campbell, and Coleridge, in the other. Many more names, both German and British, we might have cited as belonging to the last poetic era, but these are enough to show, by comparison, how much we have dwarfed in poetry. It may be that this is partly owing to the wider range of modern literature, and the greatly increased demand for ready literary ability, but the fact remains as we have stated it; and certainly there are now few among us who devote themselves exclusively to the poetic art, and fewer still who have cultivated it with anything approaching to success. First among the latter class we have ranked, and still do rank, Tennyson. He has resisted all literary temptations which might have interfered with his craft; like Wordsworth, he has refused to become a *littérateur*, and has taken his lofty stand upon minstrelsy alone. And upon that one account, if on no other, we should deeply regret to see him fail. Occasional failure, or what the world will term as such, is no more than every poet who has early developed his powers, and whose genius has met with ready recognition, must expect; for, in the absence of any universal standard, the public are wont to weigh the actions, words, and writings of each man separately, and to decide upon their merit according to previous achievement. It may be a positive misfortune to have succeeded too early. There is much more in the word "Excelsior" than meets the common eyes, or, we shrewdly apprehend, than reaches the understanding of the men who use it so freely. A man may rise to fame by one sudden effort; but unless he can leap as high, if not higher, again, he will presently be talked of as a cripple by multitudes, who, but for his first airy vault, would have regarded his second with astonishment. It is the consciousness of the universal application of this rule of individual comparison which, in all ages, has forced poets and other literary men to study variety. Having achieved decided success in one department, they doubt whether their second effort can transcend the first; and being unwilling to acknowledge discomfiture, even by themselves, they essay some new feat of intellectual gymnastics. That the world has been a gainer thereby we do not doubt. "New fields and new pastures" are as necessary to the poet as to the shepherd; only it behooves him to take care that he does not conduct us to a barren moor.

Now let us examine more particularly the poem before us. Had *Maud* been put into our hands as the work of some young unrecognized poet, we should have said that it exhibited very great promise—that it contained at least one passage of such extraordinary rhythmical music, that the sense became subordinate to the sound, a result which, except in the case of one or two of the plaintive ancient Scottish ballads, and some of the lyrics of Burns, has hardly ever been attained by any British writer of poetry

—that such passages, however, though they exhibited the remarkable powers of the author, were by no means to be considered as manifestations, or rather assurances, of his judgment, even in musical matters, since they alternated with others of positively hideous cacophony, such as we should have supposed that no man gifted with a tolerable ear and pliable fingers would have perpetrated—that sometimes a questionable taste had been exhibited in the selection of ornaments, which were rather gaudy than graceful, and often too ostentatiously exposed—that there were other grave errors against taste which we could only attribute to want of practice and study—that the objectionable and unartistic portions of the poem were, leaving the mediocre ones altogether out of the question, grossly disproportionate to the good—and that the general effect of the poem was unhappy, unwholesome, and disagreeable. Such would have been our verdict, had we not known who was the writer; and we feel a double disappointment now when forced to record it against a poet of such deserved reputation. But it is the best course to express our opinion honestly, and without reservation. Mr. Tennyson's indiscriminate admirers may possibly think it their duty to represent this, his latest production, as a magnificent triumph of genius, but they never will be able to persuade the public to adopt that view, and we trust most sincerely that the Laureate will not permit himself to be confirmed in practical error through their flatteries. We say this much because we see no reason for attributing the inferior quality of his later poems to any decay of his native or acquired powers. We believe that he can, whenever he pleases, delight the world once more with such poetry as he enunciated in his youth; but we think that he has somehow or other been led astray by poetic theories, which may be admirably adapted for the consideration of dilettanti, but which are calculated rather to spoil than to enhance the productions of a man of real genius. Theories have been ere now the curse of many poets. For example, who will deny that, but for their obstinate adherence to theory, the reputations both of Wordsworth and of Southey would have been greater than they presently are?

Maud is a monologue in six-and-twenty parts, each of them intended to depict a peculiar phase of the mind of the speaker, who is a young gentleman in decayed circumstances, and therefore morbid and misanthropical. The poem opens thus. . . .

(Thirty-two verses are here given.)

Is that poetry? Is it even respectable verse? Is it not altogether an ill-conceived and worse-expressed screed of bombast, set to a metre which has the string-halt, without even the advantage of regularity in its hobble? Do not say that we are severe, we are merely speaking the truth, and we are ready to furnish a test. Let any man who can appreciate melody, turn to "Locksley Hall," and read aloud eight or ten stanzas of that wonderful poem, until he has possessed himself with its music, then let him attempt to sound the passage which we have just quoted, and he will immediately perceive the woeful difference. The contrast between the breathings of an Æolian harp and the rasping of a blacksmith's file is scarcely more palpable. Our young misanthrope goes on to describe the ways of the world, of which he seems to entertain a very bad opinion, and finally comes to the conclusion that war upon a large scale is the only proper remedy for adulteration of comestibles, house-breaking and child-murder.

(Sixteen more verses are quoted.)

Having thus vented his bile by a wholesale objurgation of the peace-party, which shows, as Bailie Jarvie says, that "the creature has occasional glimmerings," this unhappy victim of paternal speculation suddenly bethinks himself that there are workmen at the Hall, now the property of the "millionaire" or "grey old wolf," by which endearing titles the father of Maud is designated throughout, and that the family are coming home. He remembers the little girl—

> Maud with her sweet purse-mouth when
> my father dangled the grapes,

but makes up his mind to have nothing to say to her:

> Thanks, for the fiend best knows whether
> woman or man be the worse.
> I will bury myself in my books, and the
> Devil may pipe to his own.

However, on an early day he obtains a glimpse, in a carriage, of "a cold and clear-cut face," which proves to belong to Maud, and he thus describes her—

Faultily faultless, icily regular, splendidly null,
Dead perfection, no more; nothing more, if it had not been
For a chance of travel, a paleness, an hour's defect of the rose,
Or an underlip, you may call it a little too ripe, too full,
Or the least little delicate aquiline curve in a sensitive nose,
From which I escaped heart-free, with the least little touch of
    spleen.

The thaw, however, commences. He presently hears
her singing; and, as this passage is the first in the volume
which displays a scintillation of poetic power, or reminds
us in any way of the former writings of Mr. Tennyson,
we gladly insert it:—

> A voice by the cedar tree,
> In the meadow under the Hall!
> She is singing an air that is known to me,
> A passionate ballad gallant and gay,
> A martial song like a trumpet's call!
> Singing alone in the morning of life,
> In the happy morning of life and of May,
> Singing of men that in battle array,
> Ready in heart and ready in hand,
> March with banner and bugle and fife
> To the death for their native land.
>
> Maud with her exquisite face,
> And wild voice pealing up to the sunny sky,
> And feet like sunny gems on an English green,
> Maud in the light of her youth and her grace,
> Singing of Death, and of Honour that cannot die,
> Till I well could weep for a time so sordid and mean,
> And myself so languid and base.
>
> Silence, beautiful voice!
> Be still, for you only trouble the mind
> With a joy in which I cannot rejoice,
> A glory I shall not find.

Still! I will hear you no more,
For your sweetness hardly leaves me a choice
But to move to the meadow and fall before
Her feet on the meadow grass, and adore,
Not her, who is neither courtly nor kind,
Not her, not her, but a voice.

When we read the above passage we had good hope that
the Laureate had emerged from the fog, but he again becomes indistinct and distorted.   However, the worst is
past, for we verily believe it would be impossible for in-
genuity itself to caricature the commencement.   Maud
begins to smile upon Misanthropos, who is, however, still
suspicious; for her brother has an eye to a seat for the
county, and the young lady may be a canvasser in disguise.
We should like to know what gentleman sat for the
following sketch:—

What if tho' her eye seem'd full
Of a kind intent to me,
What if that dandy-despot, he,
That jewell'd mass of millinery,
That oil'd and curl'd Assyrian Bull
Smelling of musk and of insolence,
Her brother, from whom I keep aloof,
Who wants the finer politic sense
To mask, tho' but in his own behoof,
With a glassy smile his brutal scorn—
What if he had told her yestermorn
How prettily for his own sweet sake
A face of tenderness might be feign'd,
And a moist mirage in desert eyes,
That so, when the rotten hustings shake
In another month to his brazen lies,
A wretched vote may be gain'd.

It seems, however, that a young member of the peerage, who owes his rank to black diamonds, is an admirer of Maud; whereupon the misanthropic lover again becomes abusive:—

(Thirty-four verses are here quoted.)

But, after all, Misanthropos proves too much for the titled Lord of the Mines, for he and Maud have a walk together in a wood, and the courtship commences in earnest.

* * * *

Birds in our wood sang
Ringing thro' the valleys,
Maud is here, here, here
In among the lilies.

I kiss'd her slender hand,
She took the kiss sedately;
Maud is not seventeen,
But she is tall and stately.
* * * *
Look, a horse at the door,
And little King Charles is snarling,
Go back, my lord, across the moor,
You are not her darling.

O dear, dear! what manner of stuff is this?

But that Assyrian Bull of a brother is again in the way, and treats Misanthropos cavalierly; notwithstanding which, he proposes to Maud, and is accepted. We make every allowance for the raptures of a lover on such an occasion, and admit that he is privileged to talk very great nonsense; but there must be a limit somewhere; and we submit to Mr. Tennyson whether he was justified, for his own sake, in putting a passage so outrageously silly as the following into the mouth of his hero:—

> Go not, happy day,
>   From the shining fields,
> Go not, happy day,
>   Till the maiden yields.
> Rosy is the West,
>   Rosy is the South,
> Roses are her cheeks,
>   And a rose her mouth.
> When the happy Yes
>   Falters from her lips,
> Pass and blush the news
>   Over glowing ships,
> Over blowing seas,
>   Over seas at rest,
> Pass the happy news,
>   Blush it thro' the West;
> *Till the red man dance*
>   *By his red cedar tree,*
> *And the red man's babe*
>   *Leap, beyond the sea.*
> Blush from West to East,
>   Blush from East to West,
> *Till the West is East,*
>   *Blush it thro' the West.*
> Rosy is the West,
>   Rosy is the South,
> Roses are her cheeks,
>   And a rose her mouth.

Mr. Halliwell some years ago published a collection of Nursery Rhymes. We have not the volume by us at present; but we are fully satisfied that nothing so bairnly as the above is to be found in the Breviary of the Innocents. The part which follows this is ambitiously and elaborately written, and we doubt not will find many admirers. It is eminently rhetorical, and replete with graceful imagery, but somehow there is not a line in it which haunts us. It seems to us a splendid piece of versification, but deficient in melody and passion, and much too artificial for the situation. Others, however, may think differently, and therefore we extract the conclusion:—

(Twenty-four verses are quoted.)

Then follows some namby-pamby which we shall not quote. There is to be a grand political dinner and dance at the Hall to which Misanthropos is not invited; but he intends to wait in Maud's own rose-garden until the ball is over, when he hopes to obtain an interview for a moment. Then comes a very remarkable passage, in which Mr. Tennyson gives a signal specimen of the rhythmical power which he possesses. The music of it is faultless; and we at least are not disposed to cavil at the quaintness of the imagery, which is almost Oriental in its tone. We treasure it the more, because it is the one gem of the collection—the only passage that we can read with pure unmixed delight, and with a perfect conviction that it is the strain of a true poet. Other passages there are, more ambitious and elaborate, studded all over with those metaphors, strange epithets, and conceits which are the disfigurement of modern poetry, and which we are surprised that a man of genius and experience should persist in using; but they all seem to us to want life and reality, and surely the ink was sluggish in the pen when they were written. Only in this one does the verse flash out like a golden thread upon a reel; and we feel that our hands are bound, like those of Thalaba, when the enchantress sang to him as she spun:—

Come into the garden, Maud, etc.*

Little more of story is there. The lovers are surprised in the garden by the Assyrian Bull and Lord Culm and Coke, and the former smites Misanthropos on the face. A duel ensues, when *"procumbit humi bos."* Misanthropos betakes himself to France, returns, finds that his love is dead, and goes mad. Mr. Tennyson has written a mad passage, but we must needs say that he had better have spared himself the trouble. Seven pages of what he most accurately calls "idiot gabble," are rather too much, more especially when they do not contain a touch of pathos. We weep over the disordered wits of Ophelia —we listen to the ravings of Misanthropos, and are nervous as to what may happen if the keeper should not presently appear with a strait-jacket. The case is bad enough when young poetasters essay to gain a hearing by dint of maniacal howls; but it is far worse when we find a man of undoubted genius and widespread reputa-

---

* This famous poem is given entirely but omitted here.—(The Editor.)

tion, demeaning himself by putting his name to such absolute nonsense as this:—

Not that grey old wolf, for he came not back
From the wilderness, full of wolves, where he used to lie;
He has gather'd the bones for his o'ergrown whelp to crack;
Crack them now for yourself, and howl, and die.
Prophet, curse me the blabbing lip,
And curse me the British vermin, the rat;
I know not whether he came in the Hanover ship,
But I know that he lies and listens mute
In an ancient mansion's crannies and holes:
Arsenic, arsenic, sir, would do it,
Except that now we poison our babes, poor souls!
It is all used up for that.

Can Mr. Tennyson possibly be labouring under the delusion that he is using his high talents well and wisely, and giving a valuable contribution to the poetic literature of England, by composing and publishing such gibberish? We are told that there is method in madness, and Shakespeare never lost sight of that when giving voice to the ravings of King Lear; but this is mere barbarous bedlamite jargon, without a vestige of meaning, and it is a sore humiliation to us to know that it was written by the Laureate.

At length Misanthropos recovers his senses; principally, in so far as we can gather from the poem, because the British nation has gone to war with Russia; and we expected to learn from Mr. Tennyson that he had enlisted, and gone out to the Crimea to head a forlorn hope, and perish in a hostile battery. It appears, however, that he had no such intention; and the poem closes with the following passage, which bears a *singular* resemblance to fustian:—

> Tho' many a light shall darken, and many shall weep
> For those that are crush'd in the clash of jarring claims,
> Yet God's just doom shall be wreak'd on a giant liar;
> And many a darkness into the light shall leap,
> And shine in the sudden making of splendid names,
> And noble thought be freer under the sun,
> And the heart of a people beat with one desire;
> For the long, long canker of peace is over and done,
> And now by the side of the Black and the Baltic deep,
> And deathful-grinning mouths of the fortress, flames
> The blood-red blossom of war with a heart of fire.

It must, we think, have been observed by most readers of Tennyson's poetry, that his later productions do not exhibit that felicity of diction which characterized those of an earlier period. It seems to us that he formerly bestowed great pains upon his style, which was naturally ornate, for the purpose of attaining that simplicity of expression which is the highest excellence in poetry as in every other kind of composition. By simplicity we do not mean bald diction, or baby utterance;—we use the term in its high sense, as expressive of the utmost degree of lucidity combined with energy, when all false images, far-fetched metaphors and comparisons, and mystical forms of speech, are discarded. The best of Tennyson's early poems are composed in that manner; but of late years there has been a marked alteration in his style. He gives us no longer such exquisite little gems as "Hero and Leander," which was printed in the first edition of his poems, but which seems to have been excluded, through over-fastidiousness, from the sub-sequent collection. It is many a long year since we read that poem, but we know it by heart sufficiently well to de-claim it; and we venture from memory to transcribe the opening stanza;—

> O go not yet, my love!
> The night is dark and vast,
> The moon is hid in the heaven above,
> And the waves are climbing fast;
> O kiss me, kiss me once again,
> Lest that kiss should be the last!
> O kiss me ere we part—
> Grow closer to my heart—
> My heart is warmer surely than the bosom of the main!

What can be more beautiful, musical, or exquisite than that passage? No wonder that it lingers on the mind, like the echo of a fairy strain. But turn to those simple pas-sages in *Maud*, and you find nothing but namby-pamby. We have already quoted more than one such passage, and perhaps it is unnecessary to multiply instances; but, lest it should be said that lovers' raptures, being often incompre-hensible, incoherent, and rather childish in reality, ought to be so rendered in verse, we pray the attention of the reader to the following few lines, which admit of no such plea in justification:—

> So dark a mind within me dwells,
> And I make myself such evil cheer,
> That if I be dear to some one else,
> Then some one else may have much to fear;
> But if I be dear to some one else,
> Then I should be to myself more dear.

> Shall I not take care of all that I think,
> Yea ev'n of wretched meat and drink,
> If I be dear,
> If I be dear to some one else?.

On what possible pretext can lines like these be ranked as poetry? Why should we continue to sneer at Sternhold and Hopkins, when the first poetical writer of the day is not ashamed to give such offerings to the public?

In his more ambitious attempts, Mr. Tennyson is now wordy, and very often rugged. Some of his later verses bear a strong resemblance to that kind of crambo which was invented to test the youthful powers of pronunciation; and the enigma relating to "Peter Piper," who "pecked a peck of pepper off a pewter platter," is not more execrably cacophonous than many lines which we could select from the volume before us. Here is one instance, not by any means the strongest:—

Be mine a philosopher's life in the quiet woodland ways,
Where if I cannot be gay let a passionless peace be my lot,
Far-off from the clamour of liars belied in the hubbub of lies;
From the long-neck'd geese of the world that are ever hissing
  dispraise
Because their natures are little, and, whether he heed it or not,
Where each man walks with his head in a cloud of poisonous flies.

Also it appears to us that he has become addicted to exaggeration, and an unnecessary use of very strong language. The reader must have already perceived this from the extracts we have given descriptive of Maud's brother, and of his friend; but the same violence of phraseology is exhibited when there appears no occasion for hyperbole, and then the effect becomes ludicrous. In former times, few could vie with Mr. Tennyson in the art of heightening a picture; now he has lost all discretion, and overlays his subject, whether it relates to a material or a mental image. We might pass over "daffodil skies," "gross mud-honey," "ashen-grey delights," "the delicate Arab arch" of a lady's feet, and "the grace that, bright and light as a crest of a peacock, sits on her shining head." We might, we say, pass over these things, as mere casual lapses or mannerisms; but when Mr. Tennyson, for the purpose, we presume, of indicating the morbid tendencies of his hero, makes him give vent to the following confession, we have no bowels of compassion left, and we feel a considerable degree of contempt for Maud for having condescended to listen to the addresses of such a pitiful poltroon:—

> Living alone in an empty house,
> Here half-hid in the gleaming wood,
> Where I hear the dead at mid-day moan,
> And the shrieking rush of the wainscot mouse,
> And my own sad name in corners cried,
> When the shiver of dancing leaves is thrown
> About its echoing chambers wide,
> Till a morbid hate and horror have grown
> Of a world in which I have hardly mixt,
> And a morbid eating lichen fixt
> On a heart half turned to stone.

But we have no heart to go on further; nor shall we criticise the minor poems appended to *Maud*, for there is not one of them which we consider at all worthy of the genius of the author.

A more unpleasant task than that which we have just performed in reviewing this poem, and in passing so unfavourable a judgment, has not devolved upon us for many a day. We hoped to have been able to applaud—we have been compelled, against our wish and expectation, to condemn. It may possibly be said that there was no occasion for expressing any kind of opinion; and that if, after perusing *Maud*, we found that we could not conscientiously praise it, it was in our option to let it pass unnoticed. But we cannot so deal with Mr. Tennyson. His reputation is a high one; and he has a large poetic following. In justice to others of less note, upon whose works we have commented freely, we cannot maintain silence when the Laureate has taken the field. Some of those whom we have previously noticed, may possibly think that our judgments have been harsh—for when did ever youthful poet listen complacently to an honest censor?—but they shall not have an excuse for saying that, while we spoke our mind freely with regard to them, we have allowed others of more acknowledged credit to escape, when their writings demanded condemnation. Why should we attempt reviewing at all, if we are not to be impartial in our judgments? If the opinion which we have expressed should have the effect of making Mr. Tennyson aware of the fact that he is seriously imperilling his fame by issuing poems so ill considered, crude, tawdry, and objectionable as this, then we believe that our present plainness of speech will be the cause of a great gain in the poetic literature of the country. If, on the contrary, Mr. Tennyson chooses to turn a deaf ear to our remonstrance, we cannot help it; but we have performed our duty. We have never been insensible to his merits, nor have we wilfully withheld our admiration; and it is from the very poignancy of our regret to see a man so gifted descend to platitudes like these, that we have expressed ourselves so broadly. Fain would we, like Ventidius in Dryden's play, arouse our Anthony to action; but we cannot hope to compass that by sugared words, or terms of indolent approval. We must touch him to the quick. In virtue of the laurel-wreath, he is the poetical champion of Britain, and should be prepared to maintain the lists against all comers. Is this a proper specimen of his powers? By our Lady of the Lances! we know half-a-dozen minor poets who, in his present condition, could bear him from his saddle in a canter.*

* *Blackwood's Magazine*, September, 1855. (W. E. Aytoun.)

MR. DICKENS *

THE republication of Mr. Dickens's works in a collected form affords an opportunity for offering some observations on the position which the most celebrated novelist of the day occupies, and will in future occupy, in English literature. If popularity is to be taken as the test of merit, Mr. Dickens must be ranked next to Sir Walter Scott in the list of English novelists. For more than twenty-five years he has continued to publish an unintermitting series of fictions, most of which are probably more than twice as long as those to which the author of *Waverley* owed his fame, and might have owed his fortune if he had pursued it somewhat less eagerly. Besides his larger works, Mr. Dickens is the author of a great variety of smaller tales, and the conductor of one of the most successful of the periodical publications of the day. In whatever he has undertaken he has obtained not only success, but an unbounded and enthusiastic popularity, which is manifested, whenever the opportunity offers, with all the warmth of personal affection. It is interesting to attempt to analyse the qualities which have produced such results. Nothing throws more light on the character of an age than the study of its amusements—especially its literary amusements; and Mr. Dickens has

* *The Works of Charles Dickens.* Library Edition, London: Chapman and Hall. 1858.

amused the public more successfully than any other living man.

Pickwick was first published, we believe, about the year 1832 or 1833, when the Reform Bill had just been passed, and when what Mr. Carlyle has called—with the miraculous facility for inventing nicknames, which is not the least of his gifts—the Scavenger Age, was in the first flush of its triumphant inauguration. We should be at a loss to mention any one who reflected the temper of the time in which he rose into eminence more strongly than Mr. Dickens. We feel no doubt that one principal cause of his popularity is the spirit of revolt against all established rules which pervades every one of his books, and which is displayed most strongly and freshly in his earlier productions. Just as Scott owed so much of his success to the skill with which he gave shape and colour to the great Conservative reaction against the French Revolution, Mr. Dickens is indebted to the exquisite adaptation of his own turn of mind to the peculiar state of feeling which still prevails in some classes, and which twenty years ago prevailed far more widely, with respect to all the arrangements of society. So much cant had been in fashion about the wisdom of our ancestors, the glorious constitution, the wise balance of King, Lords, and Commons, and other such topics, which are embalmed in the *Noodle's Oration,* that a large class of people were ready to hail with intense satisfaction the advent of a writer who naturally and without an effort bantered everything in the world, from elections and law courts down to Cockney sportsmen, the boots at an inn, cooks and chambermaids. Mr. Dickens had the additional advantage of doing this not only with exquisite skill, and with a sustained flow of spirit and drollery almost unequalled by any other writer, but in a style which seemed expressly intended to bring into contempt all those canons of criticism which a large proportion of people were learning to look upon as mere pedantry and imposture. *Pickwick* is throughout a sort of half-conscious parody of that style of writing which demanded balanced sentences, double-barrelled epithets, and a proper conception of the office and authority of semicolons. It is as if a saucy lad were to strut about the house in his father's court-dress, with the sleeves turned inside out and the coat-tails stuck under his arms. Whenever he can get an opportunity, Mr. Dickens rakes up the old-fashioned finery, twists it into every sort of grotesque shape, introduces it to all kinds of strange bedfellows, and contrives, with an art which is all the more ingenious because it was probably quite undesigned, to convey the impression that every one who tries to write, to think, or to act by rule, is little more than a pompous jackass. It is impossible to describe the spirit of a writer of whose best books slang is the soul without speaking his own language. Mr. Dickens is the very Avator of chaff, and bigwigs of every description are his game. The joviality, the animal spirits, and the freshness with which he acted this part in his earliest books are wonderful. We cannot mention any caricature so perfect and so ludicrous as the description of Messrs. Dodson and Fogg, and that of the trial of Bardell *v.* Pickwick. The mere skill of his workmanship would have unquestionably secured the success of such a writer; but the harmony between his own temper and that of his audience must be appreciated before we can understand the way in which approbation grew into enthusiasm.

It would, however, be a great mistake to suppose that it was merely to banter that Mr. Dickens owed his marvellous success. Mere banter soon grows wearisome; and Mr. Dickens was led by nature as much as by art to mix up a very stronge dose of sentiment with his caricature. From first to last, he has tried about as much to make his readers cry as to make them laugh; and there is a very large section of the British public—and especially of the younger, weaker, and more ignorant part of it—which considers these two functions as comprising the whole duty of novelists. It is impossible to deny that certain classes of Englishmen and Englishwomen retain all the tendencies of Prince Arthur's young gentlemen in France, who were as sad as night for very wantonness. They do not care for violent paroxyms of passion—they are disgusted by horrors. The outrageous rants, surgical operations, and *post mortem* examinations which afford such lively pleasure to Parisian readers, would be out of place here; but if anybody can get a pretty little girl to go to heaven prattling about her dolls, and her little brothers and sisters, and quoting texts of Scripture with appropriate gasps, dashes, and broken sentences, he may send half the women in London, with tears in their eyes, to Mr. Mudie's or Mr. Booth's. This kind of taste has not only been flattered, but prodigiously developed, by Mr. Dickens. He is the intellectual parent of a whole class of fictions, of which the *Heir of Redcliffe* was perhaps the most successful. No man can offer to the public so large a stock of death-beds adapted for either sex and for any age from five-and-twenty downwards. There are idiot death-beds, where the patient cries ha, ha! and points wildly at vacancy—pauper death-beds, with unfeeling nurses to match—male and female children's death-beds, where the young ladies or gentlemen sit up in bed, pray to the angels, and see golden water on the walls. In short, there never was a man to whom the King of Terrors was so useful as a lay figure.

This union of banter and sentiment appears to us to form the essence of Mr. Dickens's view of life. In the main, it is a very lovely world, a very good and a very happy world, in which we live. We ought all to be particularly fond of each other and infinitely pleased with our position. The only drawback to this charming state of things is that a great number of absurd people have got up a silly set of conventional rules, which the rest of us are foolish enough to submit to. The proper course with them is good natured ridicule and caricature, which cannot fail to make them conscious of the absurdity of their position. Here and there, no doubt, is to be found a villain who has laid aside the dagger, the bowl, and the Spanish cloak, which by rights he ought to carry, for some one of the many costumes worn by Englishmen in the nineteenth century; and there are plenty of erring brothers and sisters who have lost all but their picturesqueness, which is in itself enough to constitute the highest claim to our sympathy. It would be no uninteresting task to trace the stream downwards from the fountain-head, and to show how this view pervades the long series of works to which we have referred, though the exigencies of fecundity and an enlarged acquaintance with the world have modified it very considerably, especially by way of acidulation. We are all dear brothers and sisters in *Bleak House* and *Little Dorrit*, just as we were in *Pickwick* and *Nicholas Nickleby;* but we have reached a time of life in which family quarrels must be expected, and we have learned that good-natured banter, when kept up for a quarter of a century, is apt, with the kindest intentions in the world, to degenerate into serious and angry discussion. It is all very well to cork a man's face after a college supper-party, but if the process were kept up for five-and-twenty years, whenever he took a nap, it might come to be worth his while to require a special and serious justification for such conduct.

We cannot now attempt to trace the history of Mr. Dickens's publications, or of the various stages through which his style and his opinions have passed, but we may briefly indicate the literary position to which, in our opinion, he has attained. It does not appear to us certain that his books will live, nor do we think that his place in literary history will be by the side of such men as Defoe and Fielding, the founders of the school to which he belongs. *Pickwick* stands as far above *Tom Jones* as it stands above *Dombey and Son* or *Bleak House*. It is an exquisitely piquant caricature of the everyday life of the middle and lower classes at the time to which it refers; but the general theory of life on which it is based is not only false, but puerile. Caricature depends for its vitality almost entirely on the degree of wisdom which it veils, just as the ornaments of a dress depend for their beauty on the materials which they adorn. The wit of *Henry IV.* or the *Merry Wives of Windsor* is like spangles on rich velvet—the wit of *Pickwick* is like spangles on tinsel paper. Mr. Dickens's very highest notion of goodness does not go beyond that sort of good-nature celebrated in the old song about the fine old English gentleman who had an old estate, and kept up his old mansion at a bountiful old rate. He can only conceive of virtues and vices in their very simplest forms. The goodness of his good men is always running over their beards, like Aaron's ointment—the wickedness of his villains is always flaming and blazing like a house on fire. The mixed characters, the confusion, the incompleteness, which meet us at every step in real life, never occur in his pages. You understand what he means on the first reading far better than on any other. The only characters drawn from real observation belong to one or two classes of life. All the oddities of London he has sketched with inimitable vigour; but class characteristics and local peculiarities are of a very transient nature. Fifty years hence, most of his wit will be harder to understand than the allusions in the *Dunciad*; and our grand-children will wonder what their ancestors could have meant by putting Mr. Dickens at the head of the novelists of his day.

Though, however, we do not believe in the permanence of his reputation, it is impossible to deny that Mr. Dickens has exercised an immense influence over contemporary literature, or that his books must always be an extremely curious study on that account. Till our own days, almost every popular writer formed his style on the classical model. Even those who revolted most strongly against the canons of composition current in the eighteenth century—Coleridge, Wordsworth, Southey, Charles Lamb, and their associates—had, almost without an exception, been taught to write. They maintained that the stiffness of the style then dominant arose from a misapprehension of the true principles of the art of literature; but that it was an art they never doubted. The first person of mark who wrote entirely by the light of nature, and without the guidance of any other principle than that of expressing his meaning in the most emphatic language that he could find, was Cobbett. Though no two persons could resemble each other less in character, the position of Mr. Dickens with respect to fiction is precisely analogous to that of Cobbett with respect to political discussion. The object of the arguments of the one is to drive his opinion into the dullest understanding—the object of the narrative of the other is to paint a picture which will catch the eye of the most ignorant and least attentive observer. Mr. Dickens's writings are the apotheosis of what has been called newspaper English. He makes points everywhere, gives unfamiliar names to the commonest objects, and lavishes a marvellous quantity of language on the most ordinary incidents. Mr. William Russell and Mr. Charles Dickens have respectively risen to the very top of two closely connected branches of the same occupation. The correspondence from the Crimea is constructed upon exactly the same model as *Pickwick* and *Martin Chuzzle-wit*, and there can be no doubt that the triumphs which this style has attained in Mr. Dickens's hands have exercised and will continue to exercise, very considerable influence on the mould into which people will cast their thoughts, and indirectly upon their thoughts themselves. We cannot affect to say that we look upon the growth of this habit with much satisfaction. It appears to us to foster a pert, flippant frame of mind, in which the fancy exerts an amount of influence which does not rightfully belong to it, and in which it is very hard for people to think soberly of others, and almost impossible for them not to think a great deal too much about themselves and the effect which they are producing. There is a sex in minds as well as in bodies, and Mr. Dickens's literary progeny seem to us to be for the most part of the feminine gender, and to betray it by most unceasing flirtations, and by a very tiresome irritability of nerve.*

* *The Saturday Review*, May 8, 1858.

MR. SWINBURNE'S NEW POEMS: *POEMS AND BALLADS* *

IT is mere waste of time, and shows a curiously mistaken conception of human character, to blame an artist of any kind for working at a certain set of subjects rather than at some other set which the critic may happen to prefer. An artist, at all events an artist of such power and individuality as Mr. Swinburne, works as his character compels him. If the character of his genius drives him pretty exclusively in the direction of libidinous song, we may be very sorry, but it is of no use to advise him and to preach to him. What comes of discoursing to a fiery tropical flower of the pleasant fragrance of the rose or the fruitfulness of the fig-tree? Mr. Swinburne is much too stoutly bent on taking his own course to pay any attention to critical monitions as to the duty of the poet, or any warnings of the worse than barrenness of the field in which he has chosen to labour. He is so firmly and avowedly fixed in an attitude of revolt against the current notions of decency and dignity and social duty that to beg of him to become a little more decent, to fly a little less persistently and gleefully to the animal side of human nature, is simply to beg him to be something different from Mr. Swinburne. It is a kind of protest

* *Poems and Ballads.* By Algernon Charles Swinburne. London: E. Moxon & Co. 1866.

which his whole position makes it impossible for him to receive with anything but laughter and contempt. A rebel of his calibre is not to be brought to a better mind by solemn little sermons on the loyalty which a man owes to virtue. His warmest prayer to the gods is that they should

> Come down and redeem us from virtue.

His warmest hope for men is that they should change

> The lilies and languors of virtue
> For the raptures and roses of vice.

It is of no use, therefore, to scold Mr. Swinburne for grovelling down among the nameless shameless abominations which inspire him with such frenzied delight. They excite his imagination to its most vigorous efforts, they seem to him the themes most proper for poetic treatment, and they suggest ideas which, in his opinion, it is highly to be wished that English men and women should brood upon and make their own. He finds that these fleshly things are his strong part, so he sticks to them. Is it wonderful that he should? And at all events he deserves credit for the audacious courage with which he has revealed to the world a mind all aflame with the feverish carnality of a schoolboy over the dirtiest passages in Lemprière. It is not every poet who would ask us all to go hear him tuning his lyre in a stye. It is not everybody who would care to let the world know that he found the most delicious food for poetic reflection in the practices

of the great island of the Ægean, in the habits of Messa-
lina, of Faustina, of Pasiphaë. Yet these make up Mr.
Swinburne's version of the dreams of fair women, and
he would scorn to throw any veil over pictures which
kindle, as these do, all the fires of his imagination in
their intensest heat and glow. It is not merely "the noble,
the nude, the antique" which he strives to reproduce. If
he were a rebel against the fat-headed Philistines and
poor-blooded Puritans who insist that all poetry should
be such as may be wisely placed in the hands of girls of
eighteen, and is fit for the use of Sunday schools, he would
have all wise and enlarged readers on his side. But there
is an enormous difference between an attempt to revivify
among us the grand old pagan conceptions of Joy, and an
attempt to glorify all the bestial delights that the subtle-
ness of Greek depravity was able to contrive. It is a
good thing to vindicate passion, and the strong and large
and rightful pleasures of sense, against the narrow and
inhuman tyranny of shrivelled anchorites. It is a very
bad and silly thing to try to set up the pleasures of sense
in the seat of the reason they have dethroned. And no
language is too strong to condemn the mixed vileness and
childishness of depicting the spurious passion of a putres-
cent imagination, the unnamed lusts of sated wantons, as
if they were the crown of character and their enjoyment
the great glory of human life. The only comfort about
the present volume is that such a piece as "Anactoria" will
be unintelligible to a great many people, and so will the
fevered folly of "Hermaphroditus," as well as much else

that is nameless and abominable.   Perhaps if Mr. Swinburne can a second and a third time find a respectable publisher willing to issue a volume of the same stamp, crammed with pieces which many a professional vendor of filthy prints might blush to sell if he only knew what they meant, English readers will gradually acquire a truly delightful familiarity with these unspeakable foulnesses; and a lover will be able to present to his mistress a copy of Mr. Swinburne's latest verses with a happy confidence that she will have no difficulty in seeing the point of every allusion to Sappho or the pleasing Hermaphroditus, or the embodiment of anything else that is loathsome and horrible.   It will be very charming to hear a drawing-room discussion on such verses as these, for example:—

> Stray breaths of Sapphic song that blew
>   Through Mitylene
> Shook the fierce quivering blood in you
>   By night, Faustine.
>
> The shameless nameless love that makes
>   Hell's iron gin
> Shut on you like a trap that breaks
>   The soul, Faustine.
>
> And when your veins were void and dead,
>   What ghosts unclean
> Swarmed round the straitened barren bed
>   That hid Faustine?
>
> What sterile growths of sexless root
>   Or epicene?
> What flower of kisses without fruit
>   Of love, Faustine?

We should be sorry to be guilty of anything so offensive
to Mr. Swinburne as we are quite sure an appeal to the
morality of all the wisest and best men would be. The
passionate votary of the goddess whom he hails as
"Daughter of Death and Priapus" has got too high for
this. But it may be presumed that common sense is not
too insulting a standard by which to measure the worth
and place of his new volume. Starting from this sufficiently modest point, we may ask him whether there is
really nothing in women worth singing about except "quiv-
ering flanks" and "splendid supple thighs," "hot sweet
throats" and "hotter hands than fire," and their blood
as "hot wan wine of love"? ... Is purity to be expunged
from the catalogue of desirable qualities? Does a poet
show respect to his own genius by gloating, as Mr. Swinburne does, page after page and poem after poem, upon
a single subject, and that subject kept steadily in a single
light? Are we to believe that having exhausted hot lustfulness, and wearied the reader with a luscious and nause-
ating iteration of the same fervid scenes and fervid ideas,
he has got to the end of his tether? Has he nothing more
to say, no further poetic task but to go on again and again
about

> The white wealth of thy body made whiter
>   By the blushes of amorous blows,
> And seamed with sharp lips and fierce fingers,
>   And branded by kisses that bruise.

And to invite new Félises to

> Kiss me once hard, as though a flame
> Lay on my lips and made them fire.

Mr. Swinburne's most fanatical admirers must long for something newer than a thousand times repeated talk of

> Stinging lips wherein the hot sweet brine
> That Love was born of burns and foams like wine.

And

> Hands that sting like fire,

And of all those women,

> Swift and white,
> And subtly warm and half perverse,
> And sweet like sharp soft fruit to bite,
> And like a snake's love lithe and fierce.

This stinging and biting, all these "lithe lascivious regrets," all this talk of snakes and fire, of blood and wine and brine, of perfumes and poisons and ashes, grows sickly and oppressive on the senses. Every picture is hot and garish with this excess of flaming violent colour. Consider the following two stanzas:—

> From boy's pierced throat and girl's pierced bosom
> Drips, reddening round the blood-red blossom,
> The slow delicious bright soft blood,
> Bathing the spices and the pyre,
> Bathing the flowers and fallen fire,
> Bathing the blossom by the bud.

> Roses whose lips the flame has deadened
> Drink till the lapping leaves are reddened
> And warm wet inner petals weep;
> The flower whereof sick sleep gets leisure,
> Barren of balm and purple pleasure,
> Fumes with no native steam of sleep.

Or these, from the verses to Dolores, so admirable for their sustained power and their music, if hateful on other grounds:—

Cold eyelids that hide like a jewel
 Hard eyes that grow soft for an hour;
The heavy white limbs and the cruel
 Red mouth like a venomous flower;
When these are gone by with their glories
 What shall rest of thee then, what remain,
O mystic and sombre Dolores,
 Our Lady of Pain?
   * * *

By the ravenous teeth that have smitten
 Through the kisses that blossom and bud,
By the lips intertwisted and bitten
 Till the foam has a savour of blood,
By the pulse as it rises and falters,
 By the hands as they slacken and strain,
I adjure thee, respond from thine altars,
 Our Lady of Pain.
   * * *

Thy skin changes country and colour,
 And shrivels or swells to a snake's.
Let it brighten and bloat and grow duller,
 We know it, the flames and the flakes,
Red brands on it smitten and bitten,
 Round skies where a star is a stain,
And the leaves with thy litanies written,
 Our Lady of Pain.
   * * *

Where are they, Cotytto or Venus,
 Astarte or Ashtaroth, where?
Do their hands as we touch come between us?
 Is the breath of them hot in thy hair?
From their lips have thy lips taken fever,
 With the blood of their bodies grown red?

It was too rashly said, when *Atalanta in Calydon* appeared, that Mr. Swinburne had drunk deep at the springs
of Greek poetry, and had profoundly conceived and as-
similated the divine spirit of Greek art. *Chastelard* was
enough to show that this had been very premature. But
the new volume shows with still greater plainness how
far removed Mr. Swinburne's tone of mind is from that
of the Greek poets. Their most remarkable distinction is
their scrupulous moderation and sobriety in colour. Mr.
Swinburne riots in the profusion of colour of the most
garish and heated kind. He is like a composer who
should fill his orchestra with trumpets, or a painter who
should exclude every colour but a blaring red, and a green
as of sour fruit. There are not twenty stanzas in the
whole book which have the faintest tincture of soberness. We are in the midst of fire and serpents, wine and
ashes, blood and foam, and a hundred lurid horrors. Unsparing use of the most violent colours and the most intoxicated ideas and images is Mr. Swinburne's prime characteristic. Fascinated as everybody must be by the music
of his verse, it is doubtful whether part of the effect may
not be traced to something like a trick of words and letters, to which he resorts in season and out of season with
a persistency that any sense of artistic moderation must
have stayed. The Greek poets in their most impetuous
moods never allowed themselves to be carried on by the
swing of words, instead of by the steady, though buoyant,
flow of thoughts. Mr. Swinburne's hunting of letters,
his hunting of the same word, to death is ceaseless. We

shall have occasion by and by to quote a long passage in which several lines will be found to illustrate this. Then, again, there is something of a trick in such turns as these:—

Came flushed from the full-flushed wave.
Grows dim in thine ears and deep as the deep dim soul of a star.
White rose of the rose-white water, a silver splendour and flame.

There are few pages in the volume where we do not find conceits of this stamp doing duty for thoughts. The Greeks did not wholly disdain them, but they never allowed them to count for more than they were worth. Let anybody who compares Mr. Swinburne to the Greeks read his ode to "Our Lady of Pain," and then read the well-known scene in the *Antigone* between Antigone and the Chorus, beginning *zowc avizars puxav*, or any of the famous choruses in the *Agamemnon*, or an ode of Pindar. In the height of all their passion there is an infinite soberness of which Mr. Swinburne has not a conception.

Yet, in spite of its atrocities, the present volume gives new examples of Mr. Swinburne's forcible and vigorous imagination. The "Hymn to Proserpine" on the proclamation of the Christian faith in Rome, full as it is of much that many persons may dislike, contains passages of rare vigour:—

All delicate days and pleasant, all spirits and sorrows are cast
Far out with foam of the present that sweeps to the surf of the past:

When beyond the extreme sea-wall, and between the remote sea-
    gates,
Waste water washes, and tall ships founder, and deep death waits:
Where, mighty with deepening sides, clad about with the seas as
    with wings,
And impelled to invisible tides, and fulfilled of unspeakable
    things,
White-eyed and poisonous-finned, shark-toothed and serpentine-
    curled,
Rolls under the whitening wind of the future the wave of the
    world.
The depths stand naked in sunder behind it, the storms flee away;
In the hollow before it the thunder is taken and snared as a prey;
In its sides is the north-wind bound; and its salt is of all men's
    tears;
With light of ruin, and sound of changes and pulse of years:
With travail of day after day, and with trouble of hour upon
    hour;
And bitter as blood is the spray; and the crests are as fangs that
    devour;
And its vapour and storm of its steam as the sighing of spirits
    to be;
And its noise as the noise in a dream; and its depth as the roots
    of the sea:
And the height of its head as the utmost stars of the air:
And the ends of the earth at the might thereof tremble, and
    time is made bare.

The variety and rapidity and sustention, the revelling in
power, are not more remarkable here than in many other
passages, though even here it is not variety and rapidity
of thought. The anapæst to which Mr. Swinburne so
habitually resorts is the only foot that suffices for his
never-staying impetuosity. In the "Song in Time of
Revolution" he employs it appropriately, and with a
sweeping force as of the elements:—

The heart of the rulers is sick, and the high priest covers his head!
For this is the song of the quick that is heard in the ears of the
    dead.
The poor and the halt and the blind are keen and mighty and
    fleet:
Like the noise of the blowing of wind is the sound of the noise
    of their feet.

There are, too, sweet and picturesque lines scattered in
the midst of this red fire which the poet tosses to and fro
about his verses. Most of the poems, in his wearisomely
iterated phrase, are meant "to sting the senses like wine,"
but to some stray pictures one may apply his own exquisite phrases on certain of Victor Hugo's songs, which,
he says,

> Fell more soft than dew or snow by night,
> Or wailed as in some flooded cave
> Sobs the strong broken spirit of a wave.

For instance, there is a perfect delicacy and beauty in four
lines of the hendecasyllabics—a metre that is familiar in
the Latin line often found on clocks and sundials, *Horæ
nam pereunt et imputantur*:—

> When low light was upon the windy reaches,
> Where the flower of foam was blown, a lily
> Dropt among the sonorous fruitless furrows
> And green fields of the sea that make no pasture.

Nothing can be more simple and exquisite than

For the glass of the years is brittle wherein we gaze for a span.

Or than this:—

> In deep wet ways by grey old gardens
> Fed with sharp spring the sweet fruit hardens;
>   They know not what fruits wane or grow;
> Red summer burns to the utmost ember;
> They know not, neither can remember,
>   The old years and flowers they used to know.

Or again:—

> With stars and sea-winds for her raiment
> Night sinks on the sea.

Up to a certain point, one of the deepest and most really poetical pieces is that called the "Sundew." A couple of verses may be quoted to illustrate the graver side of the poet's mind:—

> The deep scent of the heather burns
> About it; breathless though it be,
> Bow down and worship; more than we
> Is the least flower whose life returns,
> Least weed renascent in the sea.
>   *   *   *   *
> You call it sundew: how it grows,
> If with its colour it have breath,
> If life taste sweet to it, if death
> Pain its soft petal, no man knows:
> Man has no right or sense that saith.

There is no finer effect of poetry than to recall to the minds of men the bounds that have been set to the scope of their sight and sense, to inspire their imaginations with a vivid consciousness of the size and the wonders and the strange remote companionships of the world of force and growth and form outside of man. *"Qui se considérera de la sorte,"* said Pascal, *"s'effraiera, sans doute, de se voir comme suspendu dans la masse que la nature lui a donnée entre ces deux abimes de l'infini et du néant."* And there are two ways in which a man can treat this affright that seizes his fellows as they catch interrupted glimpses of their position. He can transfigure their baseness of fear into true poetic awe, which shall underlie their lives as a lasting record of solemn rapture. Or else he can jeer and mock at them, like an unclean fiery imp from the pit. Mr. Swinburne does not at all events treat the lot of mankind in the former spirit. In his best mood, he can only brood over "the exceeding weight of God's intolerable scorn, not to be borne;" he can only ask of us, "O fools and blind, what seek ye there high up in the air," or "Will ye beat always at the Gate, Ye fools of fate." If he is not in his best mood he is in his worst—a mood of schoolboy lustfulness. The bottomless pit encompasses us on one side, and stews and bagnios on the other. He is either the vindictive and scornful apostle of a crushing iron-shod despair, or else he is the libidinous laureate of a pack of satyrs. Not all the fervour of his imagination, the beauty of his melody, the splendour of many phrases and pictures, can blind us to the absence of judgment and reason, the reckless contempt for anything like a balance, and the audacious counterfeiting of strong and noble passion by mad intoxicated sensuality. The lurid clouds of lust or of fiery despair and defiance never lift to let us see the pure and peaceful and bounteous kindly aspects of the great landscape of human life. Of enlarged *medi-tation*, the note of the highest poetry, there is not a trace, and there are too many signs that Mr. Swinburne is with-out any faculty in that direction.] Never have such boun-tifulness of imagination, such mastery of the music of verse, been yoked with such thinness of contemplation and such poverty of genuinely impassioned thought.*]

* *The Saturday Review*, August 4, 1866.   (John Morley.)

THE FLESHLY SCHOOL OF POETRY:
MR. D. G. ROSSETTI *

IF, on the occasion of any public performance of Shakespeare's great tragedy, the actors who perform the parts of Rosencranz and Guildenstern were, by a preconcerted arrangement and by means of what is technically known as "gagging," to make themselves fully as prominent as the leading character, and to indulge in soliloquies and business strictly belonging to Hamlet himself, the result would be, to say the least of it, astonishing; yet a very similar effect is produced on the unprejudiced mind when the "walking gentlemen" of the fleshly school of poetry, who bear precisely the same relation to Mr. Tennyson as Rosencranz and Guildenstern do to the Prince of Denmark in the play, obtrude their lesser identities and parade their smaller idiosyncrasies in the front rank of leading performers. In their own place, the gentlemen are interesting and useful. Pursuing still the theatrical analogy, the present drama of poetry might be cast as follows: Mr. Tennyson supporting the part of Hamlet, Mr. Matthew Arnold that of Horatio, Mr. Bailey that of Voltimand, Mr. Buchanan that of Cornelius, Messrs. Swinburne and Morris the parts of Rosencranz and Guildenstern, Mr. Rossetti that of Osric, and

* *Poems.* By Dante Gabriel Rossetti. Fifth Edition. London: F. S. Ellis.

Mr. Robert Lytton that of "A Gentleman." It will be
seen that we have left no place for Mr. Browning, who
may be said, however, to play the leading character in his
own peculiar fashion on alternate nights.

This may seem a frivolous and inadequate way of opening our remarks on a school of verse-writers which some
people regard as possessing great merits; but in good
truth, it is scarcely possible to discuss with any seriousness
the pretensions with which foolish friends and small critics
have surrounded the fleshly school, which, in spite of its
spasmodic ramifications in the erotic direction, is merely
one of the many sub-Tennysonian schools expanded to
supernatural dimensions, and endeavouring by affectations
all its own to overshadow its connection with the great
original. In the sweep of one single poem, the weird and
doubtful "Vivien," Mr. Tennyson has concentrated all
the epicene force which, wearisomely expanded, constitutes the characteristic of the writers at present under consideration; and if in "Vivien" he has indicated for them
the bounds of sensualism in art, he has in *Maud*, in the
dramatic person of the hero, afforded distinct precedent
for the hysteric tone and overloaded style which is now
so familiar to readers of Mr. Swinburne. The fleshliness
of "Vivien" may indeed be described as the distinct quality held in common by all the members of the last sub-
Tennysonian school, and it is a quality which becomes
unwholesome when there is no moral or intellectual quality to temper and control it. Fully conscious of this
themselves, the fleshly gentlemen have bound themselves
by solemn league and covenant to extol fleshliness as the

distinct and supreme end of poetic and pictorial art; to
aver that poetic expression is greater than poetic thought,
and by inference that the body is greater than the soul,
and sound superior to sense; and that the poet, properly
to develop his poetic faculty, must be an intellectual her-
maphrodite, to whom the very facts of day and night are
lost in a whirl of æsthetic terminology. After Mr. Tennyson has probed the depths of modern speculation in
a series of commanding moods, all right and interesting in
him as the reigning personage, the walking gentlemen,
knowing that something of the sort is expected from all
leading performers, bare their roseate bosoms and aver
that *they* are creedless; the only possible question here
being, if any distinterested person cares twopence whether
Rosencranz, Guildenstern, and Osric are creedless or not—
their self-revelation on that score being so perfectly gratuitous? But having gone so far, it was and is too late
to retreat. Rosencranz, Guildenstern, and Osric, finding
it impossible to risk an individual bid for the leading
business, have arranged all to play leading business together, and mutually to praise, extol, and imitate each
other; and although by these measures they have fairly
earned for themselves the title of the Mutual Admiration School, they have in a great measure succeeded in
their object—to the general stupefaction of a British audience. It is time, therefore, to ascertain whether any of
these gentlemen has actually in himself the making of a
leading performer. When the *Athenæum*—once more
cautious in such matters—advertised nearly every week
some interesting particular about Mr. Swinburne's health,

Mr. Morris's holiday-making, or Mr. Rossetti's gene-alogy, varied with such startling statements as "We are informed that Mr. Swinburne dashed off his noble ode *at a sitting*," or "Mr. Swinburne's songs have already reached a second edition," or "Good poetry seems to be in demand; the first edition of Mr. O'Shaughnessy's poems is exhausted;" when the *Academy* informed us that "Dur-ing the past year or two Mr. Swinburne has written sev-eral novels" (!), and that some review or other is to be praised for giving Mr. Rossetti's poems "the attentive study which they demand"—when we read these things we might or might not know pretty well how and where they originated; but to a provincial eye, perhaps, the whole thing really looked like leading business. It would be scarcely worth while, however, to inquire into the pre-tensions of the writers on merely literary grounds, because sooner or later all literature finds its own level, whatever criticism may say or do in the matter; but it unfortunately happens in the present case that the fleshly school of verse-writers are, so to speak, public offenders, because they are diligently spreading the seeds of disease broadcast wher-ever they are read and understood. Their complaint too is catching, and carries off many young persons. What the complaint is, and how it works, may be seen on a very slight examination of the works of Mr. Dante Gabriel Rossetti, to whom we shall confine our attention in the present article.

Mr. Rossetti has been known for many years as a painter of exceptional powers, who, for reasons best known to himself, has shrunk from publicly exhibiting his pictures, and from allowing anything like a popular estimate to be formed of their qualities. He belongs, or is said to belong, to the so-called Pre-Raphaelite school, a school which is generally considered to exhibit much genius for colour, and great indifference to perspective. It would be unfair to judge the painter by the glimpses we have had of his works, or by the photographs which are sold of the principal paintings. Judged by the photographs, he is an artist who conceives unpleasantly, and draws ill. Like Mr. Simeon Solomon, however, with whom he seems to have many points in common, he is distinctively a colourist, and of his capabilities in colour we cannot speak, though we should guess that they are great; for if there is any good quality by which his poems are specially marked, it is a great sensitiveness to hues and tints as conveyed in poetic epithet. These qualities, which impress the casual spectator of the photographs from his pictures, are to be found abundantly among his verses. There is the same thinness and transparence of design, the same combination of the simple and the grotesque, the same morbid deviation from healthy forms of life, the same sense of weary, wasting, yet exquisite sensuality; nothing virile, nothing tender, nothing completely sane; a superfluity of extreme sensibility, of delight in beautiful forms, hues, and tints, and a deep-seated indifference to all agitating forces and agencies, all tumultuous griefs and sorrows, all the thunderous stress of life, and all the straining storm of speculation. Mr. Morris is often pure, fresh, and wholesome as his own great model; Mr. Swinburne startles us more than once by some fine flash of insight; but the mind of Mr. Rossetti is like a glassy mere, broken only by the dive of some water-bird or the hum of winged insects, and brooded over by an atmosphere of insufferable closeness, with a light blue sky above it, sultry depths mirrored within it, and a surface so thickly sown with water-lilies that it retains its glassy smoothness even in the strongest wind. Judged relatively to his poetic associates, Mr. Rossetti must be pronounced inferior to either. He cannot tell a pleasant story like Mr. Morris, nor forge alliterative thunderbolts like Mr. Swinburne. It must be conceded, nevertheless, that he is neither so glibly imitative as the one, nor so transcenddently superficial as the other.

Although he has been known for many years as a poet as well as a painter—as a painter and poet idolized by his own family and personal associates—and although he has once or twice appeared in print as a contributor to magazines, Mr. Rossetti did not formally appeal to the public until rather more than a year ago, when he published a copious volume of poems, with the announcement that the book, although it contained pieces composed at intervals during a period of many years, "included nothing which the author believes to be immature." This work was inscribed to his brother, Mr. William Rossetti, who, having written much both in poetry and criticism, will perhaps be known to bibliographers as the editor of the worst edition of Shelley which has yet seen the light. No sooner had the work appeared than the chorus of eulogy began. "The book is satisfactory from end to end," wrote

Mr. Morris in the *Academy;* "I think these lyrics, with all their other merits, the most complete of their time; nor do I know what lyrics of any time are to be called *great*, if we are to deny the title to these." On the same subject Mr. Swinburne went into a hysteria of admiration: "golden affluence," "jewel-coloured words," "chastity of form," "harmonious nakedness," "consummate fleshly sculpture," and so on in Mr. Swinburne's well-known manner when reviewing his friends. Other critics, with a singular similarity of phrase, followed suit. Strange to say, moreover, no one accused Mr. Rossetti of naughtiness. What had been heinous in Mr. Swinburne was majestic exquisiteness in Mr. Rossetti. Yet we question if there is anything in the unfortunate *Poems and Ballads* quite so questionable on the score of thorough nastiness as many pieces in Mr. Rossetti's collection. Mr. Swinburne was wilder, more outrageous, more blasphemous, and his subjects were more atrocious in themselves; yet the hysterical tone slew the animalism, the furiousness of epithet lowered the sensation; and the first feeling of disgust at such themes as "Laus Veneris" and "Anactoria," faded away into comic amazement. It was only a little mad boy letting off squibs; not a great strong man, who might be really dangerous to society. "I *will* be naughty!" screamed the little boy; but, after all, what did it matter? It is quite different, however, when a grown man, with the self-control and easy audacity of actual experience, comes forward to chronicle his amorous sensations, and, first proclaiming in a loud voice his literary maturity, and consequent responsibility, shamelessly prints and publishes such a piece of writing as this sonnet on "Nuptial Sleep:"—

At length their long kiss severed, with sweet smart:
And as the last slow sudden drops are shed
From sparkling eaves when all the storm has fled,
So singly flagged the pulses of each heart.
Their bosoms sundered, with the opening start
Of married flowers to either side outspread
From the knit stem; yet still their mouths, burnt red,
Fawned on each other where they lay apart.

Sleep sank them lower than the tide of dreams,
And their dreams watched them sink, and slid away.
Slowly their souls swam up again, through gleams.
Of watered light and dull drowned waifs of day;
Till from some wonder of new woods and streams
He woke, and wondered more: for there she lay.

This, then, is "the golden affluence of words, the firm outline, the justice and chastity of form." Here is a full-grown man, presumably intelligent and cultivated, putting on record for other full-grown men to read, the most secret mysteries of sexual connection, and that with so sickening a desire to reproduce the sensual mood, so careful a choice of epithet to convey mere animal sensations, that we merely shudder at the shameless nakedness. We are no purists in such matters. We hold the sensual part of our nature to be as holy as the spiritual or intellectual part, and we believe that such things must find their equivalent in all; but it is neither poetic, nor manly, nor even human, to obtrude such things as the themes of whole poems. It is simply nasty. Nasty as it is, we are very mistaken if many readers do not think it nice. English society of one kind purchases the *Day's Doings*. English society of another kind goes into ecstasy over Mr. Solomon's pictures—pretty pieces of morality, such as "Love dying by the breath of Lust." There is not much to choose between the two objects of admiration, except that painters like Mr. Solomon lend actual genius to worthless subjects, and thereby produce veritable monsters—like the lovely devils that danced round Saint Anthony. Mr. Rossetti owes his so-called success to the same causes. In poems like "Nuptial Sleep," the man who is too sensitive to exhibit his pictures, and so modest that it takes him years to make up his mind to publish his poems, parades his private sensations before a coarse public, and is gratified by their applause.

It must not be supposed that all Mr. Rossetti's poems are made up of trash like this. Some of them are as noteworthy for delicacy of touch as others are for shamelessness of exposition. They contain some exquisite pictures of nature, occasional passages of real meaning, much beautiful phraseology, lines of peculiar sweetness, and epithets chosen with true literary cunning. But the fleshly feeling is everywhere. Sometimes, as in "The Stream's Secret," it is deliciously modulated, and adds greatly to our emotion of pleasure at perusing a finely-wrought poem; at other times, as in the "Last Confession," it is fiercely held in check by the exigencies of a powerful situation and the strength of a dramatic speaker; but it is generally in the foreground, flushing the whole poem with unhealthy rose-colour, stifling the senses with overpowering sickliness, as of too much civet.   Mr. Rossetti is never dramatic, never impersonal—always attitudinizing, posturing, and describing his own exquisite emotions.   He is the Blessed Damozel, leaning over the "gold bar of heaven," and seeing

> Time like a pulse shake fierce
> Thro' all the worlds,

he is "heaven-born Helen, Sparta's queen," whose "each twin breast is an apple sweet;" he is Lilith the first wife of Adam; he is the rosy Virgin of the poem called "Ave," and the Queen in the "Staff and Scrip;" he is "Sister Helen" melting her waxen man; he is all these, just as surely as he is Mr. Rossetti soliloquizing over Jenny in her London lodging, or the very nuptial person writing erotic sonnets to his wife.   In petticoats or pantaloons, in modern times or in the middle ages, he is just Mr. Rossetti, a fleshly person, with nothing particular to tell us or teach us, with extreme self-control, a strong sense of colour, and a careful choice of diction.   Amid all his "affluence of jewel-coloured words," he has not given us one rounded and noteworthy piece of art, though his verses are all art; not one poem which is memorable for its own sake, and quite separable from the displeasing identity of the composer.   The nearest approach to a perfect whole is the "Blessed Damozel," a peculiar poem, placed first in the book, perhaps by accident, perhaps because it is a key to the poems which follow.   This poem appeared in a rough shape many years ago in the *Germ*, an unwholesome periodical started by the Pre-Raphaelites, and suffered, after gasping through a few feeble numbers, to die the death of all such publications. In spite of its affected title, and of numberless affectations throughout the text, the "Blessed Damozel" has great merits of its own, and a few lines of real genius. We have heard it described as the record of actual grief and love, or, in simple words, the apotheosis of one actually lost by the writer; but, without having any private knowledge of the circumstance of its composition, we feel that such an account of the poem is inadmissible. It does not contain one single note of sorrow. It is a "composition," and a clever one. Read the opening stanzas:—

> The blessed damozel leaned out
>   From the gold bar of Heaven;
> Her eyes were deeper than the depth
>   Of water stilled at even;
> She had three lilies in her hand,
>   And the stars in her hair were seven.
>
> Her robe, ungirt from clasp to hem,
>   No wrought flowers did adorn,
> But a white rose of Mary's gift,
>   For service meetly worn;
> Her hair that lay along her back
>   Was yellow like ripe corn.

This is a careful sketch for a picture, which, worked into actual colour by a master, might have been worth seeing. The steadiness of hand lessens as the poem proceeds, and

although there are several passages of considerable power,
—such as that where, far down the void,

> this earth
> Spins like a fretful midge

or that other, describing how

> the curled moon
> Was like a little feather
> Fluttering far down the gulf—

the general effect is that of a queer old painting in a
missal, very affected and very odd. What moved the
British critic to ecstasy in this poem seems to us very sad
nonsense indeed, or, if not sad nonsense, very meretricious affectation. Thus, we have seen the following
verses quoted with enthusiasm, as italicized—

> And still she bowed herself and stooped
> Out of the circling charm;
> *Until her bosom must have made*
> *The bar she leaned on warm,*
> And the lilies lay as if asleep
> Along her bended arm.

> From the fixed place of Heaven she saw
> *Time like a pulse shake fierce*
> *Thro' all the worlds.* Her gaze still strove
> Within the gulf to pierce
> Its path; and now she spoke as when
> The stars sang in their spheres.

It seems to us that all these lines are very bad, with the
exception of the two admirable lines ending the first verse,

and that the italicized portions are quite without merit, and almost without meaning. On the whole, one feels disheartened and amazed at the poet who, in the nineteenth century, talks about "damozels," "citherns," and "citoles," and addresses the mother of Christ as the "Lady Mary,"—

> With her five handmaidens, whose names
> Are five sweet symphonies,
> Cecily, Gertrude, Magdalen,
> Margaret and Rosalys.

A suspicion is awakened that the writer is laughing at us. We hover uncertainly between picturesqueness and namby-pamby, and the effect, as Artemus Ward would express it, is "weakening to the intellect." The thing would have been almost too much in the shape of a picture, though the workmanship might have made amends. The truth is that literature, and more particularly poetry, is in a very bad way when one art gets hold of another, and imposes upon it its conditions and limitations. In the first few verses of the "Damozel" we have the subject, or part of the subject, of a picture, and the inventor should either have painted it or left it alone altogether; and, had he done the latter, the world would have lost nothing. Poetry is something more than painting; and an idea will not become a poem, because it is too smudgy for a picture.

In a short notice from a well-known pen, giving the best estimate we have seen of Mr. Rossetti's powers as a poet, the *North American Review* offers a certain explanation for affectation such as that of Mr. Rossetti. The writer suggests that "it may probably be the expression of genuine moods of mind in natures too little comprehensive." We would rather believe that Mr. Rossetti lacks comprehension than that he is deficient in sincerity; yet really, to paraphrase the words which Johnson applied to Thomas Sheridan, Mr. Rossetti is affected, naturally affected, but it must have taken him a great deal of trouble to become what we now see him—such an excess of affectation is not in nature.* There is very little writing in the volume spontaneous in the sense that some of Swinburne's verses are spontaneous; the poems all look as if they had taken a great deal of trouble. The grotesque mediævalism of "Stratton Water" and "Sister Helen," the mediæval classicism of "Troy Town," the false and shallow mysticism of "Eden Bower," are one and all essentially imitative, and must have cost the writer much pains. It is time, indeed, to point out that Mr. Rossetti is a poet possessing great powers of assimilation and some faculty for concealing the nutriment on which he feeds. Setting aside the *Vita Nuova* and the early Italian poems, which are familiar to many readers by his own excellent translations, Mr. Rossetti may be described as a writer who has yielded to an unusual extent to the complex influences of the literature surrounding him at the present moment.

---

* "Why, sir, Sherry is dull, *naturally* dull; but it must have taken him a *great deal of trouble* to become what we now see him—such an excess of stupidity is not in nature."

—*Boswell's Life*.

He has the painter's imitative power developed in proportion to his lack of the poet's conceiving imagination. He reproduces to a nicety the manner of an old ballad, a trick in which Mr. Swinburne is also an adept. Cultivated readers, moreover, will recognise in every one of these poems the tone of Mr. Tennyson broken up by the style of Mr. and Mrs. Browning, and disguised here and there by the eccentricities of the Pre-Raphaelites. The "Burden of Nineveh" is a philosophical edition of "Recollections of the Arabian Nights;" "A Last Confession" and "Dante at Verona" are, in the minutest trick and form of thought, suggestive of Mr. Browning; and that the sonnets have been largely moulded and inspired by Mrs. Browning can be ascertained by any critic who will compare them with the *Sonnets from the Portuguese*. Much remains, nevertheless, that is Mr. Rossetti's own. We at once recognise as his own property such passages as this:—

> I looked up
> And saw where a brown-shouldered harlot leaned
> Half through a tavern window thick with vine.
> Some man had come behind her in the room
> And caught her by her arms, and she had turned
> With that coarse empty laugh on him, as now
> He *munched her neck with kisses, while the vine*
> *Crawled in her back.*

Or this:—

> As I stooped, her own lips rising there
> *Bubbled with brimming kisses* at my mouth

Or this:—

> Have seen your lifted silken skirt
> Advertise dainties through the dirt!

Or this:—

> What more prize than love to impel thee,
> *Grip* and *lip* my limbs as I tell thee.

Passages like these are the common stock of the walking gentlemen of the fleshly school. We cannot forbear expressing our wonder, by the way, at the kind of women whom it seems the unhappy lot of these gentlemen to encounter. We have lived as long in the world as they have, but never yet came across persons of the other sex who conduct themselves in the manner described. Females who bite, scratch, scream, bubble, munch, sweat, writhe, twist, wriggle, foam, and in a general way slaver over their lovers, must surely possess some extraordinary qualities to counteract their otherwise most offensive mode of conducting themselves. It appears, however, on examination, that their poet-lovers conduct themselves in a similar manner. They, too, bite, scratch, scream, bubble, munch, sweat, writhe, twist, wriggle, foam, and slaver, in a style frightful to hear of. Let us hope that it is only their fun, and that they don't mean half they say. At times, in reading such books as this, one cannot help wishing that things had remained for ever in the asexual state described in Mr. Darwin's great chapter on Palingenesis. We get very weary of this protracted hankering after a person of the other sex; it seems meat, drink, thought, sinew, religion for the fleshly school. There is no limit to the fleshliness, and Mr. Rossetti finds in it its own religious justification much in the same way as Holy Willie:—

> Maybe thou let'st this fleshly thorn
> Perplex thy servant night and morn,
>   'Cause he's so gifted.
> If so, thy hand must e'en be borne,
>   Until thou lift it.

Whether he is writing of the holy Damozel, or of the Virgin herself, or of Lilith, or Helen, or of Dante, or of Jenny the street-walker, he is fleshly all over, from the roots of his hair to the tip of his toes; never a true lover merging his identity into that of the beloved one; never spiritual, never tender; always self-conscious and æsthetic. "Nothing," says a modern writer, "in human life is so utterly remorseless—not love, not hate, not ambition, not vanity—as the artistic or æsthetic instinct morbidly developed to the suppression of conscience and feeling;" and at no time do we feel more fully impressed with this truth than after the perusal of "Jenny," in some respects the finest poem in the volume, and in all respects the poem best indicative of the true quality of the writer's humanity. It is a production which bears signs of having been suggested by Mr. Buchanan's quasi-lyrical poems, which it copies in the style of title, and particularly by "Artist and Model;" but certainly Mr. Rossetti cannot be accused, as the Scottish writer has been accused, of maudlin

sentiment and affected tenderness. The two first lines
are perfect:—

> Lazy laughing languid Jenny,
> Fond of a kiss and fond of a guinea;

And the poem is a soliloquy of the poet—who has been
spending the evening in dancing at a casino—over his
partner, whom he has accompanied home to the usual
style of lodgings occupied by such ladies, and who has
fallen asleep with her head upon his knee, while he
wonders, in a wretched pun—

> Whose person or whose purse may be
> The lodestar of your reverie?

The soliloquy is long, and in some parts beautiful, despite a very constant suspicion that we are listening to an
emasculated Mr. Browning, whose whole tone and gesture, so to speak, is occasionally introduced with startling
fidelity; and there are here and there glimpses of actual
thought and insight, over and above the picturesque
touches which belong to the writer's true profession, such
as that where, at daybreak—

> lights creep in
> Past the gauze curtains half drawn to,
> And *the lamp's doubled shade grows blue.*

What we object to in this poem is not the subject, which
any writer may be fairly left to choose for himself; nor
anything particularly vicious in the poetic treatment of
it; nor any bad blood bursting through in special passages.

But the whole tone, without being more than usually coarse, seems heartless. [There is not a drop of piteousness in Mr. Rossetti. He is just to the outcast, even generous; severe to the seducer; sad even at the spectacle of lust in dimity and fine ribbons. Notwithstanding all this, and a certain delicacy and refinement of treatment unusual with this poet, the poem repels and revolts us, and we like Mr. Rossetti least after its perusal. We are angry with the fleshly person at last. The "Blessed Damozel" puzzled us, the "Song of the Bower" amused us, the love-sonnet depressed and sickened us, but "Jenny," though distinguished by less special viciousness of thought and style than any of these, fairly makes us lose patience. We detect its fleshliness at a glance; we perceive that the scene was fascinating less through its human tenderness than because it, like all the others, possessed an inherent quality of animalism. "The whole work" ("Jenny,") writes Mr. Swinburne, "is worthy to fill its place for ever as one of the most perfect poems of an age or generation. There is just the same life-blood and breadth of poetic interest in this episode of a London street and lodging as in the song of 'Troy Town' and the song of 'Eden Bower;' just as much, and no jot more," —to which last statement we cordially assent; for there is bad blood in all, and breadth of poetic interest in none. "Vengeance of Jenny's case," indeed!—when such a poet as this comes fawning over her, with tender compassion in one eye and æsthetic enjoyment in the other! It is time that we permitted Mr. Rossetti to speak for himself, which we will do by quoting a fairly representative poem entire:—

LOVE-LILY.

Between the hands, between the brows,
　　Between the lips of Love-Lily,
A spirit is born whose birth endows
　　My blood with fire to burn through me;
Who breathes upon my gazing eyes,
　　Who laughs and murmurs in mine ear,
At whose least touch my colour flies,
　　And whom my life grows faint to hear.

Within the voice, within the heart,
　　Within the mind of Love-Lily,
A spirit is born who lifts apart
　　His tremulous wings and looks at me;
Who on my mouth his finger lays,
　　And shows, while whispering lutes confer,
That Eden of Love's watered ways
　　Whose winds and spirits worship her.

Brows, hands, and lips, heart, mind, and voice,
　　Kisses and words of Love-Lily,—
Oh! bid me with your joy rejoice
　　Till *riotous longing rest in me!*
Ah! let not hope be still distraught,
　　But find in her its gracious goal,
Whose speech Truth knows not from her thought,
　　Nor Love her body from her soul.

With the exception of the usual "riotous longing," which seems to make Mr. Rossetti a burthen to himself, there is nothing to find fault with in the extreme fleshliness of these verses, and to many people who live in the country

they may even appear beautiful. Without pausing to
criticise a thing so trifling—as well might we dissect a
cobweb or anatomize a medusa—let us ask the reader's
attention to a peculiarity to which all the students of the
fleshly school must sooner or later give their attention—
we mean the habit of accenting the last syllable in words
which in ordinary speech are accented on the penulti-
mate:—

> Between the hands, between the brows,
> Between the lips of Love-Lil*ee!*

which may be said to give to the speaker's voice a sort of
cooing tenderness just bordering on a loving whistle.
Still better as an illustration are the lines:—

> Saturday night is market night
> Everywhere, be it dry or wet,
> And market night in the Haymar-*ket!*

which the reader may advantageously compare with Mr.
Morris's

> Then said the king
> Thanked be thou; *neither for nothing*
> Shalt thou this good deed do to me;

or Mr. Swinburne's

> In either of the twain
> Red roses full of rain;
> She hath for bondwo*men*
> All kinds **of** flowers.

It is unnecessary to multiply examples of an affectation
which disfigure all these writers—Guildenstern, Rosen-

cranz, and Osric; who, in the same spirit which prompts the ambitious nobodies that rent London theatres in the "empty" season to make up for their dullness by fearfully original "new readings," distinguish their attempt at leading business by affecting the construction of their grandfathers and great-grandfathers, and the accentuation of the poets of the court of James I. It is in all respects a sign of remarkable genius, from this point of view, to rhyme "was" with "grass," "death" with "lièth," "love" with "of," "once" with "suns," and so on *ad nauseam.* We are far from disputing the value of bad rhymes used occasionally to break up the monotony of verse, but the case is hard when such blunders become the rule and not the exception, when writers deliberately lay themselves out to be as archaic and affected as possible. Poetry is perfect human speech, and these archaisms are the mere fiddlededeeing of empty heads and hollow hearts. Bad as they are, they are the true indication of falser tricks and affectations which lie far deeper. They are trifles, light as air, showing how the wind blows. The soul's speech and the heart's speech are clear, simple, natural, and beautiful, and reject the meretricious tricks to which we have drawn attention.

It is on the score that these tricks and affectations have procured the professors a number of imitators, that the fleshly school deliver their formula that great poets are always to be known because their manner is immediately reproduced by small poets, and that a poet who finds few imitators is probably of inferior rank—by which they mean to infer that they themselves are very great poets indeed. It is quite true that they are imitated. On the stage, twenty provincial "stars" copy Charles Kean, while not one copies his father; there are dozens of actors who reproduce Mr. Charles Dillon, and not one who attempts to reproduce Macready. When we take up the poems of Mr. O'Shaughnessy,* we are face to face with a second-hand Mr. Swinburne; when we read Mr. Payne's queer allegories,† we remember Mr. Morris's early stage; and every poem of Mr. Marston's ‡ reminds us of Mr. Rossetti. But what is really most droll and puzzling in the matter is, that these imitators seem to have no difficulty whatever in writing nearly, if not quite, as well as their masters. It is not bad imitations they offer us, but poems which read just like the originals; the fact being that it is easy to reproduce sound when it has no strict connection with sense, and simple enough to cull phraseology not hopelessly interwoven with thought and spirit. The fact that these gentlemen are so easily imitated is the most damning proof of their inferiority. What merits they have lie with their faults on the surface, and can be caught by any young gentleman as easily as the measles, only they are rather more difficult to get rid of. All young gentlemen have animal faculties, though few have brains; and if animal faculties without brains will make poems, nothing is easier in the world. A great and good poet, however, is great and good irrespective of manner, and

---

* *An Epic of Women.* By Arthur W. E. O'Shaughnessy. (Hotten.)

† *The Masque of Shadows.* By John Payne. (Pickering.)

‡ *Songtide, and other Poems.* By Philip Bourke Marston. (Ellis.)

often in spite of manner; he is great because he brings great ideas and new light, because his thought is a revelation; and, although it is true that a great manner generally accompanies great matter, the manner of great matter is almost inimitable. The great poet is not Cowley, imitated and idolized and reproduced by every scribbler of his time; nor Pope, whose trick of style was so easily copied that to this day we cannot trace his own hand with any certainty in the *Iliad*; nor Donne, nor Sylvester, nor the Della Cruscans. Shakespeare's blank verse is the most difficult and Jonson's the most easy to imitate, of all the Elizabethan stock and Shakespeare's verse is the best verse, because it combines the great qualities of all contemporary verse, with no individual affectations; and so perfectly does this verse, with all its splendour, intersect with the style of contemporaries *at their best*, that we would undertake to select passage after passage which would puzzle a good judge to tell which of the Elizabethans was the author—Marlowe, Beaumont, Dekkar, Marston, Webster, or Shakespeare himself. The great poet is Dante, full of the thunder of a great Idea; and Milton, unapproachable in the serene white light of thought and sumptuous wealth of style; and Shakespeare, all poets by turns, and all men in succession; and Goethe, always innovating, and ever indifferent to innovation for its own sake; and Wordsworth, clear as crystal and deep as the sea; and Tennyson, with his vivid range, far-piercing sight, and perfect speech; and Browning, great, not by virtue of his eccentricities, but because of his close intellectual grasp. Tell *Paradise Lost*, the *Divine Com-*

edy, in naked prose; do the same by *Hamlet, Macbeth,* and *Lear;* read Mr. Hayward's translation of *Faust;* take up the *Excursion,* a great poem, though its speech is nearly prose already; turn the "Guinevere" into a mere story; reproduce Pompilia's last dying speech without a line of rhythm. Reduced to bald English, all these poems, and all great poems, lose much; but how much do they not retain? They are poems to the very roots and depths of being, poems born and delivered from the soul, and treat them as cruelly as you may, poems they will remain. So it is with all good and thorough creations, however low in their rank; so it is with the "Ballot in a Wedding" and "Clever Tom Clinch," just as much as with the "Epistle of Karsheesh," or Goethe's torso of "Prometheus;" with Shelley's "Skylark," or Alfred de Musset's "A la Lune," as well as Racine's "Athalie," Victor Hugo's "Parricide," or Hood's "Last Man." A poem is a poem, first as to the soul, next as to the form. The fleshly persons who wish to create form for its own sake are merely pronouncing their own doom. But *such* form! If the Pre-Raphaelite fervour gains ground, we shall soon have popular songs like this:—

> When winds do roar, and rains do pour,
> Hard is the life of the sail*or;*
> He scarcely as he reels can tell
> The side-lights from the binna*cle;*
> He looketh on the wild wa*ter,* &c.,

and so on, till the English speech seems the speech of raving madmen. Of a piece with other affectations is the

device of a burthen, of which the fleshly persons are very
fond for its own sake, quite apart from its relevancy.
Thus Mr. Rossetti sings:—

> Why did you melt your waxen man,
>   Sister Helen?
> To-day is the third since you began.
> The time was long, yet the time ran,
>   Little brother.
>   (*O mother, Mary mother,*
> *Three days to-day between Heaven and Hell*)

This burthen is repeated, with little or no alteration,
through thirty-four verses, and might with as much
music, and far more point, run as follows:—

> Why did you melt your waxen man,
>   Sister Helen?
> To-day is the third since you began.
> The time was long, yet the time ran,
>   Little brother.
>   (*O Mr. Dante Rossetti,*
> *What stuff is this about Heaven and Hell?*)

About as much to the point is a burthen of Mr. Swinburne's, something to the following effect:—

> We were three maidens in the green corn,
>   *Hey chickaleerie, the red cock and gray,*
> Fairer maidens were never born,
>   *One o'clock, two o'clock, off and away.*

We are not quite certain of the words, as we quote from
memory, but we are sure our version fairly represents the

original, and is quite as expressive. Productions of this sort are "silly sooth" in good earnest, though they delight some newspaper critics of the day, and are copied by young gentlemen with animal faculties morbidly developed by too much tobacco and too little exercise. Such indulgence, however, would ruin the strongest poetical constitution; and it unfortunately happens that neither masters nor pupils were naturally very healthy. In such a poem as "Eden Bower" there is not one scrap of imagination, properly so-called. It is a clever grotesque in the worst manner of Callot, unredeemed by a gleam of true poetry or humour. No good poet would have wrought into a poem the absurd tradition about Lilith; Goethe was content to glance at it merely, with a grim smile, in the great scene in the Brocken. We may remark here that poems of this unnatural and morbid kind are only tolerable when they embody a profound meaning, as do Coleridge's "Ancient Mariner" and "Cristabel." Not that we would insult the memory of Coleridge by comparing his exquisitely conscientious work with this affected rubbish about "Eden Bower" and "Sister Helen," though his influence in their composition is unmistakable. Still more unmistakable is the influence of that most unwholesome poet, Beddoes, who, with all his great powers, treated his subjects in a thoroughly insincere manner, and is now justly forgotten.

The great strong current of English poetry rolls on, ever mirroring in its bosom new prospects of fair and wholesome thought. Morbid deviations are endless and inevitable; there must be marsh and stagnant mere as well as mountain and wood. Glancing backward into the shady places of the obscure, we see the once prosperous nonsense-writers each now consigned to his own little limbo—Skelton and Gower still playing fantastic tricks with the mother-tongue; Gascoigne outlasting the applause of all, and living to see his own works buried before him; Silvester doomed to oblivion by his own fame as a translator; Carew the idol of courts, and Donne the beloved of schoolmen, both buried in the same oblivion; the fantastic Fletchers winning the wonder of collegians, and fading out through sheer poetic impotence; Cowley shaking all England with his pindarics, and perishing with them; Waller, the famous, saved from oblivion by the natural note of one single song—and so on, through league after league of a flat and desolate country which once was prosperous, till we come again to these fantastic figures of the fleshly school, with their droll mediæval garments, their funny archaic speech, and the fatal marks of literary consumption in every pale and delicate visage. Our judgment on Mr. Rossetti, to whom we in the meantime confine our judgment, is substantially that of the *North American Reviewer,* who believes that "we have in him another poetical man, and a man markedly poetical, and of a kind apparently, though not radically, different from any of our secondary writers of poetry, but that we have not in him a new poet of any weight;" and that he is "so affected, sentimental, and painfully self-conscious, that the best to be done in his case is to hope that this book of his, having unpacked his bosom of so much that is unhealthy, may have done him more good than it has given others pleasure." Such, we say, is our opinion, which might very well be wrong, and have to undergo modification, if Mr. Rossetti was younger and less self-possessed. His "maturity" is fatal.*

THOMAS MAITLAND

* *The Contemporary Review*, October, 1871. (Robert Buchanan.)

WALT WHITMAN

A STRANGELY impudent agitation has just been started with regard to what is called "Walt Whitman's Actual American Position." Whitman, it may be explained, is an American writer who some years back attracted attention by a volume of so-called poems which were chiefly remarkable for their absurd extravagance and shameless obscenity, and who has since, we are glad to say, been little heard of among decent people. It now appears that, although there is a small *coterie* of persons in this country who are not ashamed to confess their liking for Whitman's nastiness, his own countrymen have universally repudiated him. "The real truth," says an American journal, which has taken up the subject apparently in the interest of Whitman, "is that, with the exception of a very few readers, Whitman's poems in their public reception have fallen still-born in this country. They have been met, and are met to-day, with the determined denial, disgust, and scorn of orthodox American authors, publishers, and editors, and in a pecuniary and worldly sense have certainly wrecked the life of their author." "No established publishing house will publish his books. Most of the stores will not even sell them." "Repeated attempts to secure a small income by writing for the magazines during his illness have been utter failures. The *Atlantic* will not touch him. His offerings to

Scribner are returned with insulting notes; the *Galaxy* the same. *Harper's* did print a couple of his pieces two years ago, but imperative orders from headquarters have stopped anything further. All the established American poets studiously ignore Whitman." We are of course sorry that Whitman, or any other man, should be in sore distress, but we must say that we are very glad indeed to hear that his writings are unsaleable, and that no respectacle publisher or editor in America will give him countenance by printing his contributions. This fact, if it is true, shows that the moral sense of the American public is, after all, not quite so much deadened as some recent events might lead one to imagine. If the *New York Herald* will not have anything to do with Walt Whitman, it is a proof that even the *Herald* draws the line somewhere. We can only regret that the same view is not taken by all publishers on this side of the ocean, and that there is one firm at least in London which is not ashamed to advertise a "complete" edition of Whitman's works. We have no desire to pry into the details of Whitman's private life. The description which he gives of himself in his writings as "disorderly, fleshly, sensual," and fond of loafing, is not perhaps to be taken in a literal sense; and in any case we have no desire to speculate as to how far his private life may have been imprudent or irregular. The important fact is that he has found it impossible to get a living by his writings, which are everywhere shunned and rejected. Considering the character of these writings, this seems to us a very natural and desirable result, and it is difficult to understand why people should be expected to buy an article which disgusts them. Some of Mr. Whitman's friends and admirers in London have, however, worked themselves into a state of theatrical indignation with regard to the treatment of this great man by his unappreciative and ungrateful countrymen. Mr. Robert Buchanan, who has made himself the mouthpiece of this extraordinary agitation, not only claims for Whitman "literary immortality," but exalts his "ineffable goodness" and "beneficence," and declares, in a passage flavoured with a touch of blasphemy which we prefer not to quote, that "only this last consecration of Martyrdom was wanting to complete our poet's apotheosis." Mr. Buchanan, being himself a poet, naturally chafes against the restraints of ordinary prose, and we are treated to a wonderful picture, in the highest style of fine language, of a "golden eagle sick to death, worn with age and famine, or with both, passing with weary waft of wing from promontory to promontory, from peak to peak, pursued by a crowd of prosperous rooks and crows, who fall screaming back whenever the noble bird turns his indignant head, and which follow frantically once more, hooting behind him, whenever he ascends again on his way." This is all very fine no doubt in its way, but it may be thought to be hardly a fair description of the case of a dirty bird which is shunned on account of its unclean habits. Mr. Buchanan also breaks out into furious vituperation against all American publishers and men of letters, whom he abuses in the most vulgar terms; and warns the American nation collectively that its "honour will be tarnished eternally by the murder of its only remaining prophet." Mr. Buchanan concludes by what is really an insulting appeal to his own countrymen, as "loving and revering" this apostle of beastliness, to give him "a substantial proof of the honour in which he is held here in the heart of England."

From the height of this rhapsodical outburst it is a sad descent to the prosaic facts of the case. It is of course open to any one who admires, or is simply sorry for, Whitman to subscribe for his support; but it is difficult to understand why those who dislike his flagrant indecencies should be denounced because they do not feel inclined to give him any encouragement. Mr. Buchanan himself, though he does not scruple to rank Whitman with the Saviour, and declares that his teaching is "as Heavenly manna," thinks it necessary to "disclaim entire sympathy with Whitman's materialistic idealism, which seems to go too far in the direction of illuminating the execrable." Mr. Buchanan does not explain exactly what he means by "execrable," but in any sense such an admission goes far to justify the distrust and loathing with which Whitman is regarded both here and in America. Mr. Buchanan holds that "these great experiments in poetry" are "destined to exercise an extraordinary influence on the future of religion as well as poetry," and this, he says, "no one who has read his works will deny." Public opinion, however, both here and in America, has expressed itself very decisively as to these great experiments; and there is very little chance of Mr. Buchanan or any of his associates bringing the world round to a different view. It is no doubt true that there are many people who have never read Whitman's so-called poetry all through, but enough is known to show that it is an attempt to make animal brutality and indecency pass for poetry. No doubt the present effort to revive curiosity on the subject will be a useful advertisement to any bookseller who happens to have a stock of Whitman's garbage on hand. It must be remembered, however, that his earlier works have been before the public for some twenty years, and that during the whole of that time the opinion originally formed of them has been steadily sustained, and, if possible, intensified; and there is, we imagine, very little danger of this judgment being now reversed by friendly puffery and agitation, even when such great authorities as Mr. Buchanan supposes himself to be take up the matter. There are, no doubt, questions both of art and philosophy on which public opinion at times goes astray; but in the present instance the elementary instincts of mankind are sufficient to settle the question. There would indeed need to be a very remarkable change both in the moral and intellectual constitution of educated people before such writings as those of Whitman could be accepted as, in any sense, honest literature.

When Mr. Buchanan screeches about "literary outlawry," "murder," and "official persecution," he is obviously only talking nonsense. We have no desire to say anything in disparagement of American publishers, but they are no doubt not absolutely exempt from the weaknesses of other tradesmen; and we suspect that, if there really were a market anywhere for Whitman's wares, he

would have no difficulty in finding some one to retail
them for him. It is reasonable to assume that American
publishers and editors know their own business, and that
they have sufficient reasons for having nothing to do with
Mr. Whitman. He has chosen to identify himself with
unsavoury things, and whatever he might now write, his
name would be a taint to any respectable periodical. The
fact is that it was only the indecent exposure which Whitman made of himself in the first instance that attracted
passing attention to him as a sort of psychological mon-
strosity. Apart from his scandalous eccentricities, his
writings are poor stuff, and the affectation of deep philosophy is easily seen through. The assumption that a
man who sets himself to outrage public decency should
be gratefully supported by public charity is certainly a
very curious one. Mr. Buchanan asserts that his idol has
many worshippers in this country, but we venture to say
that this is a part of his delusion; and we may add that
those who are so unfortunate in their tastes as to belong to
this sect would perhaps act prudently for themselves in
not proclaiming it too loudly. The conclusion would
seem to be that the "illumination of the execrable" is not
a remunerative business; and so far the lesson is a useful
one, and may be taken to heart by any other writers who
have a weakness that way. There is also, however, a
general principle underlying Mr. Buchanan's letter which
deserves notice. He appears to imagine that society is
bound, as a matter of course, to contribute to the maintenance of any one who chooses to set up as a man of
genius. The genius may be less apparent than some other

characteristics, but society is bound all the same to accept implicitly the claimant's own assurance, and that of a few sympathetic friends, that he is a genius, and to provide for him accordingly. This, we fancy, is a favourite idea with a certain class of poets, who have usually reasons of their own for holding that their incomes ought not to be dependent merely on the popularity of their works and the respect in which they are held by those who know them. Instances can no doubt be mentioned of great poets who were not sufficiently appreciated while alive; but, on the other hand, it would be rather hazardous to undertake to provide for every one who, believing himself to be a poet, could not get a living by his works. We should then have a fine flock of hard-up "golden eagles" eager to take advantage of public charity. If the appeal on behalf of Whitman were based simply on his age and indigence, we should not think ourselves bound to say anything against it. But the plan proposed is to help him to circulate his writings, and thus implies approval of them. It is satisfactory to believe that agitation for such a purpose is likely to prove as futile as it is audacious.*

---

* *The Saturday Review*, March 18, 1876.

TESS OF THE D'URBERVILLES

By Thomas Hardy

THERE is something very graceful and instructive
in the modern practice of writing apologetic or
critical prefaces to new editions of novels. In his first
edition the author stands the fire of criticism without replying. He waits, like the British infantry of old, till
he sees the colour of his opponents' eyes, and then, in the
preface to a fresh edition, he lets fly at those assailants.
Somehow it is commonly the author of a very successful
book who thus gives us his own views of his own art and
of his critics. One would rather expect the unsuccessful
writer to stand on the defensive, but he, poor gentleman,
has no new edition, no opportunity of retaliation. Could
I write a successful novel—which is not a probable chance
—I think I might contemplate the royalties with an
avaricious grin, and quote

> *Criticus* me sibilat; at mihi plaudo
> Ipse domi simul ac nummos contemplor in arcâ

Especially if most of my critics had danced triumphantly
before me, beating cymbals and hailing the conqueror,
while only a few "hesitate"—or howled—"dislike," me-
thinks I could possess my soul in peace. But this frame
of mind is growing rare, and authors do what Buffon did
not—they reply to their reviewers. Mr. Hardy has

just answered the graceless persons—a small minority—
who did not admire without qualification his tale, *Tess of
the D'Urbervilles.* The following extract from his preface is culled out of the *Illustrated London News.* The
last sentence, of course, is not Mr. Hardy's:

In the introductory words to the first edition I suggested the
possible advent of the genteel person who would not be able to
endure the tone of these pages. That person duly appeared, mostly
mixed up with the aforesaid objectors. In another of his forms
he felt upset that it was not possible for him to read the book
through three times, owing to my not having made that critical
effort which "alone can prove the salvation of such an one." In
another, he objected to such vulgar articles as the Devil's pitch-
fork, a lodging-house carving-knife, and a shame-bought parasol
appearing in a respectable story. In another place he was a gentleman who turned Christian for half-an-hour the better to express his grief that a disrespectful phrase about the Immortals
should have been used; though the same innate gentility compelled
him to excuse the author in words of pity that one cannot be too
thankful for: "He does but give us of his best." I can assure
this great critic that to exclaim illogically against the gods,
singular or plural, is not such an original sin of mine as he seems
to imagine. True, it may have some local originality; though,
if Shakespeare were an authority on history, which, perhaps, he is
not, I could show that the sin was introduced into Wessex as early
as the Heptarchy itself. Says Glo'ster to Lear, otherwise Ina,
king of that country—
  As flies to wanton boys are we to the gods;
  They kill us for their sport.
Needless to say that the "great critic" is Mr. Andrew Lang.

Mr. Hardy's argument is logical indeed. "I said from
the first," he observes, "that the genteel person"—meaning the Snob—"would not like my book. Some people
did not like my book, therefore they are genteel persons.

Nothing can be more convincing. Then Mr. Hardy selects myself (as I signed my notice in the *New Review*), and he makes a reply which, I am sure, is only a petulant expression of annoyance, and does not seriously signify what it seems to signify. Mr. Hardy has no means of knowing what my private shade of theological dogma is. He cannot tell whether I am, as a matter of creed, a Christian or not. Nor can he really suppose that I, being, *ex hypothesi*, an unbeliever, pretended for half-an-hour to belief, in order that I might pick a hole in a phrase of his. The charge of so superfluously playing the part of Tartuffe for a critical and literary purpose is comic or melancholy according to your humour. As Mr. Hardy says, he "exclaimed illogically against the gods" in the phrase, "The President of the Immortals (in Æschylean phrase) had ended his sport with Tess." This was the moral and marrow of his romance, as I supposed, and the phrase must seem equally illogical to an Atheist and a Christian, to a Buddhist and a Bonze. For nobody in his senses now believes in a wicked malignant President of the Immortals, whatever Glo'ster may have said in his haste while Ina was a monarch of the West Saxons. No; one need not be a Christian, or pretend to be a Christian, before resenting a comment on the "President of the Immortals" which is confessed to be illogical, and which —if Mr. Hardy does not believe in a malignant "President"—is insincere and affected. And here I may add the expression of my regret that my quotation, "he does but give us of his best," has annoyed Mr. Hardy. For he always does give us of his best—of his best labour and earnest endeavour—and this is a virtue not universal among artists.

*   *   *   *   *

As to *Tess* and my own comparative distaste for that lady and her melancholy adventures, let me be unchristian for half-an-hour and give my reasons. But, first, let me confess that I am in an insignificant minority. On all sides—not only from the essays of reviewers, but from the spoken opinions of the most various kinds of readers —one learns that *Tess* is a masterpiece. One hears the same opinion from a great classical scholar, who seldom deserts the ancients for the moderns, and from a Scot living his life out in a remote savage island, which, by the way, is *not* Samoa. There is no absolute standard of taste in literature, but such a consensus of opinion comes as near being a standard as one generation can supply. So I confess myself in the wrong, as far as an exterior test can make me in the wrong; and yet a reviewer can only give his own impression, and state his reasons, as far as he knows them, for that impression. In the *Illustrated London News* of October 1 there is not only the beginning of a new tale by Mr. Hardy, but an eloquent estimate of Mr. Hardy's genius by Mr. Frederick Greenwood. Thence one might cull texts to serve in an apology for one's own sentiments about *Tess* and some other books of Mr. Hardy's, and for a disquisition on the general relations of the faults of a work of art to our final estimate of its value. Mr. Greenwood, greatly admiring, as every one must admire, the talent of Mr. Hardy, says that one of his tales (*The Hand of Ethel-*

berta) is "forbidding in conception." Now, to my private
taste—and *on n'a que soi*, even when one is a reviewer—
Tess is also "forbidding in conception." I have not read
The Hand of Ethelberta, but *Tess* is not the only one of
Mr. Hardy's novels which repels me by what is, to me,
the "forbidding" character of its "conception." There is a
tale of his about a woman who adored an effigy of a dead
lover. I gladly forget the rest. Well, "it gar me a'
grue," to quote a better writer, and the *frisson*, if new, is
none the better for that. There is *Two on a Tower*,
where the heroine, a widow, is not infrequently described
as "warm." Her child, by a second marriage, through
some legal misadventure or mischance, is to be born
without a legitimate father. So she marries a clergyman
—a bishop if my memory holds good—and imposes the
babe on that prelate. It may be my "gentility," or it may
be my partiality for a married clergy, but somehow I do
find the "conception" of *Two on a Tower* to be "forbidding." I don't like the practical joke on the clergyman;
and the "warmth" of the widow seems too conspicuously
dwelt upon.

Again, I find a similar "forbidding" quality in *Tess*, as
I do, and have always done, in *Clarissa Harlowe*. Poor
Tess, a most poetical, if not a very credible character, is
a rural Clarissa Harlowe. She is very unlike most rural
maids, but then she comes of a noble lineage. She is
not avenged by the sword of Colonel Morden, but by that
lodging-house carving-knife, which seems anything but
a trusty stiletto. She does not die, like Clarissa, as the
ermine martin dies of the stain on its snowy fur, but she

goes back to the atrocious cad who betrayed her, and wears
—not caring what she wears—the parasol of pomp and the
pretty slippers of iniquity. To say that all this is out of
character and out of keeping is only to set my theory of
human nature against Mr. Hardy's knowledge of it. I
never knew a Tess, as Mr. Thackeray was never personally
acquainted with a convict. Her behaviour does not in-
variably seem to me that of "a pure woman," but perhaps
I am no judge of purity, at all events in such extraordi-
narily disadvantageous circumstances. As to purity,
people are generally about to talk nastily when they
dwell on the word. The kind of "catastrophe" spoken of
by Mr. Hardy has been adequately treated of by St.
Augustine, in his *De Civitate Dei*. To my own gentility
it is no stumbling-block. Other girls in fiction have been
seduced with more blame, and have not lost our sympathy, or ceased to be what Mr. Hardy calls "protagon-
ists." The case of Effie Deans will occur to the studious
reader. It is not the question of "purity" that offends me,
but that of credibility in character and language. The
villain Alec and the prig Angel Clare seem to me equally
unnatural, incredible, and out of the course of experience.
But that may only prove one's experience to be fortu-
nately limited. When all these persons, whose conduct
and conversation are so far from plausible, combine in a
tale of which the whole management is, to one's own taste,
unnatural and "forbidding," how can one pretend to believe or to admire without reserve? Of course it may be
no fault in a book that it is "forbidding;" many people
even think it a merit. *Le Père Goriot* is "forbidding";

Madame Bovary is "forbidding," yet nobody in his senses denies their merit. But then, to myself, those tales are credible and real. *Tess* is not real nor credible, judged by the same personal standard. To be sure, *Tess*, unlike *Madame Bovary*, is at all events and undeniably a romance. When Angel Clare, walking in his sleep, carries the portly Tess, with all her opulent charms and "ethereal beauty" to a very considerable distance, he does what Porthos, or Guy Livingstone, could hardly have done when wide awake. It is a romantic incident, but if an otherwise romantic writer had introduced it, the critics, one fears, would have laughed. At all events, when any reader finds that a book is beyond his belief, in character, in language, and in event, the book must, for him, lose much of its interest. Again, if he be struck by such a defect of style as the use of semi-scientific phraseology out of place, he must say so; he must point out the neighbourhood of the reef on which George Eliot was wrecking her English. An example of a fault so manifest, and of such easy remedy (for nobody need write jargon), I selected and reproduce. A rustic wife is sitting in a tavern, taking her ease at her inn. "A sort of halo, an occidental glow, came over life then. Troubles and other realities took on themselves a metaphysical impalpability, sinking to mere cerebral phenomena for serene contemplation, and no longer stood as pressing concretions which chafed body and soul." "Men and hangels igsplain this," cried Jeames, on less provocation. First, one does not know whether this description of Mrs. Durbeyfield's tavern content is to be understood as her

way of "envisaging" it, or as Mr. Hardy's. It can hardly
be Mrs. Durbeyfield's, because the words "cerebral" and
"metaphysical" were probably not in her West Saxon vocabulary. So the statement must be Mr. Hardy's manner
of making clear and lucid to us the mood of Mrs. Durbeyfield. It is, apparently, a mood which the philosopher
may experimentally reproduce by eating as good a dinner
as he can get, and drinking a fair quantity of liquor, such
as his soul loves, when he is troubled and anxious. Now,
if I may venture to imagine Mr. Herbert Spencer in these
conditions, and analysing his own state of mind, after
dinner, for *Typical Developments*, he probably would,
and he legitimately might, put his results into techincal
language. But where a novelist, or a poet, deals with a
very unscientific character, like Mrs. Durbeyfield or Sir
John Falstaff, then the use of psychological terminology
seems to my sense out of place. How can a trouble, say
want of pence, become a metaphysical impalpability?
How can it sink to a cerebral phenomenon, and how is it
lightened by so sinking? Everything, all experience, is
a cerebral phenomenon. How a trouble, not being a
"gathering," can be a "pressing concretion," or wherefore
a "concretion" at all, are questions which baffle one. Intelligible or not (and I confess to being no metaphysician),
the phraseology seems inappropriate. Inappropriateness,
as far as I am able to judge, often marks the language of
Mr. Hardy's characters. To take a specimen at random.
Alec, who has been "converted" for a moment from his
profession as a rural Don Juan, meets Tess again, and
says, "Ever since you told me of that babe of ours, it is

just as if my emotions, which have been flowing in a strong stream heavenward, had suddenly found a sluice open in the direction of you through which they have at once gushed." Now "babe" is good, is part of the patois of Zion, but the rest of the statement is so expressed as to increase one's feeling of unreality, as if one were reading a morally squalid fairy tale. And this sense of unreality is exactly what I complain of in *Tess*.

* * * * *

Well, for all these reasons—for its forbidding conception, for its apparent unreality, for its defects of style, so provokingly superfluous—*Tess* failed to captivate me, in spite of the poetry and beauty and economic value of its rural descriptions, in spite of the genius which is obvious and undeniable in many charming scenes. To be more sensitive to certain faults than to great merits, to let the faults spoil for you the whole, is a critical misfortune, if not a critical crime. Here, too, all is subjective and personal; all depends on the critic's taste, and how it reacts against a particular kind of error.

As Mr. Greenwood says, "some blemish there is in *Under the Greenwood Tree,* as there is not in the Medicean Venus, and one or two other works." Modern taste perhaps regards the whole conception and treatment of the Medicean Venus as one error and blemish, if we compare it with the works of the great age. But, of course, all work has its blemishes, or almost all work. Shakespeare is as far as possible from being impeccable, and we know what Kirchhoff and Möllendorff say about the *Odyssey,* what M. Renan said about St. John's Gospel, and M. Scherer about Molière. To some tastes faults appear which to others are unapparent. But there are faults and faults, tastes and tastes. We all admit the existence of blemishes in the works which are most dear to us; there are palpable faults in *Rob Roy*, in *Tom Jones*, in *Tartuffe* (they tell me), and, they tell me, in *Vanity Fair*. The question is, how far do these faults offend the reader, and spoil, for him, the merit of the work before him? Here, again, we deal with the subjective. A man says that *Pickwick* is "low" and boisterous; well, my genteelness (or "gentility") is unoffended by *Pickwick*. He says that *Rob Roy* is prolix, that Thackeray preaches too much, that the *dénouement* of *Tartuffe* is inartistic. Perhaps—nay, very probably—these censures are just, but the faults do not spoil the merits, for me. On the other hand, I confess that what seem to me faults in *Tess*, do not exactly spoil, but leave me less patience than I could wish, to enjoy the book's many and notable merits. Yet what is all this but saying that one prefers *Far from the Madding Crowd* to *Tess* and some of Mr. Hardy's other works? Arguing about it proves nothing, especially in the face of a consensus of praise from almost everybody who is not "genteel." I might say that *Tess* is not only a romance, but a *tendenz* story, a story with a moral, or part of it, being, apparently, the malignant topsy-turviness of things, the malevolent constitution of the world, the misfortunes of virtue, the conspiracy of circumstances against the good and "pure." A lurking vein of optimism may make one distrust this conclusion (if this indeed be the conclusion), and one may be comforted by one's very powerlessness to believe; may say, like the unconsciously heterodox old woman, "After all, perhaps it is not true." And that is a consolation for oneself, but not good for the novel. So I have ventured to say my say, though I had not intended at any time to speak again about any work of Mr. Hardy's.*

* *Longman's Magazine.* November, 1892. (Andrew Lang.)

"R. L. S." *

MR. GRAHAM BALFOUR has done his best; and his best should rank decently among official biographies. He is loving, he is discreet, he has much knowledge. Indeed, almost the worst that can be said of him is that he is a day or so after the fair. We live so fast, and our reading is so many weeks ahead of death any time, that the moment for the official biography of Robert Lewis Stevenson seems already one with dead Yesterday, if not the day before that. That is as may be. As to Mr. Balfour's tact and piety (a most service-able blend), there cannot be two opinions: he has written lovingly of his dead cousin, and, according to his lights, he has written well. I mean, he has done his best for the Stevenson of legend and his best for the Stevenson of life. So far as I can see, he does not distinguish the one from the other: his predilections are all with rumour and report; and if they be not, at least he can govern his tongue. On the whole, I may congratulate him on his result.

Yet I confess that "it do not over stimilate." I cannot lay a finger on any point in this biography, excepting here and there whereat I have a peculiar interest, and say that Mr. Balfour has not done his utmost, and is not, as an official biographer, entirely successful. Yet am I dis-

* *The Life of Robert Lewis Stevenson.* By Graham Balfour. In Two Volumes. London: Methuen & Co., 1901.

232

contented, dissatisfied, still looking for more. I daresay
the feeling is personal; that I cannot judge equably, for
I know too much. So be it. 'Tis a fact that, recalling
what I can recall, I can only take Mr. Balfour's book as a
solemn and serious essay in that kind of make-believe
in which the biographee (if one may use so flippant a
neologism in so august a connexion) did all his life rejoice,
and was exceeding glad. I read; and as I read I am
oppressed by the thought that here is Lewis Stevenson
very much as he may well have wanted to be, but that
here is not Lewis Stevenson at all. At any rate, here is
not the Lewis Stevenson I knew. At this place let me
take refuge in an analogy. Mr. Balfour's first volume is
prefaced by a portrait. It is not unlike in certain ways,
yet it set me wondering how and when and by whom that
brilliant face had been thus commonly transfigured. I
looked for information, and then I saw why this very feminine view of a very masculine creature had got itself such
currency as print can give.* I do not want to make Mr.
Graham Balfour blush for his loyalty; but I can't help
the reflection that, even as the portrait is smooth, and
smiling, and ladylike, and unexceptionable, so, in less
degree, is his *Life.* What astonishes me, what commands
my admiration, is that he has done so well that even I can
read him with interest, and can recommend him to all

---

* It (the portrait) is merely amateur and inexpressive and
sentimental; yet it tells me in plain terms why Rodin was not
permitted to make that bust of Stevenson he wished so much to
sign. All the same, Messrs. Methuen could and should have
given us a better thing, especially in Stevenson's biography. It is
not fair to him that he should go forth, officially, as *that.*

them that would still be sentimentalizing about R. L. S. *

For me there were two Stevensons: the Stevenson who went to America in '87; and the Stevenson who never came back. The first I knew, and loved; the other I lost touch with, and, though I admired him, did not greatly esteem. My relation to him was that of a man with a grievance; and for that reason, perhaps—that reason and others—I am by no means disposed to take all Mr. Balfour says for gospel, nor willing to forget, on the showing of what is after all an official statement, the knowledge gained in an absolute intimacy of give-and-take which lasted for thirteen years, and includes so many of the circumstances of those thirteen years that, as I believe, none living now can pretend to speak of them with any such authority as mine. This, however, is not to say that

---

* This notwithstanding, I do not know that, apart from Mr. Graham Balfour's views, and some few details which I do not remember reading before, it gives us anything important or new. Stevenson, indeed, has been fortunate in his critics and biographers: from himself—an artist in speech, selection, presentation—onwards. To *The Dictionary of National Biography* Mr. Sidney Colvin contributed a model summary of his life and achievement; M. Marcel Schwob's note in *The New Review* is as illuminating and ingenious a piece of criticism as can be read; Mr. Raleigh's lecture (Edwin Arnold), none the worse for being touched with a certain romantic enthusiasm, is a thing to read, and read again—once for his subject's sake, and once (at least) for its author's; Mr. Cope Cornford, in that little handbook of his (Blackwood), to which I was privileged to contribute a note or two, appears to me to have said as much about Stevenson the man as need now be told, and all about Stevenson the artist that can be said for twenty years. Mr. Balfour does but complement these things: he neither abolishes nor replaces them.

Mr. Balfour's view of his famous cousin is not warranted
to the letter, so far as he saw and knew. I mean no more
than that the Stevenson he knew was not the Stevenson
who came to me (that good angel, Mr. Leslie Stephen,
aiding) in the old Edinburgh Infirmary; nor the Stevenson I nursed in secret, hard by the old Bristo Port, till he
could make shift to paddle the *Arethusa*; nor the Stevenson who stayed with me at Acton after selling Modestine,*
nor even the Stevenson who booked a steerage berth to
New York, and thence trained it "across the plains," and
ended for the time being as a married man and a Silverado
squatter; though I confess that in this last avatar the
Stevenson of Mr. Balfour's dream had begun, however
faintly and vaguely, to adumbrate himself, and might
have been looked for as a certainty by persons less affec-
tionate and uninquiring than those by whom he was then
approached. Mr. Balfour does me the honour of quoting
the sonnet into which I crammed my impressions of my
companion and friend; and, since he has done so, I may as
well own that "the Shorter Catechist" of the last verse
was an afterthought. In those days he was in abeyance,
to say the least; and if, even then, *il allait poindre à
l'horizon* (as the composition, in secret and as if ashamed,
of *Lay Morals* persuades me to believe he did), I, at any
rate, was too short-sighted to suspect his whereabouts.

* It was now, I think, that he made the immense discovery
that a girl on a certain level of life has eyes for nothing masculine a plane or two below that level. At all events, he wore his
tourist's raiment, and was infinitely gratified to be able to report,
after one of his rambles, that a casual wayfarer had asked him
for a fill of tobacco, and had called him "Sir."

When I realized it, I completed my sonnet; but this was not till years had come and gone, and the Shorter Catechist, already detested by more than one, was fully revealed to me.

I will say at once that I do not love the Shorter Catechist, in anybody, and that I loved him less in Stevenson than anywhere that I have ever found him. He is too selfish and too self-righteous a beast for me. He makes ideals for himself with a resolute regard for his own salvation; but he is all-too apt to damn the rest of the world for declining to live up to them, and he is all-too ready to make a lapse of his own the occasion for a rule of conduct for himself and the lasting pretext for a highly moral deliverance to such backsliding Erastians as, having memories and a certain concern for facts, would like him to wear his rue with a difference. At bottom Stevenson was an excellent fellow. But he was of his essence what the French call *personnel*. He was, that is, incessantly and passionately interested in Stevenson. He could not be in the same room with a mirror but he must invite its confidences every time he passed it; to him there was nothing obvious in time and eternity, and the smallest of his discoveries, his most trivial apprehensions, were all by way of being revelations, and as revelations must be thrust upon the world; he was never so much in earnest, never so well pleased (this were he happy or wretched), never so irresistible, as when he wrote about himself.*

---

* Mr. Raleigh notes with a just delight the faultless tact by which these utterances are marked. But here came in the man of letters. The man of talk was neither so convincing nor anything like so discreet.

Withal, if he wanted a thing, he went after it with an entire contempt for consequences. For these, indeed, the Shorter Catechist was ever prepared to answer; so that, whether he did well or ill, he was safe to come out unabashed and cheerful. He detested Mr. Gladstone, I am pleased to say; but his gift of self-persuasion was scarce second to that statesman's own.* He gave himself out for the most open-minded of men: to him one point of view was as good as another; Age's was respectable, but so was Youth's; the Fox that had a tail was no whit more considerable than the Fox whose tail was lost. *Et patati, et patata.* 'Twas all "as easy as lying" to him, for 'twas all in the run of his humanity. But in the event it was academic: for where he was grossly interested, he could see but one side of the debate; and there are people yet living (I am not one of them) who, knowing him intimately, have not hesitated to describe him in a word of three letters, the suspicion of which might well make him turn in his grave. And yet, I do not know. He ever took himself so seriously—or rather he ever played at life with such a solemn grace—that perhaps, after all, he would scarce stir where he lies for the dread vocable. For he was a humourist and a thinker, and could he hear it, he would certainly smile, fall (like the Faquir of story) to considering himself umbilically, and, finding in the

---

* Mr. Balfour again reminds us of what he thought of Gordon, and how he would fain have joined the Curtins, and fought with them the obscure and bloody tyranny which then lay over Ireland. 'Tis at least as pleasant to recall that once, after a certain famous victory, he would not allow himself to be addressed for days, except as "Mr. Peiwar Kotal Stevenson."

end that he had fairly earned it, go back to sleep, with a glow of satisfaction for that this part also had been well played. No better histrion ever lived. But in the South Seas the mask got set, the "lines became a little stereotyped." Plainly the Shorter Catechist was what was wanted. And here we are: with Stevenson's later letters and Mr. Graham Balfour's estimate.

'Tis as that of an angel clean from heaven, and I for my part flatly refuse to recognise it. Not, if I can help it, shall this faultless, or very nearly faultless, monster go down to after years as the Lewis I knew, and loved, and laboured with and for, with all my heart and strength and understanding.* In days to come I may write as much as can be told of him. Till those days come, this protest must suffice. If it convey the impression that I take a view of Stevenson which is my own, and which declines to be concerned with this Seraph in Chocolate, this barley-sugar effigy of a real man; that the best and

---

* I published his first sustained achievement in fiction (*The New Arabian Nights*); I procured him the first cheque for an hundred pounds he ever earned; I did my best for his works, in fact, until he asked me to take a commission of five per cent. on the receipts. I refused, and he went for some time in his own way. Then Mr. Charles Baxter, an infinitely better business man than I, and with (I am sure he will agree) a far more marketable commodity to sell than I had had, came on; and Stevenson, beginning with a pound a month, from his parents, ended by spending something between £4,000 and £5,000 a year. How he spent it Heaven and Mr. Baxter alone know. Mr. Balfour gives the figures; but one needn't go further than to rejoice in them. To finish with myself: I was (I can say it now) for something in the contrivance of the *Edinburgh Edition*; so that first and last I may claim to have done my part.

the most interesting part of Stevenson's life will never get written—even by me; and that the Shorter Catechist of Vailima, however brilliant and distinguished as a writer of stories, however, authorized and acceptable as an artist in morals, is not my old, riotous, intrepid, scornful Stevenson at all—suffice it will.

For the rest I think he has written himself down in terms that may not be mistaken, nor improved, in a fragment of an essay on morals printed in the *Appendix* to the *Edinburgh Edition*. "An unconscious, easy, selfish person," he remarks, "shocks less, and is more easily loved, than one who is laboriously and egotistically unselfish. There is at least no fuss about the first; but the other parades his sacrifices, and so sells his favours too dear. Selfishness is calm, a force of nature: you might say the trees are selfish. But egoism is a piece of vanity; it must always take you into its confidence; it is uneasy, troublesome, searching; it can do good, but not handsomely; it is uglier, because less dignified than selfishness itself. But here," he goes on, with that careful candour which he so often has, "here I perhaps exaggerate to myself, because I am the one more than the other, and feel it like a hook in my mouth at every step I take. *Do what I will, this seems to spoil all.*" This, as it seems to me, describes him so exactly that, if you allow for histrionics (no inconsiderable thing, remember!), you need no more description. It was said of him, once, that when he wrote of anything, he wrote of it with such an implacable lucidity as left it beggared of mystery. This is what he has done in this passage; and who runs may read him in it as he was. 'Tis to this anxious and uncloistered egotism of his that we are indebted for so much good writing in the matter of confession and self-revelation. To this the circumstance is due that when the Amateur Emigrant asked his friend, the Blacksmith, how—speaking as man to man; as one in the steerage to another—he had behaved on the voyage, he was staggered by the reply that he had done not so badly "on the whole." 'Tis to this that we are indebted for the prayers, the supplications for valour, the vocalizings about duty (which the most of us do as a matter of course), by which that part of the world which reads Stevenson—(and that part of it which does not is happily the smaller)—has long been, and is still being, joyously edified.

Mr. Balfour notes with tender admiration that, when Stevenson had quarrelled with anybody, he was always trying to do that person a service in secret. But if this be not the hero of my quotation all over: salving his conscience for a possible injustice, done in heat and apprehended too late for anything but a frank avowal and a complete apology; which, in the circumstances, the Shorter Catechist finds abhorrent, and therefore immoral: then self-analysis is of no moment, and confession means nothing, and no virtue is left in words. And in the manner of his giving, as exampled by Mr. Balfour, the Anxious Egotist is characteristically and not pleasantly apparent. "I hereby authorize you," he writes, "to pay when necessary £—— to Z——: if I give him more, it would only lead to his starting a gig and keeping a Pomeranian dog." 'Tis wittily put, of course; but it scarce becomes the lips of a man who had several kennels of Pomeranians, kept gigs innumerable, reported that brilliant and taking little talk between Count Spada and the General of the Jesuits, realized the place in God's economy of "The Singer on the garden seat," and held as an essential gospel that an act may be forgiven of the Deities, but that to neglect an opportunity, to hang back, to do nothing when something might be done—this, this is the Unpardonable Sin. Alas! there be special sorts of gigs, and who shall number the varieties of the Pomeranian dog? And from my heart I wish that Mr. Balfour had left that utterance of one who bred Pomeranians and kept gigs— sometimes, it may be, with a moral aim, but always as seemed good to him—unguessed and unreported. But to your Anxious Egotist, your trained and cultured Shorter Catechist, what magnificence in the matter of self-approval, self-oblivion, self-righteousness could come amiss? Stevenson's world was ever "a brave gymnasium," more or less; but if there were room in it for "the singer on the garden seat," it was only as a romantic object. He had no real part in this philosopher's economy of things, since he might dare nothing at this philosopher's cost. In a "brave gymnasium" ordered on these lines the gigs and the Pomeranians all went one way; and that, despite all Stevenson's protestings, was not the way of Stevenson's *bénéficiaires.* 'Tis the oddest of revelations; but 'tis of Mr. Balfour's making, not Stevenson's. He, I am sure, would cheerfully have gone to the stake, like the good and constant histrion he was, or ever he would have given it to the world in what he used to call "cold, hard print."

But I must call a truce, and leave cavilling. I long to say that 'tis wonderful to me, who have forgot so much, to find so much of myself in Stevenson and in Stevenson's biographer. I take up a volume of the *Edinburgh Edition*, and I read that, included in the plenishing of his ideal house are, "a Canaletto print or two;" and I recall the circumstance that his taste for Canaletto prints, even as his Canaletto prints themselves, came through and from me. I bought them, I remember, in the Knightsbridge Road, and he paid me what I gave for them, which was some six or seven shillings apiece. I turn the page, and read of "Piranesi etchings on the walls;" and I remember who placed them there, and the blessed hours I've had in their neighbourhood.* I turn the page again, and I come on the *Moral Emblems* and *Not I*; and once more the Muse of Memory is too much for me, and, as in a dream, I see myself touting in the interest of these works, taking sixpence of this one and eightpence of that other, and embezzling these receipts: for I neither paid the laborious graver-poet † the price of his endeavour, nor delivered the works for which I was acting as agent.‡ But, return-

---

* Since everything pertaining to Stevenson is of perdurable interest, it is fair and fit to note that in Mr. Colvin's "reminiscences of the office in Edinburgh of his old friend Mr. Charles Baxter," you should read, not "office," but "dining-room." Thus, though, history is written.

† Or should it be poet-graver? So much rubbish has been written of both that I leave the question to his true-lovers. Of course I don't refer to the poet of Underwoods.

‡ My friend, Mr. Austin Dobson, may speak, and he will, with feeling on this point; for these ridiculous exercises have now, I believe, a monetary value, and are quoted by collectors at long

ing to Mr. Balfour's book, I open it at random; I read
that "Bob Stevenson came, and I can never be grateful
enough for what he did for me then;" and the Muse once
more awakens me. I recall the despairing telegram which
reached me late one night; the call on my good friend,
the late Constantine Ionides, for ready money;* the jour-
ney through Westbourne Grove (the blazing central
telegraph office by the way) to St. John's Wood, where
Bob and his wife resided. I think it was in Acacia Road.
But I know that I blundered: that I went to the wrong
house, and, by appealing to a bell, disturbed a lady (whom
I imagine to have been but parcel-dressed) in the practice
of her avocations. Over a garden-wall, and with a gar-
den-door between, I explained the nature of my errand to
her; was dismissed in terms whose frostiness still hangs
glittering about my remembrance; groped my way till I
found the house I wanted; and, after knocking and ringing till my heart went into my stomach, and Lewis's death
in a foreign land was merely a matter of hours to me,
roused Bob from his bed, intimated my views, and produced "the wherewithal." His eyes were heavy with
sleep, but he started next day. Or it is a casual mention
of "Z——": a very casual mention. Again the Muse
appeals to me, and recalls how "Z——" chucked his practice and went to Hyères at a dozen hours' notice, did his
best—(I wish I could write what it was)—and suddenly
became a person in the Stevensonian Hierarchy; but presently, saying or doing something somebody or other did

prices. So that I have swindled him for quite a substantial sum.
* There was no time to send to Edinburgh.

not like, was disseated, cast into outer darkness, and not so much as named—(such is the Anxious Egotist!)—among the innumerable doctors who figure, with Dr. Scott, of Bournemouth, at the head of them, in the dedication of one of Stevenson's books. With what an instancy the circumstances of that dispatch—the how, the when, the whence—leap to my pen's end as I write! For the moment I forget myself; and 'tis something of an effort to recall that Stevenson is dead, but "Z——" is yet in complete and cheerful activity, recking naught of his exclusion from Stevenson's list, and doing his best for low and high, as he was doing it when he came into my life these some and twenty years ago.

A sentence in the Dedication (suppressed; but finally printed in the *Edinburgh Edition*) of *The Master of Ballantrae*, reminds me of a certain *Ballade Stevenson*, for which I am responsible, and which I preferred (and so, I think, did he), above the sonnet. "I would have all literature bald," so the sentence goes, *"and all authors (if you like) but one."* That brings back my ballade, with its refrain, "A bald and cullid-headed man;" and that refrain in its turn brings back the days of what the two Stevensons, Bob and Lewis, knew as "jink."* The begin-

---

* Mr. Balfour prints a fragment—prints it for the first time, I believe—in which Stevenson essays to give an idea of the conditions and ideals of "jink," and of the state of mind which made "jink" excellent. 'Tis a spirited piece, so far as it goes; but as the writer ignores some essential elements, it conveys but a faint and feeble impression of the facts, as they were afterwards reported to me. The writer, also, is pleased to leave in doubt the identity of the only true begetter of the name "John Libbel."

ning is a sentence in Artemus Ward. It runs (I must quote from memory) thus:—"'Twas the lone sunset hour. Three bald-headed cullid men was playing monte; all was peas;" and it so took hold upon the two Stevensons that, first of all, "bald-headed and cullid," and then, by a natural transition, "bald and cullid-headed" became their favourite description of any and everything preferred by them—a passage in Shakespeare, an achievement in whisky and sheep's head, a good talk, a notable drunk, a fair woman. This I remembered, and hence my refrain. How I wish I could recall those three octaves and that envoy! Why did Mr. Balfour not resuscitate this dead and forgotten masterpiece? 'Tis as good of its kind as any of my nicknames for him: Fastidious Brisk and (especially) the *in*delicate Ariel. Another nickname, by the way, which Mr. Balfour does not quote, came from the Parliament House. "Here," quoth the jolly creature who invented it (he was afterwards, and perhaps still is, a sheriff-substitute somewhere or other)—"Here comes the Gifted Boy." Thus, and not otherwise, Peter Robertson took on, as they say, "Peveril of the Peak," and was instantly retorted upon as "Peter of the Painch." In Stevenson's case there was no response. The nickname troubled him for a moment; but he had nothing to say to it.

That begetter was not himself, it was his cousin; and I do not doubt that the scheme for depositing goods in Libbel's name at all the *monts-de-piété* in the known world, with a view to bewildering the German historian of the year 2001, was likewise his cousin's. It is absolutely like Bob, and it is utterly unlike Lewis, whose conceptions were never on so vast and secular a scale.

In truth, he loved not to be thus attacked, and was in such cases sometimes at a loss for words. He shone in debate, and he excelled in talk. But in both talk and debate he was strung to his highest pitch—alert, daring of an inextinguishable gaiety, quick and resourceful to the nth degree; and to try a fall with him then was to get badly handled, if not utterly suppressed. But he was not averse from monologue—far from it; and I have sometimes thought that he ran his temperament too hard.* Also, was he what the world calls "a wit"? I do not think he was. After all, a wit is a man of phrases: consciously, sometimes, he waits, he thinks, he condenses his thought, and out comes his witticism; or he waits not, nor thinks, nor condenses, but says something, and by no sort of effort he retorts in the only possible way. Mr. Thackeray † has noted the difference between old Mr. Congreve,

* I mean that, on accasion, he would play the fool (none ever did it better), when his audience was tired of laughter. Then he became a buffoon, and a buffoon to whom you could not show the door. At these times, I think, he got down to hysteria. In any case his temperament was amazingly fresh, vigorous, and assertive; and to have him in the house "When doleful Dumps his heart did wound, And griping Griefs," etc., was no light infliction.

† I have quoted Thackeray: not because he was historically correct; for, after all, Congreve the talker may have been as lively as Sheridan or Colman, as Byron reports them, but: because, being an artist, in Fielding and Congreve he has formulated, whether well or ill, two types of talker, and set them face to face. To neither, I take it, does Thackeray, whose method is small, and whose resentments are smaller—(whose theory of talk, too, does not commend itself to the Average Talker)—do justice. Still, he thought for himself; there is a sense in which

inventing his epigrams in a corner, and young Mr. Harry
Fielding, who pours out everything he has in his heart,
and is, in effect, as brilliant, as engaging, and as arresting
a talker as Colonel Esmond has known. In print Stevenson was now and then witty enough for seven; but in talk
his way was, not Congreve's but, Harry Fielding's. No;
he was certainly not a wit, in the sense that
Congreve was a wit. Perhaps he was nearer than
he knew to that Jack Fletcher—(he talked comedies, his
printer says)—for whom, having begun his later life, and
being somewhat stricken with respectability, he could find
no better description to me than "a dirty dog"; perhaps
(of the Samoan Stevenson I will say at once that I do
not for one moment think so) he would have relished
Fielding, and found himself, so to speak, in that most gal-
lant, cheerful practical-artist soul. But Fielding and
Fletcher certainly, and Congreve probably, would have
had a retort, or courteous or the other thing, for the
author of that rather marking phrase—"The Gifted Boy."
And Stevenson, who was not a wit, but something a thousand times better, had none. No "Peter of the Painch"
occurred to this new Peveril of the Peak; and that was
Lewis's way. Give him all that Mrs. Battle asked, and
he was almost inimitable. Come to him suddenly: "prop
him on the nose," as it were: and he was tame. And so
much now for that far-glancing, variously coloured, in-
tensely romantic and flagrantly humorous expression of
life—the talk of R. L. S.

he wrote for himself; and I am glad to have so great a man from
whom to illustrate my point.

Follow the Henley-Stevenson plays. But how to deal with them? Mr. Balfour gives us a list of those projected and those done; and, having forgotten all about it, I find that list most interesting. It reads well, even now; for I fear that one of our first cares was to find a good name for the still unattempted piece; and Mr. Balfour's quotation, if it show nothing else, will show that in this endeavour we were not wholly unsuccessful. *Honour and Arms*—is not that a canorous and inspiriting title? And *The King of Clubs*—reader, does that promise nothing? And *The Tragedy of Hester Noble*—how is that for a playbill? *Ajax* I pass, though (coming after Sophocles)* we never made so good a play. But *Farmer George* (of which I remember nothing whatever) at any rate sounds

---

* I suggested, one day, in the course of talk, that the tragic motives had changed not since the beginning, and that we might save ourselves a world of pains if we thieved our "passionate moral problems" from the Greeks. Stevenson was instantly attracted; and we sketched, and partly wrote, our *Ajax*: whose hero is one Sir Robert Trelawney, an elderly Anglo-Indian engineer, who—brave, honest, magnificent—plays the unconscious criminal as one of several directors in a fraudulent bank. It was, though I say it who should not, a good play; and the character of Tecmessa, carefully modernized and terribly intensified, would I believe, have persuaded an actress, whose first thought was not for her gowns, to have tried to be a player. But we never finished our work; for by that time the Actor, that immitigable compound of imbecility and authority, that expression of temperament without mind which is the nearest one can get in decent phraseology to its feminine analogue, the Mere Woman, had come to stink in our nostrils; and such ideas as we may have had of the *Philoctetes*, and the *Oresteia*, and the *Alcestis*, and the rest were not referred to any more. But I still think that, with Salvini and Duse (say), our *Ajax* might have been proved a play.

well. Comes *The Mother-in-Law*; and that would have been a tragedy. As to *Madame Fate and Madame Destiny*, I cannot recall a single particular; but I *do* remember that the first touch was mine, and that the second title is merely an improvement on the first. To go back a little: *Honour and Arms* is of its essence English, Jacobitish, romantic; the hero is sorely tried; love is too much for duty; and if I remember aright, he emerges ill from his trial. But his father (Sir Austin Fielding), is a noble old boy; his mistress (Jean Lorimer: Jean—or is it Barbara?) is a noble young girl. And when I tell you that William of Orange is the *deus ex machina*; that Harry Fielding was broke and sentenced to be shot; that Sir Austin pleaded with the King, with Ginkel, and the Scots soldier of fortune who had witnessed Harry's failure; that then the Lorimers came in, and the *scène-à-faire* was (in our strong conceit) as good as done; so that Harry took back his sword and married his Barbara (or his Jean), and Sir Austin (he was really Tom Stevenson) played the Scottish Father, and even Dutch William was moved to a genial saying—reader mine, if I tell you that much, won't you be sorry, sorry while life is in you, that you will never see that play? And may I, if you aren't—may I, with or without offence, at once assert that you know nothing about plays? Well, well . . . in those days, as Mr. Balfour very justly puts it, we—I and Lewis— knew nothing neither. All the same, it was a golden time. I stole the idea of *The King of Clubs* from *The Old Curiosity Shop*, and found more to thieve years afterwards in *Old St. Paul's*; it was invented for that excellent actor, Mr. Shiel Barry; a chief character was called the Hon. Aquila Breckenridge (if anything could be more American than that name, I'd like to see it); the scene was New Orleans somewhere about 1830. It was all so taking and extreme, and Barry was so exactly what we wanted, that I wonder now that it never got written. That it and the rest were left in the shape of Good Intentions, to crawl the floor of hell with the good Bishop's span-long babes, was owing, I think, to the fact that both collaborators wanted money, and had got sick and tired of the Abstract Actor. Had we been men of substance— men able to take a theatre and pay their players to do as they were told—we might possibly have persisted, and done what was in us to re-create the Romantic Drama in the terms of prose. But we were not men of substance; and our consideration of the Abstract Actor very soon convinced us that, if he had anything to do with it, men of substance we should never be. "Et voilà pourquoi votre fille est muette"; that is why the Muse of Romantic Drama, the Muse of *Anthony* and *Carmosine*, of *On ne badine pas avec l'amour* and *la Tour de Nesle*, stands where and as she did, before we scrimmaged for her favours.

Lewis the musician, too—how much I saw of him! how often have I ministered to his artless and homely needs! Like his cousin, Stevenson had no ear for intervals: his one tune for many years was *Auld Lang Syne*, which he sang, in the belief that it was a genuine Scots melody, to all manner of verses, decent sometimes, improvised or

recalled as occasion or inspiration served.* Yet had he an
aery and delicate sense of rhythm; and I have ever regretted that he did not study music from the first. Not,
of course, for creation's sake; for at the best he could
never have been anything but what his cousin used to
call a Mus. Doc.—a plodder equally uninspired, uninteresting, and superfluous: not, I say, for music's sake, but
for that of his own vigilant, inquiring, far-wandering,
extremely technical mind, which might often and for
long spaces of time have found in Bach and Beethoven,
or even in Purcell and Lulli and Couperin, the refresh-
ment it had to seek, and did, in Xavier de Montépin and
Fortuné du Boisgobey. I, for my part, know nothing of
the mathematics of music; but in those days I strummed
the piano a little, and I was, as they say, "no mean performer" on the tin whistle:—

> Once again,
> O thou, Orpheus and Herakles, the Bard
> And the Deliverer, touch the stops again:—

so that it fell to me to teach him the difference between
The Mill, Mill, O and (say) *Fra Poco,* both of which
come very fairly well on the humbler instrument, and on
the other to shadow forth some vague yet painful hints of
the enormous and distressing suggestiveness which Beethoven expressed into the slow movements of his sonatas.

---

* A special favourite (on the tin whistle) was the melody of
The Thorn; but in this case he was overcome by the humour
of the words. Had he—had we—but known that they are the
work of Robert Burns!

Gluck, too, was a household word with us; so were Handel and Mozart; and as for jigs and reels——! Well, well; it's all over now, and I've made no attempt at making music since seven years. But we are told that the mathematics of music, as they appeared to Stevenson's imagination, whether technical or creative, were at once a solace to him, and a great distraction; and I love to think that I helped him, insistently helped him, to venture outside his art, and to carve out for his mind this tiny brigand-state in an immense enchanted kingdom, where, had he not been himself, he had no business at all to be.

I have said nothing of Stevenson the artist in this garrulous and egotistic pronouncement on his official *Life;* for the very simple reason that I have nothing to say. To tell the truth, his books are none of mine: I mean, that if I want reading, I do not go for it to the *Edinburgh Edition.* I am not interested in remarks about morals; in and out of letters I have lived a full and varied life, and my opinions are my own. So, if I crave the enchantment of romance, I ask it of bigger men than he, and of bigger books than his: of *Esmond* (say) and *Great Expectations*, of *Redgauntlet* and *Old Mortality*, of *La Reine Margot* and *Bragelonne*, of *David Copperfield* and *A Tale of Two Cities*: while, if good writing and some other things be in my appetite, are there not always Hazlitt and Lamb—to say nothing of that "globe of miraculous continents" which is known to us as Shakespeare? There is his style, you will say; and it is a fact that it is rare, and in the last times better, because much simpler, than in the first. But after all, his style is so perfectly achieved that the achievement gets obvious: and when achievement gets obvious, is it not by way of becoming uninteresting? And is there not something to be said for the person who wrote that Stevenson always reminded him of a young man dressed the best he ever saw for the Burlington Arcade? Stevenson's work in letters does not now take me much, and I decline to enter on the question of its immortality; since that, despite what any can say, will get itself settled, soon or late, for all time. No; when I care to think of Stevenson it is not of "R. L. S.": R. L. S. "the renowned, the accomplished, Executing his difficult solo:" but of the "Lewis" that I knew, and loved, and wrought for, and worked with for so long. The successful man of letters does not greatly interest me: I read his careful prayers, and pass on, with the certainty that, well as they read, they were not written for print; I learn of his nameless prodigalities—and recall some instances of conduct in another vein. I remember, rather, the unmarried and irresponsible Lewis: the friend, the comrade, the *charmeur*.* Truly that last word, French as it is, is the only one that is worthy of him. I shall ever remember him as that. The impression of his writings disappears; the impression of himself and his talk is ever a possession.

---

* By the way, the only lesson in writing I ever had from him was conveyed in this sentence:—"Dites-moi ça vertement." And Mr. Balfour is very much mistaken in saying that Stevenson had anything whatever to do with his cousin's invasion of letters, of which the worries and pains were wholly mine. I have another case in mind; but I will not adduce it. I will but say that Stevenson's interest in other people's writing—writing well or writing ill—was small.

He had, as I have said elsewhere, all the gifts (he and his cousin, he and Bob) that qualify the talker's temperament —"As voice and eye and laugh, look and gesture, humour and fantasy, audacity and agility of mind, a lively and most impudent invention, a copious vocabulary, a right gift of foolery, a just inevitable sense of right and wrong" (this though I've blamed him for a tendency to monologue, and a trick of depending too much on his temperament). And I take leave to repeat what I've said elsewhere, that those who know him only by his books—(I think our Fleeming Jenkin, were he alive, would back me here)—know but the poorest of him. Forasmuch as he was primarily a talker, his printed works, like those of others after his kind, are but a sop for posterity:—"A last dying speech and confession (as it were) to show that not for nothing were they held rare fellows in their day."

A last word. I have everywhere read that we must praise him now and always for that, being a stricken man, he would live out his life. Are we not all stricken men, and do we not all do that? And why, because he wrote better than any one, should he have praise and fame for doing that which many a poor, consumptive sempstress does: cheerfully, faithfully, with no eloquent appeals to God, nor so much as a paragraph in the evening papers? That a man writes well at death's door is sure no reason for making him a hero; for, after all, there is as much virtue in making a shirt, or finishing a gross of matchboxes, in the very act of mortality, as there is in polishing a verse, or completing a chapter in a novel. As much, I say; but is there not an immense deal more? In the one case, the sufferer does the thing he loves best in life. In the other, well—who that has not made shirts, or finished match-boxes, shall speak? Stevenson, for all his vocalizings, was a brave man, with a fine, buoyant spirit; and he took the mystery of life and time and death as seemed best to him. But we are mortals all; and, so far as I have seen, there are few of us but strive to keep a decent face for the Arch-Discomforter. There is no wonder that Stevenson wrote his best in the shadow of the Shade; for writing his best was very life to him. Why, then, all this crawling astonishment—this voluble admiration? If it meant anything, it would mean that we have forgotten how to live, and that none of us is prepared to die; and that were an outrage on the innumerable unstoried martyrdoms of humanity. Let this be said of him, once for all: "He was a good man, good at many things, and now this also he has attained to, to be at rest." That covers Sophocles and Shakespeare, Marlborough and Bonaparte. Let it serve for Stevenson; and, for ourselves, let us live and die uninsulted, as we lived and died before his books began to sell and his personality was a marketable thing.*

* *Pall Mall Magazine,* December, 1901. (W. E. Henley.)

THE END